The Modern Novel

Blackwell Introductions to Literature

This series sets out to provide concise and stimulating introductions to literary subjects. It offers books on major authors (from John Milton to James Joyce), as well as key periods and movements (from Anglo-Saxon literature to the contemporary). Coverage is also afforded to such specific topics as "Arthurian Romance." While some of the volumes are classed as "short" introductions (under 200 pages), others are slightly longer books (around 250 pages). All are written by outstanding scholars as texts to inspire newcomers and others: non-specialists wishing to revisit a topic, or general readers. The prospective overall aim is to ground and prepare students and readers of whatever kind in their pursuit of wider reading.

Published

The Modern Novel
A Short Introduction

Jesse Matz

Blackwell
Publishing

350 Main Street, Malden, MA 02148-5020, USA
108 Cowley Road, Oxford OX4 1JF, UK
550 Swanston Street, Carlton, Victoria 3053, Australia

First published 2004 by Blackwell Publishing Ltd

Library of Congress Cataloging-in-Publication Data

Matz, Jesse.
The modern novel : a short introduction / Jesse Matz.
p. cm. – (Blackwell introductions to literature)
Includes bibliographical references (p.) and index.
ISBN 1-4051-0048-6 (hardcover : alk. paper) –
ISBN 1-4051-0049-4 (pbk. : alk. paper)
1. English fiction – 20th century – History and criticism.
2. Modernism (Literature) – Great Britain.   3. American fiction –
20th century – History and criticism.   4. Modernism (Literature) –
United States.   I. Title.   II. Series.
PR888.M63M37 2004
809.3′04 – dc22
2003018399

A catalogue record for this title is available from the British Library.

Set in 10 on 13 pt Meridian
by SNP Best-set Typesetter Ltd, Hong Kong
Printed and bound in the United Kingdom
by T.J. International Ltd, Padstow, Cornwall

For further information on
Blackwell Publishing, visit our website:
http://www.blackwellpublishing.com

Contents

Acknowledgments

Writing this book was made possible by Kenyon College and by the editorial team at Blackwell Publishing. Kenyon, the marvelous place where I work and teach, provided the financial resources, the moral support, and the inspiration. The wonderful people at Blackwell – Emma Bennett, Jennifer Hunt, Karen Wilson, and Fiona Sewell – provided vital guidance at every step along the way, from the conception of the book through its revisions to its final touches. Thanks are due also to my friends and colleagues at Kenyon (particularly Owen Beetham, my research assistant, and Jeff Bowman, my main sounding board); to Brian Shaffer, who gave helpful advice on an early draft; and above all to Blackwell Publisher Andrew McNeillie, whose vision, ingenuity, and enthusiasm are a true gift to the study of literature.

Introduction:
Modern *How?*

[I]n 1900, the continuity snapped.
                    Henry Adams

[O]n or about 1910, human character changed.
                    Virginia Woolf

The world broke in two in 1922 or thereabouts.
                    Willa Cather

The novel has always been modern – always concerned mainly
with contemporary life, and, as the name suggests, always after the
new thing. But some time around 1900 (or 1910, or 1922), to be
modern meant something more, because suddenly modernity
meant everything. It seemed to break the world in two, snapping
all continuities with the past, putting human character and life itself
into a state of constant change. To keep up, the novel also had to snap
and to split – to change. And so it became "the modern novel," breaking with the past, making itself new, to pursue modernity into the
future.

Why and how it did so is the subject of this book. The book is an
introduction to the forms and functions of the modern novel – its
motives, techniques, problems, and development. The book begins
with a working definition and with short sketches of the main intentions of the first modern novelists. It then describes the traits that make
a novel modern, through reference to some of the most important
examples. Questions and criticisms follow, and then the book moves

on to see what has become of the modern novel since the days of 1910 and 1922 – how later developments have outdated or enhanced it, and how it has continued on into *our* modern times.

All this will be *truly* introductory. The book is a sketch, meant to map in bold and plain lines a territory readers might later explore more fully, over the course of a semester or over the course of years. Things are necessarily left out (full historical contexts, many important writers, novels in languages other than English), but all in the hope of drawing the clearest possible profile of the modern novel itself. And all in the hope of rendering it more accessible. To be modern often meant to be difficult; the result has often been daunting. This introduction hopes to make it less so – to explain the modern novel in such a way as to give everyone a way in.

Our first way in will be some leading moments – four of the modern novel's first breakthroughs, and what they might tell us about it. We start with the opening sentence of James Joyce's *Portrait of the Artist as a Young Man* (1916). Second is a story – the story of how Gertrude Stein came by the strange style of writing that made her infamous. Third is the fragmented form of Jean Toomer's *Cane* (1923), and fourth is a debate – the debate about the very nature of reality that led Virginia Woolf to say that human character (and with it, the novel) had changed forever.

A Portrait of the Artist as a Young Man tells a familiar story: that of a boy growing to young manhood and finding a vocation. But the way the book begins is a surprise:

> Once upon a time and a very good time it was there was a moocow coming down along the road and this moocow that was coming down along the road met a nicens little boy named baby tuckoo.

The first words here are familiar enough. What could be more traditional than beginning, "once upon a time"? But what follows was (in 1916) new and strange: the words seem to be said and heard directly from life itself, without planning or purpose; they let silly baby-talk cheapen the language of literature; they make a joke of storytelling customs, and they plunge us directly into an unfamiliar world, without the kind of preparation (scene-setting, introductory explanations) that might normally ease us in. Gone is any welcoming narrator, any clear or "objective" descriptions – any proper beginning.

Why would Joyce have wanted to do without these things? For the sake of the truth, the vitality, and the new eloquence he would get in exchange. Starting without preparatory narration makes *Portrait* more like life, which never prepares us for what is to come. Starting in the voice of someone involved in the story (rather than that of an objective narrator) makes us feel more present to the action, and allowing that voice its own strange lingo enlivens the language of literature. Joyce's improper beginning breaks with convention for the sake of these greater realities, this more intense engagement with life itself, which proper form would perhaps disallow.

Twenty years earlier, in 1896, Gertrude Stein was a student at Radcliffe College. As part of a course in psychology, she did some experiments, to test what people could do *automatically* – without conscious control over their actions. The experiment went like this: she gave her test subjects a book and a "planchette" (a glass plate mounted on metal balls); she then had them place a hand on the planchette and get engrossed in the book; and she found that as they read, her subjects moved their planchettes even while paying no attention to them at all. They moved their hands automatically. And not only that: when pencils were attached to the planchettes, as the subjects moved them, they *wrote*. Here was "spontaneous automatic writing," which probably should have been nonsensical, but was instead fairly cogent and very revealing. What it revealed (to the young Gertrude Stein) was the presence of a "second personality," a deeper self speaking some primal language from the bottom of the human mind.

Something very much like that language appeared a few years later in Stein's *Tender Buttons* (1914). The book was replete with sentences unlike any that had ever appeared in prose. Random and repetitious, baffling and abstract, Stein's new sentences came in part from that "automatic self," the self at work deep beneath the conscious mind:

> A kind in glass and a cousin, a spectacle and nothing strange a single hurt color and an arrangement in a system to pointing. All this and not ordinary, not unordered in not resembling. The difference is spreading.

These are utterly perplexing sentences, mainly because they do not seem to represent anything at all. They do not try to describe anything real, and they give us none of the information we typically expect from prose. They may express some "automatic self," but why would Stein have wanted to let that self take over literature – especially if it meant deranging writing to this degree?

Stein liked automatic writing for its newness, its difficulty, and its impracticality. Like many modern writers, she wanted to see modern discoveries have an impact on literature, and she was eager to see experiment transfer over from psychology to fiction. She did not mind the strangeness of what resulted; much to the contrary, she wanted to challenge people's presumptions about meaningful language. And she wanted to see what would happen if language became useless – if it ceased to serve ordinary purposes and became instead something for us to wonder at.

To challenge presumptions: is this why Jean Toomer made *Cane* a jumble of fragments? Written amid the Harlem Renaissance (the explosion of African-American cultural activity in New York in the 1920s), Toomer's book jumbles together bits of stories, short and long, together with poems and songs and sketches. The title suggests that these fragments all pertain to the sugar-cane crop in the American South and its ties to racist exploitation, but the sense of coherence ends there, and for the most part the novel (if it is one) hardly tries to hang together. Why let things fall apart this way? Why would Toomer not try to make his book whole?

The Harlem Renaissance was a time both of excitement and of crisis, of opportunity and of regret, as centuries of pent-up creativity and anger together burst upon the cultural scene. The combination was particularly volatile for Toomer, who, as a biracial man, felt the strains of social change with peculiar intensity. And so he expressed the extremes of African-American modernity by making his novel a mer-curial mix of elements. His fragments express the fragmentation of modern life – the way new freedoms and opportunities were break-ing old rules, the way modern chaos was shattering traditional insti-tutions and customs. So the formlessness of *Cane* is a meaningful reflection of an increasingly formless world. And when *Cane*'s main protagonist describes the state of his soul, we see how a "twisted" form might be needed to reflect a painful modern reality:

> Th form thats burned int my soul is some twisted awful thing that crept in from a dream, a godam nightmare, an wont stay still unless I feed it. An it lives on words. Not beautiful words. God Almighty no. Misshapen, split-gut, tortured, twisted words.

Here we have a kind of explanation for the writing of a fragmentary book like *Cane*: modern crisis has burned itself into the soul, making the soul a troubled thing that needs new words for its salvation – not the fine words that might once have done the job, but "misshapen, split-gut" ones, twisted forms of expression to match a twisted world. The shape of *Cane* is as "tortured" as the form of life it evokes. So the shape itself is significant – meaningful precisely because it seems incoherent, a broken mirror only better able to reflect a shattered culture.

Finally, one last example: the debate that followed publication of Virginia Woolf's *Jacob's Room* (1922). The novel was based on the life of Woolf's brother, who had died very young. But only loosely based, since Woolf did not really mean to tell any traditional life story. Jacob is not portrayed directly or completely. No narrator describes him fully, and he does not express himself in such a way as to give us an authoritative account of his character. Instead, we come to know him provisionally, as he appears to his friends and family, through his essential gestures, in terms of the impressions he makes. *Jacob's Room* circles around him and slowly builds gathered impressions into a new kind of characterization – one based on the belief that a person's character is always a mysterious thing, changing with time and circumstance, and impossible simply to sum up.

Dynamic and artful, the result was also, to some readers, too insubstantial. Arnold Bennett (a best-selling novelist of the day) accused Woolf of creating characters so elusive they seemed nothing like real people: "[*Jacob's Room*] is packed and bursting with originality, and it is exquisitely written. But the characters do not vitally survive in the mind."[1] To Bennett, Woolf's characters lacked "reality." But she answered back by saying that what "reality" itself meant had changed. Bennett's ideas about character were outdated, she wrote, because modern reality itself had become a question: "He says that it is only if the characters are real that the novel has any chance of surviving. Otherwise, die it must. But, I ask myself, what is reality? And who are the judges of reality?"[2] With reality itself now in question, Woolf felt characterization had to be a matter of speculation rather than assertion, of dynamic experiment rather than standard procedure. So despite Bennett's criticism, she continued to try to "catch the phantom" of modern personality.

But what made Woolf see "reality" this way? It was open to question, she felt, because by 1922 there was no consensus about what really mattered. Once, it had seemed that religion, government, and the rules of social life dictated a certain set of priorities, beliefs, and habits, and these in turn made people see the world similarly. Now, Woolf felt, all relations between people and their institutions had changed, had become diverse, so that there was no longer any common habit of seeing and thinking to keep "reality" clear. Always now reality would be a question – a matter of specific individual perspective and circumstance, something a novelist would need to inquire into rather than presume. Not only Woolf, but all modern novelists, would now make reality itself no longer a given background to fiction but the object of its speculations.

Putting reality in question and falling into fragments; "automatic" sentences and "subjective" voices: these were a few of the things that made the novel modern. What, then, do they tell us about the nature and purpose of the modern novel? First of all, that modern novelists start with the belief that modernization has changed the very nature of reality, and that fiction also has to change its very nature in order to survive. They tell us that the modern novel therefore does things differently – that it sets itself against literary norms and conventions. Experiment, innovation, and improvisation are its hallmarks. New styles and structures are the result, and these are often shocking, surprising, and difficult. But the difficulty has its reasons: often, it makes fiction more like life, or makes the modern reality more subject to awareness, scrutiny, and understanding. Or it aims at making fiction itself as complex, as interesting, and as strange as modern experience. These are some of the fundamental tendencies of the modern novel – some of the reasons for the strange first sentence we find at the beginning of *A Portrait of the Artist*, for the fragmentation of *Cane*, for the new kind of character we find in the pages of *Jacob's Room*.

"The modern novel," then, does not just refer to any and all fiction written in modern times, or to fiction that is recent or new. It refers to something more specific: fiction that experiments with ways to contend with modernity. It refers to fiction that tries for new techniques, new theories, new languages – for the kind of radical "formal" innovation we see in the sentences and structures of Joyce and Toomer, for the new philosophies and psychologies we see in Woolf and Stein. And it refers to fiction that tries for these innovations out of a sense that modernity demands them. With the modern soul in fragments, with human character in question, with the mind a mystery, and with authority now uncertain, fiction had to change, and "the modern novel" refers to fiction that does so gladly, radically, and even with the hope of making a difference. So we might begin here with a simple, tentative definition: "the modern novel" means fiction that tries for something new, in the face of modernity, to reflect, to fathom, or even to redeem modern life.

Now this definition might seem too simple, or too vague. Don't all novels try for something new? Hasn't modernity been provoking them to do so all along? What *is* "modernity," exactly? Why would it make such a difference – and how could *fiction* really "redeem" it?

"Modernity" is the world of the present, adrift from tradition and bound for the future, traumatized by conflict and wracked by doubt; but it is above all a world of change. It is, as the poet Charles Baudelaire put it, "the transient, the fleeting, the contingent."[3] It puts life into perpetual flux, moving it ever onward to new inventions, new ideas, new ways of living, making any moment seem potentially critical. Science and technology every day create new ways to see, work, and think; shifting global politics creates ever new cultures and new conflicts; new generations gladly leave traditions behind. Stable forces are gone: God has died long ago, it seems, and aristocracies have vanished – leaving in place of their traditions only faith in change. Henry Adams – a late descendant of an important American aristocracy – summed up this transition when he wrote of himself, "when he came to ask himself what he truly thought, he felt that he had no Faith . . . That the idea of one Form, Law, Order, or Sequence had no more value for him than the idea of none; that what he valued most was Motion, and that what attracted his mind was Change."[4] This shift from order and stability to change and movement: this was mainly what modernity meant, and it was both alarming and inspiring. Would this new pattern for existence enrich human culture, or destroy it? Would it bring constant progress, dynamic freedom, pure possibility – or shocks and trauma, disaster, conflict, and war? Once it destroyed traditional practices, ceremonies, and habits, and once it broke the sequence of culture, what would replace them? What would follow?

In *All That Is Solid Melts Into Air: The Experience of Modernity*, Marshall Berman puts all this in a stark paradox: "To be modern is to find ourselves in an environment that promises us adventure, power, joy, growth, transformation of ourselves and the world – and, at the same time, that threatens to destroy everything we have, everything we know, everything we are."[5] This environment is precisely what the modern novel tries to map. It charts that environment's new psychological adventures, its transformation of social classes, the joy of its dynamic urban life – but above all the very pattern of change and the new consciousness it creates. For "modernity" had been around for a long time; what was new was the way we now "find ourselves" within it, how "being modern" means keen and all-consuming awareness that life is change, that anything is possible, that destruction might be imminent, and that something new must be created through which to make sense of it all.

To make sense of it all – to celebrate the joy of transformation, to warn against the threat of destruction, to lament what has been lost – modern novelists felt they had to try for something new. Not just new plots and new stories, but new *forms*: not the *what*, but the *how*, is what sets the modern novel apart. As Stephen Spender put it in his *The Struggle of the Modern*,

> The moderns are therefore those who start off by thinking that human nature has changed: or if not human nature, then the relationship of the individual to the environment, forever being metamorphosized . . . This change, recorded by the seismographic senses of the artist, has also to change all relations within arrangements of words or marks on canvas which make a poem or novel, or a painting.[6]

Cultural change demanded also changes in verbal arrangements, in basic styles of expression, and more. The modern novel experiments with everything – and it does so perpetually, out of a sense that forms must keep changing in order to match modernity, to keep people freshly and actively aware of it, and to discover every new possibility modernity might create.

The "formal" difference here is clearest in the way the first modern novels were meant to differ from the norm. To the modern novelist, most of the fiction written around 1900 or 1910 had become stale and pointless, for many reasons. It seemed to take things at the slow and steady pace of a bygone way of life; it seemed to stay on the surface, never going into psychological depth; it seemed inefficient, larded over with verbiage that kept reality away; it told its stories from on high, from the point of view of some impossible, all-knowing, godlike observer; it pretended to tell a seamless story from start to finish; and it always put a positive last spin on things, in neat and tidy endings. Modern novelists wanted to break with these stale traditions. They did not think that *all* novels of the past were pointless: "our quarrel is not with the classics," Virginia Woolf noted, but with the played-out novel of the recent past, since it had failed to keep up with real life. The general consensus among the younger novelists around 1910 was that fiction had to give up on its false coherence, its conventional complacency, its unmodern outlook, if it were to regain meaning and relevance.

So they took the novel and sped up its pace, or made it ebb and flow like real life; they made its sentences as slippery as the movements of the human mind; they let plot go random, told their stories from changing points of view, and began or ended them abruptly. They wrote things like the first line of *Portrait of the Artist*, where Joyce plays with the "once upon a time" beginning to give the feel of life in process, and they wrote books like *Jacob's Room*, which builds character through dynamic impressions rather than slow, objective analysis. They tried everything from automatic diction to bleak new philosophies, from untested narrators to hybrid genres to revolutionary theories of human psychology. All this they did to make the novel a match for modernity not only in its subject-matter and in its themes, but in its very "forms" of perception and expression.

To match modernity, however, was only part of the point, for the modern novelist also wanted to resist it – or even redeem it. The quintessentially modern novel tends to have some redemptive hope within it, some wish to restore meaning or wholeness or beauty to the modern world. Spender called this tendency a "pattern of hope," an "idea that modern art might transform the contemporary environment, and hence, by pacifying and ennobling its inhabitants, revolutionize the world." The hope was that new forms might become new public powers of seeing, new strong ways of feeling despite modernity's technological coldness, or new critical abilities, through which people might see through modernity's lies. Or the hope was that the novel's fine new forms might be a retreat or refuge from modernity – shelter from its destruction. Or perhaps that the novel's new linguistic vigor would give people the words to describe their modern predicaments, or ask for needed changes. What many modern novelists have in common is a tendency to write as if lives depended upon it – as if truthful, meaningful life needed the novelist's imagination, as if true insight into the human mind depended upon the depths into which it can reach, and as if modern freedom could only fully emerge in the rushed and fragmented sentences through which fiction enacts it.

Such a "pattern of hope" is behind what D. H. Lawrence said about the "help" the novel gives:

> The novel is the one bright book of life. Books are not life. They are only tremulations on the ether. But the novel as a tremulation *can* make the whole man-alive tremble . . . To be alive, to be man alive, to be whole man alive: that is the point. And at its best, the novel, and the novel supremely, can help you. It can help you not to be dead man in life.[8]

This redemptive conviction is typical. Not universal: many modern novelists do not necessarily put the "pattern of hope" into their fiction. But for the most part to write modern novels meant to face modernity with a sense that literary form could redeem it – that it could make a supreme difference to the very life of human culture.

Thus our working definition: the modern novel tries for something new, in the face of modernity, with a "pattern of hope" for redemption. There remains much to say, of course, and it will take the rest of this book to begin to explore the modern novel's new forms and its designs upon modern life. But even then our definition might seem questionable, for as we will see, modern novels often fit the definition only in partial or peculiar ways. Some that try to make a difference to modern life hardly seem new in form at all; some that are new in form have little interest in providing the sort of "help" Lawrence describes. And still others are wildly experimental for reasons that seem to have little to do with "modernity." Moreover, as the years pass, some modern novels go unconventional by breaking the conventions of the modern novel itself – by refusing the terms of our preliminary definition. So our definition might at times seem too restrictive. Then again, it might also seem too broad. Perhaps these tendencies are not at all unique to the modern novel. Perhaps fiction of all kinds has always had such motives, and perhaps other forms of art (poetry, film) are even better at carrying them out. We may need more specificity, which can only come in the details of the chapters that follow. But we can

get some more specificity here, if we augment our conceptual definition with a historical one, and see what defines the modern novel's
place in the history of culture.

As we have seen, the novel has always been modern, since it has
always set its sights on the present moment, since it has always gone
for novelty, and since it has always had strong practical impact on the
way people live their lives. *Don Quixote* (1605), often called the first
novel, questions reality, too, and Samuel Richardson's *Pamela* (1740),
an early novel told in the form of letters, immerses us in life's process
at least as much as *Portrait* or *Jacob's Room*. But there came a time when
such tendencies became more deliberate, more self-conscious, and
more essential to the vocation and reputation of novel-writing. In
Portrait and *Jacob's Room* there developed a more deliberate *modernism*
– a concerted and widespread effort to "make it new," and to modernize the practice of fiction. Earlier novels may have been experimental and innovative, but now innovation became the priority, the
requisite sign of a novel's contribution to the vital work of modern
culture.

The modern novel begins in Modernism – but just *when* this beginning took place is open to debate. Some people make it as early as
1857, the year of two foundational works of French Modernism:
Baudelaire's *Les Fleurs du Mal* and Gustave Flaubert's *Madame Bovary*.
Some make it 1901, the year Queen Victoria died, taking with her the
allegedly stultifying traditions of Victorian culture. And some make it
as late as 1914, thinking that World War I was the cataclysmic rupture
that separated the civilized past from a future of chaos. Virginia Woolf
dated the change to 1910, and Cather dated it to 1922, but in any case
it is clear that Modernism (and the modern novel) was in full swing
by the 1922 publication of *Ulysses*, the book that was Joyce's master-
piece and the very encyclopedia of modernist forms.

The "apotheosis" came in 1922: that was Modernism's high point,
and the twenty years or so that followed saw the ascendancy the
modern novel. The 1920s were its most dynamic moment of creativity and influence, as the most surprising and inspiring new works by
Joyce, Toomer, Woolf, and others scandalized and inspired worlds of
readers, scholars, and imitators. The 1930s saw a first backlash, as
political demands called for more hard-headed realism, and writers
scrambled to find ways to make fiction more publicly responsible. And
then with World War II, the worst of modernity seemed to triumph,

leaving novels little recourse. So what peaked in 1922, some people say, did not last long. The "pattern of hope," with its faith in artful experiment, and its belief that modernity could be made subject to literary revision – some people think it did not make it past the horrors of World War II. For who could maintain confidence in the power of art, after what the war taught the world about the power of chaos? Or if the war didn't kill the modern impulse, the job was finished by the postwar culture of nuclear standoffs, rampant commercialism, and dizzying global diversity – all of which had to prove that fiction could hardly face modernity down. This view dates the end of the modern novel roughly to 1939, or 1965, and calls the fiction that follows by other names.

But did the modern impulse really die out around 1939, or 1965? Even if the time for Modernism passed (since Modernism was a specific historical formation, a juncture of specific events and opportunities), might it not be possible that modern fiction could have survived the change, and even drawn strength from it? These are important questions, because some people think that what seemed like endings (the war's horrors, global shifts, anti-aesthetic attitudes, new technologies, "post"modernism) may well have been corrections and new beginnings. Perhaps these things did not kill as much as correct the modern impulse – making it more fully effective, artistic, and responsive. For World War II also changed the map of the world, so that new novels from Africa, India, and elsewhere could begin to frame *their* modernity in new ways, revitalizing fiction and advancing the modern novel by other means. And postmodernism, whose very name seems to mean the end of the modern impulse, may also have meant its replenishment. At first sheerly negative and unserious, very much out of sync with the modern "pattern of hope," postmodernism soon became a resource for the most exuberant imaginings, and perhaps helped to complete projects modern fiction had left unfinished. Perhaps these and other endings were in fact new beginnings; perhaps the modern novel still exists today, not as the dominant thing it was when Modernism held sway, but still active, with many of the same motives, purposes, and effects that have characterized it from the start.

So was it 1857 to 1939 – or is it still going on even today? This book will test both possibilities, by striking a kind of compromise. We will begin right around World War I, when it became fully clear to writers of all kinds that a changing world demanded a new kind of fiction. But to enter this world, we will see it first from the point of view of a writer who stood on the threshold of the old and the new. Henry James published some of the watershed works of modern fiction as early as the 1870s; in 1914, he wrote an essay called "The new novel," in which he surveyed the fiction of the day and predicted the problems in its future. We will begin with James – his foundations and his prognostications – and then widen out to take in the first "modernist" phase of the modern novel, which took it through to the middle of the century, in the works of novelists including Joyce, Woolf, Cather, Toomer, and Stein. These experiments, those done roughly 1914–31, will be our main focus. Once we have learned to appreciate the modern novel's vast array of possibilities, we will learn to question them. And then we will see how they are likewise questioned, transformed, and replenished in the novels of future moments. In the fiction of George Orwell, Christopher Isherwood, and John Steinbeck, the fiction of the 1930s and 1940s, we will see how politics questioned aesthetic hopes and stressed the novel's realism; in fiction by Jean Rhys, V. S. Naipaul, and Chinua Achebe, the fiction of the 1950s and 1960s, we will see how new political awakenings made the modern novel more fully responsive to whole worlds of change. We will see Modernism's technical and philosophical experiments redouble in postmodern writing by Samuel Beckett, Thomas Pynchon, Jeanette Winterson, Salman Rushdie, and others; and we will follow less extreme trends as well, in which the modern novel refined and renewed its powers of ethical exploration, its effects on social justice, its essential rebelliousness, and its powers to vie with modernity.

But before we begin, one last recapitulation of what it means for a novel to be modern. It means facing the problems and possibilities of modernity – the technological wonders, the social disorder, the psychological mysteries, the pattern of change – and making them fiction's main challenge and inspiration. It means facing modernity in new experimental forms of writing, and it tends to mean doing so with faith that aesthetic forms can make a difference to the way people see, think, and live. It probably means something now paradoxically old – something that began almost two hundred years ago (when modernity first seemed to have become a total problem), peaked in 1922 with *Ulysses* and other modernist triumphs, and ended once aesthetic idealism proved no match for postwar modern life. But it may mean something still: as we will see, novels might yet be modern, or the forms of the old modern novel might yet be vital to culture today.

CHAPTER 1

When and Why: The Rise of the Modern Novel

The "New Novel," circa 1914

He was "the master": that was what young writers called Henry James, who was, by 1900 or so, master of the art of fiction. Not only had he mastered the art; in a sense, he also made it, by helping to prove that fiction was in fact an art-form. It hadn't always been so: before the day of James's early novels – *Washington Square* and *The Portrait of a Lady*, for example, published in 1880–1 – people did not tend to put fiction on a par with poetry, music, or painting. Those were serious arts; the novel, by contrast, was something less – entertaining, and edifying in its way, but not art. But by the 1880s this had begun to change, particularly in the work of one writer often called the father of modern fiction: Gustave Flaubert. In *Madame Bovary* (1857) and other works, Flaubert showed James and the rest of the world that fiction could become a matter of fine artistic planning and execution – of stories intensely imagined, carefully framed, ambiguous in meaning, and intricate in their philosophical designs. This deliberate artistry was of course also at work elsewhere, for example in the Russian writer Ivan Turgenev, whose *Fathers and Sons* (1862) brought to the novel a new intensity of emotion, a newly precise kind of observation, a perfect combination of the complex and the simple, and a bracing nihilism; in the English novelist George Eliot, whose *Middlemarch* (1871) made society's structures an object of keen scientific and moral scrutiny; in the American writer Nathaniel Hawthorne, whose *The Scarlet Letter* (1850) gave fiction's emotional life rich new symbolic and dramatic power. These and other self-consciously artful writers were great influences on Henry James when he set out to elevate fiction to the higher status it would enjoy as a form of modern art. Which he did not just by writing beautiful books, but by explaining exactly how fiction could *transform* life.

In an essay called "The art of fiction" (1884), James wrote that fiction could even create reality, or add to its significance, and that it deserved "aesthetic" status. He insisted that "fiction is one of the *fine* arts, deserving in its turn all the honours and emoluments that have been hitherto reserved for the successful profession of music, poetry, painting, architecture," and by saying why and how, he reflected a turning point in the history of fiction.[1] Specifically, he pushed the point implied in the imaginative intensity and fine scrutiny of Flaubert, Eliot, and others: that fiction was not just an entertaining description of life, but something that could "compete with life" and improve upon it, capture life for finer purposes. This exaltation – this new mission for the fictional imagination – was crucial to the birth of the modern novel, because it meant fiction could redeem life, by refining, enriching, or intensifying it. As others came to agree with James, or to come to similar conclusions by other means, the novel would transform, from a familiar form of entertainment into a forum for new realities.

What James himself did toward this end was enrich the "consciousness" of the novel. Never before had a novelist ventured so far into the heads of characters, and never had a novelist so much to report about the complexity, subtlety, and limitlessness of what he found there. Less artful fiction would spend much less time with characters' thoughts and feelings, and far more time on plot. Indeed, thoughts and feelings would come up only insofar as they could advance the story. But in James's fiction, "consciousness" was itself the important story. For him – and for many novelists of the future – fiction had meaning only to the extent that its characters were "finely aware and richly responsible," and only to the extent that the novelist could trace all the details of their fine mental awareness. "Their being finely aware . . . *makes* absolutely the intensity of their adventure, gives the maximum of sense to what befalls them," and endows the novel with the richest reality.[2]

One provocation of James's interest in consciousness was contemporary psychology's new theory of mind. Psychology had begun to see thought in a new way, less as a matter of deliberate units of attention and more as an unconscious, mixed flow. In *Principles of Psychology* (1890) by William James (Henry's brother, and Gertrude Stein's teacher), consciousness is described as "of a teeming multiplicity of objects and relations," flowing like a stream: "Consciousness, then, does not appear to itself chopped up in bits . . . It is nothing jointed; it flows. A 'river' or a 'stream' are the metaphors by which it is most naturally described. *In talking of it hereafter, let us call it the stream of thought, of consciousness, or of subjective life.*"[3] This way of thinking about consciousness influenced Henry James's sense of its complexity (though the influence probably worked in the other direction as well), and as we will see it would later encourage writers to write in a "stream of consciousness" style. And this way of thinking became the dominant one in psychology, which now saw mental life as something far more obscure and fluid, far less even and coherent, than people had presumed it to be. Thoughts built themselves up out of sensations and perceptions in precarious ways; desires were often unknown to those who felt them, or likely to change in unpredictable ways. As Judith Ryan says in *The Vanishing Subject: Early Psychology and Literary Modernism*, although it had once seemed stable, now "the self [was] no more than a bundle of sensory impressions precariously grouped together and constantly threatened with possible dissolution."[4] These new psychological discoveries posed a problem: if the mind was now less subject to coherent and straightforward explanations, how did you describe it? Fiction gave an answer. Fiction, in fact, seemed in some ways to be the best place to develop the styles and perspectives necessary to illustrate and communicate the strange life of the mind.

The modern novel developed new ways to dramatize thought, to pattern out slippery sequences of feeling, to get behind eyes limited by moral blindness or keen with insight; it developed the new styles and tactics necessary to do justice to the mind's "dissolving" complexity. These James brought to bear – in *The Ambassadors* (1903), for example, one of his last great works. The plot of *The Ambassadors* is fairly simple. A young American man has gone to Europe and, to the dismay of his family, not come back. Another man is sent to retrieve him (to serve, that is, as the family's ambassador). The second man, however, is bewitched by Europe as well, and does not do his job: he stays too.

Beyond this minimal plot, however, there is a maximum of psychological inquiry. Motivations, feelings, decisions, and speculations come in for descriptions of endless nuance.

For example, early in the novel, when Lambert Strether has first arrived in Europe, he meets an old friend, and through "deep consciousness of the bearing of his companion," comes to a series of "finely aware" realizations. What he perceives about her is her "expensive subdued suitability" – the way she seems to have made excellent choices, which tell Strether he might do the same. Just before this moment, he has been newly aware of the need to put himself together; after it, he senses he will know better how to do so:

> Nothing could have been odder than Strether's sense of himself as at that moment launched in something of which the sense would be quite disconnected from the sense of his past and which was literally beginning there and then. It had begun in fact already . . . with a sharper survey of the elements of Appearance than he had for a long time been moved to make. He had during those moments felt these elements to be not so much to his hand as he should have liked, and then had fallen back on the thought that they were precisely a matter as to which help was supposed to come for what he was about to do. He was about to go up to London, so that hat and necktie might wait. What had come as straight to him as a ball in a well-played game – and caught moreover not less neatly – was just the air, in the person of his friend, of having seen and chosen, the air of achieved possession of those vague qualities and quantities that collectively figured to him as the advantage snatched from lucky chances.

Strether's fine consciousness catches the air of his friend's perfection and plans some more perfect future for himself; major changes happen in minute discriminations. These movements in his mind are much more important than his real trip to London. The voyages of consciousness replace any real journeys as the focus of the story, and James proves his point about the art of fiction, for once the "real" story gets replaced by plots of the mind, fiction becomes a more aesthetically intense "adventure."

But the "real" story does not really get replaced. It is just that the sense of what is "real" has changed. James's novels are not mental fantasies; in fact, in the depths of the human mind, they find a more profound reality. This is typical: the modern novel begins here as an effort not only to make fiction an art, but to make the art of fiction a better measure of reality. For James, this combination mainly meant "consciousness," and how it could refine psychological truth. Art got finer, and reality richer, each in turn. For James's contemporaries, this same kind of combination happened in different ways.

Joseph Conrad also widened the scope of the novel in these opposite directions, but for him the result was a kind of fiction more aesthetically vivid and more actively political. Conrad took the novel to Africa, to Malaysia, to South America, and used it as a way of reporting back on imperialism's corruption of western ideals. Most famously in *Heart of Darkness* (1902), Conrad revealed the evils of imperial exploitation and aggression, showing how principles that seemed fine "at home" were annihilating forces for corruption in the imperial powers' "outposts of progress." But these bracingly modern revelations would not have made for modern novels were it not for the particular approach Conrad cultivated. He felt that too much fiction lacked vivacity. He thought that its job, first and foremost, was to describe true physical and sensory life in vivid detail – and that everything else could only follow from that. He felt that fiction demanded "a single-minded attempt to render the highest kind of justice to the visible universe, by bringing to light the truth, manifold and one, underlying its every aspect"; his task, he wrote, was "by the power of the written word, to make you hear, to make you feel – it is, before all, to make you *see*." Only if a novelist really tried to "make you see" could he make you understand and believe, and so Conrad paid elaborate attention to the conjuring of vivid sensory images. These, he felt, could not only make you understand and believe, but also make you feel that you belong. They could produce in the world of readers a sense of *solidarity* – of human togetherness, that "latent feeling of fellowship with all creation" – and perhaps in that way fiction could counteract (in its form) the problems of evil Conrad saw around the world. It was in this combination of political content and sensory form – vivid seeing resulting in "solidarity" – that Conrad's fiction set out to reflect the modern world and yet also to shape it.[5]

What "outposts of progress" were to Conrad, the world of wealth was to Edith Wharton. In a very different place, she too saw corruption and annihilation: in elite America, where all values seemed to have given way to that of money alone. In *The House of Mirth* (1905), a beautiful young woman waits a little too long to get married.

Marriage for Lily Bart is a pressing concern, however, because she does not have much money, and her elite social world demands it. But she stalls, not wanting to marry for money, and she stalls too long, with disastrous results: bad luck not only keeps her unwed, but sinks her into poverty, and brings her to the point of fully tragic desperation. Having her ideal young woman fall so low, Wharton stresses the inhumanity and the danger in this economic system, and the particular vulnerability of women, for whom the dangers are greatest. Wharton takes on the modern problem of "materialism," a frequent preoccupation of modern novelists worried about the dehumanizing effects of modern economic forces. But her criticisms are not entirely realistic: "art" comes in here, too, as she clashes together two different *forms* of life. In *The House of Mirth*, a world of grace runs up against a materialist fatalism. On the one hand, Lily is "like some rare flower grown for exhibition, a flower from which every bud had been nipped except the crowning blossom of her beauty," but on the other hand she is a "mere spindrift in the whirling surface of existence." She is beauty made subject to the machine; and it is this combining of forms – the unlikely subjection of high beauty to low mechanism – that makes a modern novel out of the horror of modern materialism.

What we see here in the beginnings of the modern novel, then, are not just life's new, modern realities. Although the modern realities of psychology, of imperialism, of materialism did provoke James, Conrad, and Wharton to write their books, these writers tried to reimagine those things, and to change fiction, too, in the process. Here again is this *balance*, which we might now describe as something essential to the modern novel: a *dialectical* relationship, a fundamental back-and-forth, in which the realities of modernity make the novel more artful, and then the artful techniques developed give back new realities.

What James, Conrad, and Wharton helped begin, other writers were eager to follow up. The future of the novel looked good: so James himself thought, in 1914, when he wrote an essay about "The new novel" of the moment. And yet James also felt that he had reason to worry about the future of fiction. The new fiction seemed to him marvelously rich in new, modern detail, in new realities, but something seemed to be missing. He praised the new fiction because "it gives us the 'new' . . . as an appetite for closer notation, a sharper specification of the signs of life, of consciousness, of the human scene"; but it also prompted him to ask: "where is the interest itself?" In other words, there was an impressive "appetite for notation," a powerful way of "hugging the shore of the real," and this made the new fiction more exciting and more real than fiction had ever been before. But it lacked the "higher reference" necessary to be meaningful, purposeful, and artistic. It was all just details – realities unchanged by, unsubjected to, the imaginative forms of art.[6] The *dialectic* was not clearly there, and without it, fiction writers were letting modernity swamp fiction and undo its "higher" duties. James hit upon the problem that would trouble the modern novel for all the years to come. As modernity multiplies new, strange, fascinating realities, how should the novel take them all in without losing shape? How to balance life with art – imagination with reality? As experimentation and change take over, how do you guarantee that the novel does not lose touch with a "higher" purpose? Or does it really matter if it does?

These questions lead us to the modern novel's characteristic middle ground. It is possible to say that modernity essentially unbalances things that once went harmoniously together. We might use James's terms and call these things "appetite for notation" (on the one hand) and the need for "higher reference" on the other – life's details and its meaning, the realities and the ideals. These opposites have become more and more distant from each other as modernity has advanced. Faith, meaning, and other idealisms become less available; the realities and details of life become, at the other end, less manageable and less explicable. As these aspects of life draw further away, and draw further apart, it becomes ever more difficult to reconcile the extremes of human thought, feeling, and culture.

This is where the modern novel comes in. According to one very influential theory of fiction, it has always been the mission of the novel to suggest ways of reconciliation, to teach us "how to do justice to a chaotic, viscously contingent reality, and yet redeem it." In *The Sense of an Ending*, Frank Kermode speaks of a "tension between paradigmatic form and contingent reality" – to describe just this problem in which practical realities are hard to reconcile with ideal paradigms. And he says that narrative fiction exists to find the balance between the two patterns of human life: the pattern of *contingencies* (things that happen by chance, due to real circumstances) and the pattern of *providence* (order, larger purpose, ideal rules). According to Kermode, the balance shifts in different directions, depending upon the moods of the times. For the modern novel, the balance became far harder to strike, for the reasons we have already noted. "Contingencies" were so much more extreme, plentiful, and chancy; "providence" was so much harder to find, believe in, or conceptualize. Nevertheless, the modern novel tries to explore each and to put each in touch with the other. The modern novel tries to build bridges, to make art and life enrich each other, to find providence in contingency, and to ground ideals in reality. It tries for what we might call a *redemptive dialectic*, a reciprocal linkage of art and life, that might keep modernity from breaking our worlds apart.[7]

Seven Modern Novelists

Henry James's comments on the future of the novel came, of course, the year that future got off to a perilous start. World War I put modernity into crisis – or showed how terrible a crisis modernity could be. New powers of technological destruction made themselves shockingly and horribly felt, and old traditions seemed powerless to stop them. Just a few years before, culture had seemed to reach new heights of civilization, inspiring advances in all areas of human endeavor, making peace and prosperity seem permanent. But World War I changed all that, proving that modernity's civilized side was well matched by potential for great chaos and evil. The war's violence was unprecedented, its causes absurd, and the result was profound disillusionment. As Paul Fussell writes in *The Great War and Modern Memory*, the war even "reversed the Idea of Progress," leading Henry James to say that "the plunge of civilization into this abyss of blood and darkness . . . is a thing that so gives away the whole long age during which we supposed the world to be . . . gradually bettering."[8] In *Rites of Spring: The Great War and the Birth of the Modern Age*, Modris Eksteins notes that even "the integrity of the 'real' world, the visible and ordered world, was undermined."[9] Everything was called into question, not just the war itself but all ideals, and even reality itself. For the war made it all seem like a lie. "Civilization" was false, modernity was dangerous, and truth seemed to demand some new way of seeing and understanding the world.

This need was perhaps the primary cause of the modern novel's radical innovations. Fiction would have to change utterly, if the very integrity of the real world had been undermined. But there were also positive reasons for change; people found reason to delight in modernity's opportunities. Old rules – about sex and race, about home life, art, and propriety – were giving way to new ones, in which freedom, self-realization, and creativity seemed more possible. This change was what Virginia Woolf had in mind when she said that "human character changed": "All human relations have shifted – those between masters and servants, husbands and wives, parents and children. And when human relations change there is at the same time a change in religion, conduct, politics, and literature." An example, Woolf said, was "in the character of one's cook," who used to be confined to the basement kitchen, but was now "a creature of sunshine and fresh air" – now far more free.[10] And another example might be the new life for African Americans, described by Alain Locke as the "dramatic flowering of a new race-spirit," in which "Negro life is not only establishing new contacts and founding new centers, it is finding a new soul."[11] Such positive changes were at issue, too, and they were equally the cause of the modern novel's radical new forms.

Because the world had utterly changed, writing could not go on as before; due to the war and to new social relations, "even basic descriptive nouns . . . had lost all power to capture reality."[12] Old plots could not include the new experiences modernity offered up, and old styles of description could not get at the feelings and landscapes modernity created. Hypocrisies needed to be exposed, technological developments had to be interpreted, and even the very basis of civilization had to be rethought. New questions, new subjects, new perceptions had to remake fiction, and new forms were needed to make the changes possible. For airplanes now flew overhead, sometimes dropping bombs, sometimes writing in the sky, but fiction still went on as if life's sounds and spectacles were those of the nineteenth century. The eye now had to take in all the fragments and all the faces crushed together in the modern metropolis, but fiction still went on as if life put things and people all in their proper places. So fiction had to change. It had to *modernize*, and find ways to say what the modern eye now saw, to interpret modern experience, and perhaps even to help shape its chaos into better forms of life.

What would it mean to modernize fiction? How would you make it more responsive to these aspects of modern life? One of the first writers to attempt to answer these questions was Virginia Woolf, whose essays on modern fiction tried to explain how novels might capture modern realities. We will turn now to her sense of how fiction ought to change, and that of some of her fellow modernists, surveying quickly their main ideas and major novels, in preparation for the more detailed explanations that come in the chapters that follow.

When she wrote "Modern fiction" (1919), Woolf had just begun writing novels herself, but had found no good models for writing about the new world around her. What existed, she felt, were books still working with the conventions of a bygone era, wholly unsuited to the new rhythms and textures of life. In particular, it seemed to her, these books just concerned themselves pointlessly with *material things*. To describe a modern person, most fiction just wrong-headedly ticked off all the things in that person's environment, as if this sort of thoroughness were all. Most books were full of houses and clothes and furniture but empty of *life*; they did nothing to convey the feel of modern life ongoing, the definitive quality of a person, or the changing forms of human relationships. Modern life had become so much more a matter of speed and dynamic change; people had become so different, and so much more mysterious to each other; what people meant to each other bore little relationship to what they had meant even a few years before. Life had changed so much – indeed, had come to be *about* change – but fiction had not. It was stale, and worst of all it was so weighted down with things that it could not at all convey the fleeting, transient feel the world had taken on. The typical novel of 1910 made Woolf ask, is "life . . . like this after all?" She answered "no," and insisted that the modern novel now had to try to render the *impressions* that had made life a matter of change, confusion, and fantastic new intensity:

> The mind, exposed to the ordinary course of life, receives upon its surface a myriad impressions – trivial, fantastic, evanescent, or engraved with the sharpness of steel. From all sides they come, an incessant shower of innumerable atoms, composing in their sum what we might venture to call life itself . . . Is it not perhaps the chief task of the novelist to convey this incessantly varying spirit?[13]

Straight facts and fixed things would have to surrender to impressions and essences, to the dynamic feel of life in process, and to a sense of the way "life itself" animates human being.

Impressions and essences enliven facts and things in Woolf's *Mrs Dalloway* (1925). For the most part the novel's factual story is minimal: it is just an ordinary life on an ordinary day – specifically, daily life on the day that Clarissa Dalloway is throwing a party. Not much happens, on the outside. Mrs Dalloway makes her preparations, and as these put her in contact with family, friends, and strangers, we follow their daily lives as well. But beneath and around ordinary facts and things, impressions and essences swirl. There, nothing is ordinary, for dynamic changes and intense feelings convey the intensity of modern life. As she makes her way about London, Mrs Dalloway becomes a super-sensitive register of a world in flux. In her first plunge into the streets of London, for example, we see Woolf's way of giving impressions of life:

> For having lived in Westminster – how many years now? over twenty, – one feels even in the midst of the traffic, or waking at night, Clarissa was positive, a particular hush, or solemnity; an indescribable pause; a suspense (but that might be her heart, affected, they said, by influenza) before Big Ben strikes. There! Out it boomed. First a warning, musical; then the hour, irrevocable. The leaden circles dissolved in the air. Such fools we are, she thought, crossing Victoria Street. For Heaven only knows why one loves it so, how one sees it so, making it up, building it round one, tumbling it, creating it every moment afresh . . . In people's eyes, in the swing, tramp, and trudge; in the bellow and the uproar; the carriages, motor cars, omnibuses, vans, sandwich men shuffling and swinging; brass bands; barrel organs; in the triumph and the jingle and the strange high singing of some aeroplane overhead was what she loved; life; London; this moment of June.

The impressions Mrs Dalloway gets, and the essential meanings she discovers in the movements and mysteries of an "ordinary" day, lay bare the essential forms of modern life, the psychological realities beneath it. Felt life, the sense of the moment, dynamic imaginings, "how one sees it so" – these experiential bearings are Woolf's way of freeing fiction from the needless documentation, the inert details, the false judgments to her so dissatisfying in the typical novel of 1910.

Another writer eager to make modern fiction more true to life was Ford Madox Ford. Ford also found too much fiction deplorably fake.

In particular, he felt that too many novels failed to tell stories the way stories are really told: "The novelist from, say, Richardson to Meredith thought he had done his job when he had set down a simple tale beginning with the birth of his hero or his heroine and ending when the ring of marriage bells completed the simple convention. But the curious thing was that he never gave a thought to how stories are actually told."[14] The novelist had tended to tell stories evenly and clearly from start to finish, but when we tell stories, we jump around in time and space, single out some things and neglect others, and often describe our wishes rather than what has actually happened. Ford wanted to make fiction better reflect that actuality, and so he made it more "the record of the impression of a moment" than a "corrected chronicle," of momentary feelings rather than objective realities, all in narratives that haphazardly followed the looping and jagged paths of memory and desire.[15]

Ford's most famous book, *The Good Soldier* (1915), tells its story through the point of view of a man who, sadly, gets it all wrong. He has thought himself a happy man in a happy marriage. As his story unfolds, however, it becomes clear that he has been tragically mistaken, and that the appearance of decency has masked a reality of deceit. His problem is he cannot get things straight, and this is clear in the difficulty he has even telling his story: "I don't know how it is best to put this thing down – whether it would be better to try and tell the story from the beginning, as if it were a story; or whether to tell it from this distance of time." He decides to *try* to tell it from the beginning, but of course, since life is a matter of impressions rather than "corrected chronicles," the story we get is wholly out of order, wholly confused, and, as a result, completely true to life.

There were other ways to make fiction more vital. D. H. Lawrence, for example, thought that the new reality of the novel ought to be the real life of the body – its visceral, sexual, and even violent feelings and experiences. He felt that modern humanity had lost its vitality because it had lost touch with physical being; people had become divided: "I carry a whole waste-paper basket of ideas at the top of my head, and in some other part of my anatomy, the dark continent of my self, I have a whole stormy chaos of 'feelings.'" Lawrence felt that fiction could help solve this problem by grounding itself in felt life. Grounded in more basic physical feeling, the novel could aid in undoing what Lawrence saw as the fundamental modern mistake: the excess rationality, separating mind from body, which had detached intellectual life from its embodied sources: "How shall we ever begin to educate ourselves in the feelings? . . . [W]e can look in the real novels, and there listen in. Not listen to the didactic statements of the author, but to the low, calling cries of the characters, as they wander in the dark woods of their destiny."[16] Stressing embodiment – in its imagery, its description of motives, its sexual detail – the modern novel could undo this bad "dualism," and thereby be both a new source of redemption and a return to primitive authenticity.

These redemptive links among the primitive, the physical, the irrational are the modern framework of Lawrence's *Women in Love* (1920). The novel's apparent concerns are traditional enough: sisters fall in love and try to balance the claims of their relationships with their need for independence; their lovers try in various ways to claim them, and compete with each other; and in the process Lawrence explores the psychology of love and desire. Desire, however, is here far more brutal than it had been in traditional fiction. Brutality is attractive, love is irrational, violence seems sexual – and this is good. For example, when one of the sisters first sees her future lover, "she experienced a keen paroxysm, a transport, as if she had made some incredible discovery, known to nobody else on earth. A strange transport took possession of her, all her veins were in a paroxysm of violent sensation." At first strange, this becomes clearly a sign of those "low, calling cries" of the body Lawrence thinks we must learn to heed. And then as the novel proceeds Lawrence implies that true human motives are often destructive, sadistic, and perverse, and that honest modern fiction ought to present them that way without flinching. To modernize fiction meant to make it more primitive, out of a sense that modernity's worst effect was its "dissociation of sensibility" – the way it detached people's minds from their physical and emotional motivations.

Not all of the first modern novelists saw modernity as cause to welcome in confusion, disorder, or unreason. Willa Cather – the American writer whose novels most often glorified the American West – saw modern life more simply as an opportunity to "defurnish" fiction. In 1924, she wrote an essay, "The novel démeublé," in which she declared that "the novel, for a long while, has been overfurnished," overstuffed with things that blocked its vision. And to make such things as the American landscape once again open to view, Cather held, it would be necessary to "throw all the furniture out of the window," to get back to the bare essentials, so that "out of the teeming, gleaming stream of the present" fiction could "select the essential materials of art."[17] Like Woolf and Ford, she felt fiction needed to pare away the conventions of writing that could no longer get stories across, and this selectivity was an essential motivation for many writers of the moment. Writers who wanted to make a difference agreed that the clutter had to be cleared; that it was time to get back to basics; and that only by being light, quick, or flexible, and even fragmentary, incomplete, or spare, could fiction get into the kind of shape necessary for it to vie with modernity.

Sometimes, this meant making modern writing more *simple*. Ernest Hemingway is best known for paring sentences down, and making the barest bones the sparest embodiment of modern life. His approach to the modern meant sentences like these (from "Up in Michigan" [1923]):

> Liz liked Jim very much. She liked it the way he walked over from the shop and often went to the kitchen door to watch for him to start down the road. She liked it about his mustache. She liked it about how white his teeth were when he smiled. She liked it very much that he didn't look like a blacksmith.

Here, modernization means sharp and simple clarity. For the most part, however, to be modern meant to be difficult. As T. S. Eliot put it, "Our civilization comprehends great variety and complexity, and this variety and complexity, playing upon a refined sensibility, must produce various and complex results," so that literature of the modern moment "must be difficult."[18] To shake the world out of its complacency, to force it to see things in new ways, many writers felt it was necessary to make it hard for readers to find easy pleasure in fiction. Or even more importantly, they felt it necessary to make the language of fiction as complex as the chaos of modern life. They thought that the experience of reading, even the very relationship among the words on a page, should mimic the disorienting experience of modern living. And so we get the broken, obscure, streaming stories of William Faulkner, whose *The Sound and the Fury* (1929) is a model of modern difficulty.

In Faulkner's novel, the Compson family has fallen to pieces: long in decline from its genteel Southern eminence, wrecked by scandal,

drink, and madness, it has devolved into a generation of brothers des-
perately obsessed in one way or another with the past, and with the
disgrace of their sister. Each section of the book takes us into the head
of a different brother, into psychic worlds of mental retardation, sui-
cidal depression, and vengeful mania, with such immediacy that the
reading becomes as difficult as these states themselves. Faulkner knew
that an immediate relation to modern madness would mean that
fiction would have to risk insane literary structures. He had to have
the groundwork of his story "laid by the idiot, who was incapable of
relevancy,"[19] even if it meant obscuring his story in utter difficulty.
Form would have to follow content, even into incomprehensibility, if
the novel were to truly become as strange as what it would describe.

Faulkner's difficulty had psychological justifications. Sometimes, the
justifications for difficulty in the modern novel were more social, or
more aesthetic. They were social in Jean Toomer's *Cane* (1922), one of
the most experimental works of literature published during the Harlem
Renaissance, that explosion of creative activity that remade black
America in the 1920s. As we have seen, *Cane* jumbles together diverse
forms of writing and diverse stories, images, and moods, containing
them all in a loose plot of migration among the geographic spaces of
African-American life. Things hang together very little because the elements of African-American identity cannot be unified in art: this is the
problem finally described by the novel's only real protagonist, as he
laments the disorganization in his soul. Difficult form follows social
trouble, as the dislocation of black identity becomes a matter of literary disintegration. To modernize the novel here meant making it
disintegrate to match African-American culture, so that the gaps,
fragments, and ambiguities of the one would directly express those of
the other.

In *Cane*, *The Sound and the Fury*, *Mrs Dalloway*, and others, we have
an initial sampling of the intentions behind some of the first modern
novels. Before we turn now to explore more fully the forms and techniques these intentions created, we need to pause over one last
example. The quintessential modern novel – the one that combines all
of these intentions, and others – is James Joyce's *Ulysses* (1922). To
reflect the intensity, dynamism, and confusion of ordinary life; to catch
its fleeting impressions; to get at the essence of life, too, and to return
to the more physical realities; to explore the psychologies of madness
and desire; to break fiction into fragments, to defurnish it, and yet also

to make it as difficult as modernity: *Ulysses* shares these intentions with its contemporaries, but then also makes these intentions achieve the modern novel's two most overarching goals. *Ulysses* was in many ways the book that started it all – inspiring *Mrs Dalloway*, for example, and encouraging modern writers everywhere as it appeared serially from 1918 to 1922 and then in new editions for decades afterwards. It was also a book that right away reached the farthest poles of modernist ambition, evoking realities more intense than any novel had yet achieved, and designing new forms more original than novels had yet imagined.

Ulysses is, like *Mrs Dalloway*, relatively plotless. Over the course of its thousand pages it narrates nothing very dramatic; it is a story of Dublin life on an ordinary day, focused mainly through the thoughts of two men. Stephen Dedalus (a young, intense intellectual, idealistic but disaffected, impressive but lost) and Leopold Bloom (his older counterpart, a Jewish outsider, engaged by his job in advertising but alienated from his wife, who cheats on him this very day) wander about Dublin, from work to the streets to the bars, encountering various Dubliners in various establishments and finally striking up a friendship before heading home. In strong contrast to the heroics of the epic poem from which *Ulysses* gets its name, these ordinary activities show us just how far modern culture has fallen from the greatness of cultures past. But then again the ordinary activities become epic in their own way. This ordinary day takes in all of life, all of language; it is encyclopedic, comprehensive, and insofar as Dedalus and Bloom survive it, they are real heroes after all. Each chapter of the novel finds a new way to describe a world of explosive possibility; each chapter, that is, is like a modern novel of its own, focused on an aspect of modernity and formed in some new style. This scope makes *Ulysses* the epitome of the modern novel's two overarching goals: taking in new realities so comprehensively, *Ulysses* epitomizes the modern novel's effort to reflect modern life; doing so with such encyclopedic attention to many forms of writing, it epitomizes the modern novel's aesthetic renewal. Comprehensively real and exhaustively reflexive, *Ulysses* sums up modern fiction, and marks a good place to sum up this first pass at what it meant for fiction to modernize. Mainly, it meant making fiction capacious enough to take in the full chaos of modern life, but then also making it artful enough to ensure that literature could be equal to the reality.

Exactly how it meant all this – and how *Ulysses* and other novels show it – will be the concern of the next three chapters of this book. We will turn now to see exactly how Joyce, Woolf, Faulkner, Cather, Ford, Lawrence, Toomer, and a host of other writers modernized specific aspects of the novel. We will go from questions of plotting, closure, and realism to questions of character and symbolism; to the modes of narration for representing modern consciousness, the way time fragments in modern fiction, and the specific things that make this fiction productively difficult; and finally we will get to open questions, the uncertainties and unfinished business of the modern novel in its first forms, in preparation for what forms come next.

CHAPTER 2

"What is Reality?": The New Questions

When the moderns took it up, the novel had long been a form of *realism*. Its main goal had been to create the illusion of real life in action. As Ian Watt writes in his study of "the rise of the novel," it aimed at a "full and authentic report of human experience," an "air of total authenticity," with "verisimilitude" as its proof of success.[1] But this "formal realism" (this making form mimic reality) had really always really been a set of conventions. That is, the novel may have seemed just to present reality directly, but it always did so based on some shared set of norms, some customary way of seeing, particular to the times. Modernity exposed this "conventionality": it became clear to writers like Woolf, Cather, and Lawrence that "realism" was arbitrary – not some sure, timeless, perfect way to describe life in action, but odd techniques dependent on the priorities and preferences of the moment. Moreover, modernity put the priorities and preferences of the modern moment into a perpetual state of change. In the past, traditional social, religious, and scientific frameworks might have given reality a certain backing – enough consensus to make "human experience" seem regular and knowable. But modernity had replaced them with change, and replaced consensus with questions.

So whereas writers of the past might have thought they could take a certain "reality" for granted and get right to the work of writing, modern writers had to pause at the outset and self-consciously ask: what *is* "reality," exactly – and how do we know it? And how do we go about providing a "full and authentic report" of it?

These questions about reality might be clarified in a metaphor. Stendhal (the nineteenth-century French author of *The Red and the*

Black [1830]) once described the novel as a kind of *mirror*, passing along a road and reflecting the life around it: "A novel is a mirror carried along a high road. At one moment it reflects the blue skies, at another the mud of the puddles at your feet." The modern novelist wanted to carry on this tradition of broad reflection, but became even more concerned with questioning it. How did this reflection work? Could the mirror reflect reality perfectly? Might it not be more interesting, and more necessary, to examine the mirror itself rather than carry it with a confidence modernity would no longer permit?

Even in Stendhal's day such questions began to be asked, but with the rise of the modern novel it became fully clear that the questions were themselves the thing. They *remained* questions, meant not to be answered but enacted, in fiction that almost always devotes itself to posing reality not as a fact but as a problem. As Eugene Jolas (1927) put it, "we are no longer interested in the photography of events," but in exploring the process of picturing, the way events are framed.[2] Whatever the particular plot or theme of any particular modern novel, beneath it all is this fundamental questioning – this interest in wondering what makes things real to us. Questioning reality transformed realism in the modern novel, producing a *new* realism based strangely on doubt about reality itself.

Three fundamental attitudes follow from this fundamental questioning: *skepticism, relativism,* and *irony.* Skepticism here does not necessarily mean doubt (although doubt is a major mood of the modern novel). It means testing truths, inquiring into fundamentals, never resting content with explanations. It means not accepting givens – not presuming that life works a certain way – but resisting presumptions, scrutinizing what is given, looking beneath foundations. Skepticism means that the modern novel tends almost to work backwards. It does not proceed from some given starting point into a story; rather, it works back from the starting point to see how we got there, to see what has led to the "reality" from which our stories depart. This is not to say that modern novels are always "philosophical." It means that they are mainly about the problem of knowing what reality matters most, and why. And it also means that they no longer presume that there are any "absolute" truths. Truth, now, is relative – not a transcendent, permanent, god-given certainty, but a matter of how you see it.

And at worst, if truth recedes entirely, if there is a great difference between lost truths and bad realities, irony results. Irony – the bleak difference between what is and what ought to be, the wry gap between what is said on the surface and what is really meant – is often the end-point of the modern novel, where questioning and skepticism lead ultimately to the dismal discovery that things are very much not what they seem.

Beneath all the drama of *The Good Soldier*, for example, is the basic question: how do we know the truth about our lives? What is the reality – and what is illusion? Whose truth is the real truth? Such questions come up when John Dowell is forced to revisit what he thought had been a happy life. When that apparently good life turns out to have been rotten at the core, Dowell has to wonder: what is the reality – the way things seemed, or the way they were? He asks: "If for nine years I have possessed a goodly apple that is rotten at the core and discover its rottenness only in nine years and six months less four days, isn't it true to say that for nine years I possessed a goodly apple?" This kind of question really becomes the point of the novel. *The Good Soldier* may be about adultery, betrayal, hypocrisy, but more fundamentally it is about reality itself and how we make it up. It is about how truths vary, depending upon different perspectives, and how life is essentially the process of testing them.

Such testing tends to happen in the modern novel in four key ways. Modern novelists tend, first of all, to concern themselves with the difference between *appearance and reality*. Second, they tend to wonder about the difference between *subjective and objective* perception. They search for *essential* meanings, in the hope that these might replace the structures of belief and custom that modernity has destroyed. And finally modern novelists begin to become self-conscious about the way fiction works as a form for the *mediation* or interpretation of reality.

At one point in *Ulysses*, Stephen Dedalus does an experiment: he closes his eyes, and tries to see what becomes of reality once it no longer appears to him. He tries, in other words, to see if there is a reality apart from appearances. First, he considers how much the visual is our primary way of perceiving: "Ineluctable modality of the visible: at least that if no more, thought through my eyes. Signatures of all things I am here to read." Then, he closes his eyes, to "see" what the world is like without seeing: "Stephen closed his eyes to hear his boots crush crackling wrack and shells. You are walking through it howsomever. I am, a stride at a time." And finally he opens his eyes, wondering, "has all vanished since?," but finding it is "there all the time without you: and ever shall be, world without end." There is a reality beyond appearances, and yet still appearances are our reality. How can both things be true?

This kind of question, this kind of experiment, happens in one way or another in much of modern fiction. Writers test the difference between they way things seem and what actually turns out to be true. They wonder how the surfaces of things reveal – or hide – what is behind them. These experiments can lead in very different directions. Sometimes, they lead to despair, if appearances turn out to have little to do with reality. Sometimes, they lead to joy, as glimpses of things lead to revelations. Despair is the result in *The Good Soldier*, as John Dowell discovers beneath the appearance of civility a terrible truth: "No, by God, it is false! It wasn't a minuet that we stepped; it was a prison – a prison full of screaming hysterics." Joy comes in Woolf's fiction, where even the oddest perceptions have profound connection to vital truths, if characters are able to let the connections come:

> She [Clarissa Dalloway] pursed her lips when she looked in the glass. It was to give her face point. That was her self – pointed; dartlike; definite. That was her self when some effort, some call on her to be her self, drew the parts together, she alone knew how different, how incompatible and composed so for the world only into one center, one diamond, one woman who sat in her drawing-room and made a meeting-point, a radiancy no doubt in some dull lives, a refuge for the lonely.

Seeing her appearance in the mirror, Clarissa also sees her essential self, so that in this case, even a superficial appearance opens the way to crystalline insight.

These writers also test reality by showing how much it is "subjective." In modern fiction there are few objective realities: little is permanently, universally the same for everyone who perceives it. Modern novels therefore rarely describe things objectively; they tend to give the personal "point of view" of particular characters. Such subjective seeing enables the modern writer to test different versions of reality – and to show how reality gets made up in particular cases. In *The Sound and the Fury*, for example, we never get any objective account of what has brought such misery to the Compson family. Instead, we get it from four different subjective points of view: the first section gives us the point of view of Benjy, the family's mentally retarded sibling; the second gives us the point of view of Quentin, years earlier, at Harvard – and so on. Faulkner described these variations negatively: "I wrote the Benjy part first. That wasn't good enough so I wrote the Quentin part. That still wasn't good enough. I let Jason try it. That still wasn't enough. I let Faulkner try it and that still wasn't enough."[3] No single view here is enough, but in the different tries, we get compensation for those failures: we get not only different ways of seeing the Compson family, but different ways of seeing reality in general. One character's reality is tragic regret; another's is shaped by paranoia. There is, finally, no single reality, as Faulkner takes more of an interest in the ways realities subjectively develop.

How can this amount to a "new realism," if reality is so much in question? Reality now becomes not a thing, but a process. It is not something out there, for sure, that the novelist must describe. It is a process of engagement, a set of subjective acts, a psychological performance, something always ongoing. And once it has shifted from thing to process, the novelist has a lot more to do, and a lot more to say. For this process must be the "essence" of our lives. If reality is not something already given, but something we are always making, then the novelist has a crucial job to do: he or she can show us how this process works, dramatizing the essence of reality, and making fiction something perhaps more necessary than it had been before.

Here we come to the fourth and final way reality tends to get questioned in the modern novel. Interested less in what is real than in what we do to make it so, modern novelists become interested in the acts of interpretation or *mediation* through which we transform the vast world of experience into what matters to us. The novelists focus on the means of mediation – what we put before us to bring the world to us – and in so doing they discover just how vital their own writing can be. If reality is a fiction we make, then fiction is the key to reality, and novels self-conscious about fiction's function can become the expositor of life itself. Or they can become testament of failure – of the way our fictions delude and misguide us, and the way irony results. The modern novel tends to operate with this mixed sense of mission, confident it is vital, but unhappy about the ironies its perpetual questions often reveal.

Virginia Woolf knew that modernizing the novel meant some reckless destruction. Writers were "led to destroy the very foundations and rules of literary society." The "smashing and crashing" had begun, she said; "it is the sound of their axes that we hear," and there would have to be a "season of failures and fragments" before new building could begin.[4] This smashing and crashing, this iconoclasm, was Modernism's founding gesture: especially in the early years, everything had to be broken down and made anew. The primary impulse here was violent change – an impulse nicely exaggerated in the attitude of the "futur-ist" poet F. T. Marinetti: "Up to now literature has exalted a pensive immobility, ecstasy, and sleep. We intend to exalt aggressive action, a feverish insomnia, the racer's stride, the mortal leap, the punch and the slap."[5] In this spirit of aggressive action, the modern novel defined itself as a slap in the face of "literary society." It broke all the rules: if good literary form seemed to demand order and decency, regularity and clarity, the modern novel would deliver instead rough disorder, eccentricity and confusion. It would deliberately deform fiction, in perpetual rebellion against customary techniques, plots, styles, and expectations.

But before we see how, we ought to get some perspective on this "ideology of revolt." Modern writers thought they were smashing and crashing and making something wholly new – but were they? Did they really make the difference that Woolf and Marinetti expected? And was it really as necessary as they claimed? Or was this all largely a matter of what one critic has called "the *myth* of the modern"? Perry Meisel has argued that the modern was not the vital and radical break Woolf and Marinetti celebrated. They and other writers needed to think it was, however, so they would not have to worry that every-thing had already been done: "The will to modernity we commonly equate with the structure of modernism as a whole is largely a defen-sive response to the increasingly intolerable burdens of coming late in a tradition."[6] Did these modern writers worry about being belated arrivals to an overcrowded literary tradition, and did they therefore fake their revolution? Even if we conclude that they did not – even as we now go on to see how their "aggressive action" *did* make major differences – we should keep in mind the possibility that the new forms we are about to cover were not all quite as new as the "myth of the modern" might have us believe.

Of the differences the modern novel made, the main one was this: fiction, now, would have less *plot*. Strong plots now seemed unlikely. Full of romance, intrigue, adventure, and incident, they were at once predictable and artificial. "Good stories" were false stories, too well shaped by triumph and tragedy, marriage and death. The feel of life fell out of books too fully plotted. They smoothed out life's rough edges, faked conclusions and coincidences, and they overlooked the ordinary adventures modern life now seemed to enact. Wanting to be more attentive to the true texture of real experience, modern writers preferred things uneventful. They could not do without plot entirely, of course, but their plots were deliberately minimal, often relatively pointless, largely anti-climactic, and loose enough to allow for the random openness of human existence.

E. M. Forster expressed a typical dissatisfaction with plot in his *Aspects of the Novel*: "Yes – oh, dear, yes – the novel tells a story. That is the fundamental aspect without which it could not exist. That is the highest factor common to all novels, and I wish that it was not so, that it could be something different – melody, or perception of the truth, not this low atavistic form."[7] Forster found the need to plot a story a hindrance to fiction's higher arts; it seemed like a throwback to times of more rudimentary entertainments. Gustave Flaubert expressed a similar impatience when he expressed a desire to write "a book about nothing, a book dependent on nothing external, which would he held together by the internal strength of its style . . . a book which would have almost no subject, or at least in which the subject would be almost invisible, if such a thing is possible."[8] It may not have been possible (as Forster also admitted), but modern writers still tried for "something different" – to make the novel less dependent on the sort of stories and subjects that lost truth and loosened the hold of style.

Think again of Mrs Dalloway simply preparing for her party, or Joyce's characters wandering the streets of Dublin. Or think of the purposeless wanderings of Gertrude Stein's *Melanctha* (1908): Stein's heroine is a woman whose life never seems to change, who comes and goes and begins and ends relationships with little difference made, whose existence is entirely tied to a merely passing present. Finally, she dies, but the death is a non-event – just a stopping point in a narrative that never develops much at all: "Melanctha went back to the hospital, and there the Doctor told her she had the consumption, and before long she would surely die. They sent her where she would be taken care of, a home for poor consumptives, and there Melanctha stayed until she died." What could have been a dramatic climax is left alone, to keep from giving a pointless life a falsely climactic finish.

Stein's refusal to let plot thicken is extreme. Many modern novels retain plots of no small drama, and even the relatively plotless novels of Woolf and Joyce gather to moments of great intensity and eventful change. Or what seems like plotlessness is a shift in attention to the small-scale plots of everyday life. But even in these cases, and more generally, modern novels decrease substantially the role played by plot in fiction's designs.

Moreover, they decrease fiction's tendency toward any consistent patterns. Regular movements from one event to the next, strong links and connections among situations, characters, and places, careful inclusion of all relevant information: these, too, proved too artificial for the modern novelist. Rather than have things flow evenly through series of events well-related to each other, modern novelists chose randomness, inconsistency, deviation, omission. Jagged, jumpy, and erratic, their stories aimed to reflect the incoherence and incongruity of real life, in which things seldom go at any regular pace or hang fully together. Splintered and split, these stories aimed to reflect the diversity in modern experience, due to the fact that broken communities and lost traditions had made it impossible to thread together the diverse outlooks and activities of the modern world. Set structures gave way to "aleatory" ones – to patterns of random circumstance and inconsistent motivation.

Inconsistency broke the modern novel into fragments. Whereas novelists of the past might have tried to pattern a story's different elements into shapely coherence, modern writers often tried deliberately for fragmentation. Sometimes, this fragmentation is visible even on the printed page, where breaks and ellipses shatter sentences and paragraphs into pieces; sometimes, it is a matter of incomplete connections among the chapters, descriptions, and events that make up the book as a whole. Or sometimes it is psychological – a kind of schizophrenic dissociation of the thoughts and observations of characters through whom we see the world. It is all of these things in *Manhattan Transfer* (1925) by John Dos Passos. To capture the disintegration and dynamism of modern urban life, Dos Passos deliberately fragments his characters' experiences, even to the point of letting inner lives become as chaotically mixed as outer landscapes:

Moi monsieur je suis anarchiste . . . *And three times round went our gallant ship, and three times round went* . . . goddam it between that and money . . . *And she sank to the bottom of the sea* . . . we're in a treadmill for fair

> J'ai fait trois fois le tour du monde
> Dans mes voy . . . ages

Declaration of war . . . rumble of drums . . . beefeaters march in red after the flashing baton of a drummajor in a hat like a longhaired muff, silver knob spins flashing grump, grump, grump . . . in the face of revolution mondiale. Commencement of hostilities in a long parade through the empty rainlashed streets. Extra, extra, extra. Santa Claus shoots daughter he has tried to attack. SLAYS SELF WITH SHOTGUN . . . put the gun under his chin and pulled the trigger with his big toe. The stars look down on Fredericktown. Workers of the world, unite. Vive le sang, vive le sang.

These fragments bespeak a broken culture – a disintegration caused by modern war and anarchy, destructive to the modern mind, and reproduced on the page by writers out to give startling formal proof of the way the world has gone out of joint.

But these fragments also reflect something positive. In their brokenness, they generate a new kind of energy, which in turn reflects the vitality brought on by modernization. They may be less coherent than information normally presented, but they are also more dynamic, and more exhilarating. Is this contradictory – to call fragmentation both a bad disintegration and a good dynamicism? It may be, but if so, the contradiction is built into the modern novel itself. When "things fall apart" in the modern novel, they may do so because the world has fallen into chaos, but also because modernization has invigorated life and broken it free of old restraints. The fragmented page might be an incoherent one, but it might also represent a form of thought open to new experiences.

Fragmentation and plotlessness typically end in defiance of *closure*. As we have seen, books that end too happily in marriage or dramatically in death came to seem artless and false, and this was often because of their tendency to tie up all loose ends. Real life never gives full last explanations; its stories always continue, and some details always remain extraneous. In recognition of this continuance, of the necessity of loose ends, modern novels stay open-ended. Plots end abruptly, with questions unanswered and expectations unfulfilled. If closure comes, it tends to come ironically, or as a total surprise.

Ernest Hemingway's *The Sun Also Rises* (1926), for example, has last words that ironize the whole possibility of entertaining satisfying last thoughts. Jake, the novel's protagonist, distrusts stories that hang together. And from beginning to end Jake's story is adrift, since it is the haphazard story of dissolute Americans killing time abroad. Brawling drunkenness, violence, and aimless mistakes are the norm throughout, keeping things open even as the story draws to its close. And then at its close even the smallest amount of closure gets undone. Jake's former lover tries to put a positive last spin on their relationship, but to her sentimental closing words he responds, "Isn't it pretty to think so." Even this amount of closure, he suggests, is just false prettiness, and the truth is that no last or lasting comforts can be taken.

Even when reassurance does come, it comes as a question, as it does at the endings both of *Ulysses* and *Mrs Dalloway*. *Ulysses* ends with Leopold Bloom apparently received back into his marital bed. Thinking of him beside her as she lies awake, Molly Bloom recalls the day she accepted his proposal of marriage, and then finally comes to what seems like a powerful last affirmation of their life together. Although the novel as a whole has been fairly negative, her last thought is "yes," and it seems we are meant to take this as a strong assertion of closure: "then he asked me would I yes to say yes my mountain flower and first I put my arms around him yes and drew him down to me so he could feel my breasts and all perfume yes and his heart was going like mad and yes I said yes I will Yes." In no uncertain terms, it seems, Bloom's quest has ended. But can these words reverse so many prior pages' doubt and irony? And since Molly's last thoughts are orgasmic, don't we have to question the staying power of this final affirmation? Joyce gives us closure, but then also demands that we wonder about it. Similarly, at the end of *Mrs Dalloway* we get what sounds like a powerful final statement. Mrs Dalloway appears, at the end of her party, at the top of the stairs, and a friend thinks, admiringly, "for there she was." A very strong affirmation, this last sentence is also an open question, for it only extends what has been the novel's question all along: what does it mean, simply, to *be*?

To reject closure, plot, consistency, and unity may seem destructive –
"smashing and crashing," spitefully to make fiction as disappointing as
modern life. But these rejections were meant more to improve fiction's
subtler powers of verisimilitude and inquiry, to make it a better register of actuality. Plotless, fragmentary, unresolved fiction might seem
likely to be clumsy, unilluminating, and inartistic, but in fact it could
have a finer grain of plain incident, patient questioning, and free
exploration. It could come at life unshaped by conventional expectations, and let life itself provoke whatever form might be necessary to
communicate its truth.

Modern fiction could, in other words, pay better attention to ordinary reality. And *ordinary* reality – lived experience, in rich detail,
intensely seen – has been the modern writer's main concern. Before,
it seemed, novels only cared to deal with things in some way special,
exemplary, or dramatic, things that could be the basis for a lesson, for
excitement, for social criticism. To the modern novelist, this focus had
too often failed to provide insight into aspects of more fundamental
human existence; moreover, it made fiction insensitive to changes in
the fundamental nature of experience – especially those made by modernization. It seemed important to shift the focus and bring out what
mattered about ordinary things and events, to get more directly at the
substance of simple existence, to pay close attention to modernity's
effects on basic human relationships. It seemed important to write
fiction more true to daily life, primary feelings, deep desires, and subtle
changes, and to reveal what Aldous Huxley called "the astonishing-
ness of the most obvious things."[9]

Such was the focus of *Mrs Dalloway* and of *Ulysses*, both of which
take place on a single ordinary day, and do so largely to weave the
texture of dailiness. Unusual things happen in both books, of course,
and both are as far as possible from ordinary, but they linger longest
over what might otherwise be the most commonplace of acts and feelings. In these, they find much to wonder at. For as Leopold Bloom and
Clarissa Dalloway walk the streets of Dublin and London – hearing and
seeing the sounds and spectacles of modernity – their ordinary reac-
tions can be presented in ways that show us astonishing things about
the world and about human character. Ordinary life becomes extraordinary in its own way. Fiction's habit of description changes, focusing
now on matters of minor detail, but with the rhetoric of reverence,
wonder, or intensity ordinarily reserved for great things and high

ideals. Indeed, the modern novel tends to reverse the relation between the ordinary and the extraordinary, prompting us always to ask, when Joyce or Woolf treat things that seem not to matter, how apparently insignificant things disclose greater truth and finer beauty than things that might seem far more critical or conclusive.

The reversal also changed the nature of *symbolism* in the novel. Unlikely things, now, could be taken for wonders symbolical of transcendent meaning. An example from Willa Cather's *My Antonia* (1918) shows how. One day, at sunset, the novel's protagonists sit looking at the sky when "a great black figure suddenly appeared on the face of the sun." The figure turns out to be just a plow, made to look huge by the way the setting sun throws it into silhouette:

> On some upland farm, a plough had been left standing in the field. The sun was sinking just behind it. Magnified across the distance by the horizontal light, it stood out against the sun, was exactly contained within the circle of the disk; the handles, the tongue, the share – black against the molten red. There it was, heroic in size, a picture writing on the sun.

The plow made vast and heroic symbolizes the greatness of the ordinary. What had seemed to be something of mythic proportion turns out to be a simple thing – and so what seems to be simple and ordinary gets the attention necessary to reveal to us its real grandeur. Things are "strengthened and simplified," in a type of symbolism that is, as the symbolist poet Arthur Symons put it, an "endeavor to disengage the ultimate essence, the soul, of whatever exists and can be realised by the consciousness ... [a] dutiful waiting upon every symbol by which the soul of things can be made visible."[10] Such symbolism was not itself new; poets had long preferred it. But such a waiting upon "whatever exists," for the purpose of laying bare the "soul of things," was fairly new for fiction, where ordinary realism had tended to distinguish "souls" and "things."

In a way, these new priorities – this interest in the ordinary, the unplotted, the open – all have to do with the new way of seeing "reality." For older generations of novelists, reality had been what was established, what drove the social and natural worlds, in full factual detail. But modernity had flooded those worlds with so much new experience and new incident that a new, smaller, sidelong focus seemed necessary. Reality came to lie in the perplexed, individual experience of random, ordinary things. So the subject-matter of fiction changed, but then so did its organization, and so did its proximity to the things it described. Whereas before the emphasis had often been on an orderly telling of important events, now it fell on a haphazard wondering at lower-level experiences.

The main difference here, perhaps, is between *telling* and *showing*. What the modern writers tried for, above all, was a style that would enact life rather than just describe it. The way to give readers a real experience, it seemed, was to break down the artificial structures built up by efforts to tell a good (rather than a real) story. And above all it was vital to keep telling from becoming *preaching*, and to keep the writer's own "ideas" out of fiction altogether. "Don't be viewy" was Ford Madox Ford's advice; William Carlos Williams claimed that there should be "no ideas but in things." Didacticism was the mortal enemy of modern fiction, which tried for direct showing rather than intrusive, explanatory telling.

The technical term for this style of showing is *mimesis* (direct imitation of reality). This central change – away from stories neatly told to realities directly shown – accounts for the other changes we have been considering here. It undid plot, frayed endings, and gave to fiction the more ordinary shapes of life's everyday experiences. But this did not mean that it weakened fiction's powers of expression. Much to the contrary: this effort to give readers the feel of immediate realities demanded new powers of precision, sensitivity, and evocation. And nor did this change mean that fiction could no longer get at higher truths. It simply meant that these would be grounded, now, in real experience – much the way Cather's epic silhouette begins in a plow on the land.

CHAPTER 3

New Forms: Reshaping the Novel

If giving the feel of immediate reality meant reshaping fiction's plots and procedures, it also meant taking a new approach to *character*. Character changed, we have noted, along with "reality": once writers saw reality as something made up differently by different kinds of people, they put character into flux, for it became necessary to explore the very foundations of selfhood. Character became a question of the strange processes of consciousness, the unclear boundaries of the self, the vagaries of human perception. No certainties could say what constituted character, and so it, too, became subject to "smashing and crashing." Its foundations – in heroism, stereotype, virtue, social norms – were attacked, too, and replaced by uncertainties more true to modern experience.

Characters in modern novels are not heroes: they are rarely singled out for their superior traits, and they rarely achieve much. If anything, they are worse than normal – less beautiful, less accomplished, less intelligent, and less likely than the average person to overcome adversity. In the larger scheme of things, there is a long and steep descent from the epic heroes of myth and legend to the *anti-heroes* of modern fiction. The former were far better than average, superior to their environments, and destined for triumph; the latter are weak, disaffected, and passive, undone by circumstance, and lucky to make it through at all. Quentin Compson, in Faulkner's *The Sound and the Fury*, is a good example. In some sense, he is the hero of his family: smart enough to go to Harvard and noble in outlook, he seems good enough material for a heroical story. But in fact his advantages are disadvantages, because his intelligence and sensitivity make him tortured and passive, and ultimately he is so beset by troubles that he takes his own life. He is an anti-hero – remarkable not for his positive traits and accomplishments but for his negative ones.

Being an anti-hero, however, does not make a character unlikable, uninteresting, or absurd. There is real heroism in anti-heroism, in an unheroic world. As Lionel Trilling puts it, "Nothing is more characteristic of the literature of our time than the replacement of the hero by what has come to be called the anti-hero, in whose indifference to or hatred of ethical nobility there is presumed to lie a special authenticity."[1] If the modern world disallows heroic action – and that is one way to define the problem of modernity – then truth demands unheroic characters. Moreover, it champions them, because it sees the heroism in even the simplest daily acts of survival. And so modern writers see heroism in ordinary thoughts and actions. In, for example, the ordinary thoughts and actions of Leopold Bloom, Joyce gives us the modern version of the epic heroism of Ulysses. Bloom is a kind of *everyman*: he is no better or worse than anyone else. He submits unimpressively to the fact that his wife is cheating on him; he takes embarrassing pleasure in the base physical activities of eating and excreting; he shies away from tough situations, and seems well disliked by many of his fellow Dubliners. But all this makes him a modern kind of hero; modern writers began to find much to like in just such passivity, weakness, and failure. These traits came to seem more truly heroical, in a way, than classic heroical ones, because they showed people shouldering the stranger burden of modern futility.

And so we get a host of other such anti-heroes, in the boozing irresponsibility of Jake in *The Sun Also Rises,* or the arrogant violence of the men in *Women in Love.* Compared to the bullfighters he heroicizes, Jake is not much of a man; he drinks and brawls and cries, has been somehow castrated by a war-wound, and is well summed up by a friend who says, "You drink yourself to death. You become obsessed with sex. You spend all your time talking, not working." But there is tragic modern glory in all this inadequacy. And in *Women in Love*, there is a new kind of heroism in aggressive postures that once might have been a sign of villainy. In one famous scene, Gerald Crich forces his horse to stand close to a passing train. It bucks in terror, but he holds it fast, "his face shining with fixed amusement," with a "mechanical relentlessess," "calm as a ray of cold sunshine." His cruelty reflect a new kind of anti-heroism: one in which brutal urges are recognized for their particular integrity.

In a way, all modern characters are anti-heroes, because no modern character can connect perfectly to society as a whole. To be a hero in the old sense, a character not only has to represent his or her culture's best powers and features. He or she must live in a world in which individuals belong, in which the individual's needs can match up with those of society at large. But with the coming of modernity such a relationship became more and more difficult. A sense of connection gave way to a sense of *alienation*. Social norms seemed out of sync with individual needs, as social wholes grew more vast, impersonal, mechanistic, and oppressive. Individual character, it seemed, could no longer be defined in terms of its affiliation with the group. Instead, alienation became definitive; character came to be something defined in terms of opposition to society.

Alienation was both a good and a bad thing. On the one hand, the individual came to feel less a part of the social whole, as fiction writers saw it, because the whole had lost touch with its ideals and better values. Social life had gone cold, materialistic, haphazard, and so the decent person could only feel isolated from it. In *Portrait of the Artist*, for example, Stephen Dedalus feels always that "his sensitive nature" is poorly served by an "undivined and squalid way of life," that "his soul was still disquieted and cast down by the dull phenomenon of Dublin." But then again this alienation is also an effect of modern freedom. Modern prosperity, modern psychology, and modern art had enabled and justified unprecedented self-determination and self-esteem. And so Stephen Dedalus can also fancy himself estranged in a good way – a kind of cultural savior. He leaves Dublin at the end of *Portrait* because he cannot stay there, but he goes to find in the wide world the means to redeem what he leaves behind: "Welcome, O life! I go to encounter for the millionth time the reality of experience and to forge in the smithy of my soul the uncreated conscience of my race." Presenting individual potential this way, too, modern fiction writers have a kind of double view of modern estrangement. Characters became more isolated, alienated, detached, and had more and more to be defined internally: less affiliated with outer social doings, they could no longer be well defined by them. But by that same token they could become heroical in new ways. Almost just by being, they were rebels, fighting the system, and they took on the glamor and power always associated with people who do so.

And then their plots were different, too. Novels of the past were very often concerned to show how such rebels eventually and positively can fit back into society – how, for example, a headstrong young woman would ultimately decide to soften, conform, and marry. But modern novels had to show just how much more difficult such reconciliations had become. More and more they had to emphasize the impossibility of reconciliation – stressing instead the widening breadth of the gap between the individual and society.

The plot most critically changed was that of the *bildungsroman*. A bildungsroman is a story of a protagonist's growth from youth to adulthood, with emphasis on how rebellious individualism gives way to mature, productive, responsible participation in society. As Franco Moretti notes in *The Way of the World: The Bildungsroman in European Culture*, it is all about "the conflict between the ideal of self-determination and the equally imperious demands of socialization," usually with the former leading to and enriching the latter.[2] The plot of the bildungsroman had been crucial to novels of the past, if and when individuals could happily grow up to become a secure part of some social whole. When it no longer seemed that an individual could do so – once we enter the modern world of alienation – then the plot of the bildungsroman comes to seem false and forced. In the modern reversal of the bildungsroman, characters often grow from conformity to rebellion, and end not in happy oneness with society at large but in intense and often destructive rejections of it.

Such is the plot of Sherwood Anderson's *Winesburg, Ohio* (1919). Anderson tells a connected group of stories about modern small-town life. What once might have been a happy community is now a stultified one, bleak and repressive and full of people whose frustrations have turned them into grotesques. Threaded through the stories are the experiences of Tom Willard – a boy not yet beaten down by the drudgeries and miseries that have wrecked the adults around him. Ultimately, Tom escapes, and that outcome makes *Winesburg, Ohio* a kind of bildungsroman in reverse. For the standard plot would have had the rebellious Tom mature into someone able to find a happy place in his world. But in fact he only becomes more certain that inevitable alienation must drive him away. He finally "[takes] hold of the thing that makes the mature life of men and women in the modern world possible," but this means he must leave. Maturity here means departure, and as Tom sits on the train that will take him to Chicago or New York, "the town of Winesburg had disappeared and his life there had become but a background on which to paint the dreams of his manhood."

Such alienation is at its most extreme when even selfhood is in question – when, for example, insanity is at issue. *Madness* is a prominent feature of the modern novel, and one reason for its prominence is the modern wish to push modern alienation to its most revelatory and most painful extremes. Septimus Smith, the anti-hero of *Mrs Dalloway*, has been shell-shocked by his experiences fighting in World War I. Now he has become unable to see the world plainly. But Septimus's extreme condition only emphasizes the typical difference between society's conventions and the true experiences of the modern self. And his madness is not all bad. Ironically, it makes him a kind of visionary. The world's beauty literally explodes all around him; his thoughts run to pure poetry; his estrangement enables him to see through things, and to see the realities behind appearances, so that he seems to understand things other people cannot. "He lay very high, on the back of the world. The earth thrilled beneath him. Red flowers grew through his flesh"; when he hears the simple word, "time," "the word . . . split its husk; poured its riches over him; and from his lips fell like shells, like shavings from a plane, without his making them, hard, white, imperishable words, and flew to attach themselves to their places in an ode to Time; an immortal ode to Time." This is a psychotic break – but it is also genius, of a kind, due to the way a modern novelist like Woolf might associate madness with creativity. In this case, madness is also a positive kind of rebellion against norms, and it is the psychological epitome of the enterprise of the modern novel.

This interest in the estranged individual partakes of the modern novel's general need to question reality. Modern novels never want to go with received wisdom, consensus, or old ideas. A main part of their effort at experimental innovation is a belief that conventions get things wrong, and that the individual mind, the mind posed against society's definitions of the good, the heroical, the worthwhile, is more likely to be right, exciting, and interesting. We take this kind of thinking so much for granted now that it is easy to forget that it has not always been with us – that the modernist outlook (building upon Romantic anti-heroism) largely created it. Modern novels tend to suggest that personal truth outdoes received wisdom; and they tend to take pains to show how the painful struggle of anti-heroical *subjective* consciousness leads to the greatest insights, the truest truths.

There are problems, however, with this fondness for the subjective, anti-social mind of the estranged individual. If it goes too far, it can lead to *solipsism* – the situation in which the individual self has no awareness or knowledge of anything beyond itself. If it goes too far in another direction, it can create a *dispersed* self, in which no stable identity can take hold. And finally it can lead to characters that seem hardly to exist at all.

Solipsism separates a character so much from the outer world that subjective reality becomes no reality at all. Able to know only itself, the solipsistic self winnows away. Even modern novels rarely take things to this extreme, but some readers have thought that they come too close. That is, to some readers, *subjective* characters are too often defined too much in terms of their own dubious perceptions rather than their relations to others and to society at large. The protagonist of *The Good Soldier*, for example, verges on solipsism, when he concludes finally that he has little chance of knowing anything true about the world around him: "I know nothing – nothing in the world – of the hearts of men. I only know that I am alone – horribly alone." To some readers, Ford here has taken things to an extreme – exaggerating the extent to which reality is an exclusively subjective phenomenon.

When emphasis on the subjective qualities of character seem to imply that selfhood is always changing, always in flux, then another problem arises: there seems no basis for character at all, since identity is exploded by the sheer diversity that makes up the self. Selfhood gets so dispersed – through the changing phases of subjective perceptions, moods, and situations – that it has no constant character. Some readers accuse Woolf's novels of this excessive dispersal of selfhood, and they say that it makes her characters too vague, too elusive, too thin; traditional character is too thoroughly destroyed. Her people, that is, are not at all characters in the conventional sense – and to some readers they are so much like essences that they seem to have no existence at all. But there was a powerful justification for this approach. Dissolving selfhood seemed a fact of modern life, as one writer painfully reflected: Hugo Von Hofmannsthal expressed the very popular sense that the human self had broken up and dispersed, that although he had once felt whole and "everywhere. . . . at the center," now "everything fell into fragments for me, the fragments into further fragments, until it seemed possible to contain anything at all within a single concept."[3] If modern character no longer seemed to "contain anything," it was because so many writers felt this "limitless transmutation," this loss of integrity.

Here we come to the farthest extremes of modern character – these ghostly presences so dispersed or solipsistic that they hardly seem alive. Along with anti-heroes, everymen, and outsiders, they people the extreme reaches of the modern novel. Under new conditions of estrangement, madness, rebellion, and subjectivity, they feature forth the new possibilities for identity and self-destruction that the modern novel helped to make available to the world.

Perfect heroes, artificial plots, false endings, and excessive detail were banished from the modern novel, but there was one thing many modern writers were even more eager to rule out: the *omniscient narrator*. For years the typical narrator had been a detached *third-person* voice, all-knowing and all seeing, able to tell a perfect story. But in a world of subjective realities, skeptical questions, and false appearances, who could really know everything? Who could realistically be objective or omniscient – and how could a story told in such a fashion immerse a reader in real experience? Wouldn't it be far more realistic and far more effective to have the story told from within? Better yet, wouldn't it be most intense and immediate to do without a narrator – and just directly present the lives and thoughts of characters without any mediator at all?

Rather than try for objectivity, modern novels emphasized *perspective*. Rather than try for some fully correct, neutral, finished version of a story, they limited their stories to some haphazard, incomplete, mistaken, or limited point of view. They did so in order to get at experiential truth. An objective narrator – apart from the action, fully informed – might get the whole truth, but the truth could not feel real, because no real person ever gets the whole truth. Much better to give the partial truth, because in real life truth is always only partial. So the omniscient, panoramic, impersonal standpoint gave way to the limited, focused, personal point of view. Objectivity gave way to focalization; the flawed perspective became the hallmark of truth.

Faulkner announced the change most boldly by beginning *The Sound and the Fury* from the point of view of the mentally retarded Benjy Compson:

> Through the fence, between the curling flower spaces, I could see them hitting. They were coming toward where the flag was and I went along the fence. Luster was hunting in the grass by the flower tree. They took the flag out, and they were hitting. Then they put the flag back and they went to the table, and he hit and the other hit. Then they went on, and I went along the fence . . . and they stopped and we stopped and I looked through the fence while Luster was hunting in the grass.

The information we get is hopelessly limited. Nothing could be further from omniscience, there is no measure of distance from the experience in question, and the story that results has nothing of the form an objective narrator could provide. But it feels real. We feel we are getting Benjy's experience directly, without mediation, and to the modern novelist, that kind of truth was far more important than the "real," objective truth of the situation.

Another advantage in perspective is the fact that it can be multiple. It can, in other words, combine individual experience with something like the fuller knowledge of omniscience, by presenting the perspectives of many different characters. In *The Sound and the Fury*, we may begin in the very deficient perspective of Benjy, but then we proceed to other points of view, and something like omniscient narration develops, because we get the different facets with which to piece together a whole story. But we still get unmediated experiences, and we also get involved in the process of narration. For we have to do the work an omniscient narrator would otherwise have done for us, and the participation gives objective knowledge the feel of subjective involvement.

In *Mrs Dalloway*, the narrator at first seems very much to be objective, omniscient, but soon it becomes clear that the narrator presents the world from Mrs Dalloway's point of view. And then it becomes clear that the narrator migrates into the heads of other characters, as well; Woolf's narrator is detached just enough to leap from mind to mind, but never so detached that objectivity mutes experience. So we get a full range of perspectives, woven together into a kind of web, and as in the case of Faulkner the web ultimately combines the advantages of objective and subjective report. There is a fullness of information, and a panoramic view, but then also the feel of immediate experience, and the individuation that perspective provides.

There are different motivations at work here. The main one is *epistemological*: Woolf, Faulkner, and other perspectival writers want to find a better way to show how knowledge, understanding, and perception really take place. But the motivation is also *aesthetic*. Omniscient narration, it seems, was too clumsy and bland; perspectival narration, by contrast, encouraged subtle variations and graceful nuance. And finally there is the *ethical* motivation – which, to some people, is ultimately the most important. For us truly to understand, sympathize with, and appreciate other kinds of people, and for us really to appreciate what it is that makes them different from us, perspectival narration may be essential. It may be the means through which narrative can make us put aside our own ways of thinking and seeing and take on those of people truly unlike ourselves. In *Mimesis: The Representation of Reality in Western Literature*, Erich Auerbach goes as far as to say that these effects of perspectival narration (as he saw them in Woolf's *To the Lighthouse* [1927]) are vitally linked to true democracy in politics: "It is still a long way to a common life of mankind on earth, but the goal begins to be visible. And it is most concretely visible now in the unprejudiced, precise, interior and exterior representations of the random moment in the lives of different people."[4]

Precise interior representations demanded new reaches into "consciousness." As we have noted, the modern novel mainly began with new efforts to explore the depths of the human mind. In Flaubert and in James, novelistic realism became a matter of psychological realism, of close focus on the "fine awareness" of minds immersed in the complexities of modern life. Psychological realism intensified as the modern novel developed; "internality" seemed more and more to become the main location of modern fiction, as writers continued to transform narration in whatever ways necessary to get fully inside the mind.

This movement into the depths of consciousness arrived finally at modern fiction's most characteristic narrative style: *stream of consciousness*. William James, we have seen, had influentially redefined the mind, as a site of plural flows rather than units of thought. This new view – and others like it – changed the way writers described what went on in the heads of their characters. It meant that interior life demanded styles of description very different from those practiced upon the exterior world. Interior life was all flux, all seamless minglings of memories, perceptions, and desires – always "going on," as James put it, and remaking personal identity at every moment. To evoke this flux of interior life, novelists had to innovate similarly dynamic styles of attention, and do so in defiance of those norms of grammar, logic, and sentence structure that give false, coherent shape to consciousness. The result was stream of consciousness: when writers let free associations run roughshod over the divisions and distinctions of standard punctuation, when they let outer reality dissolve into the chaos of real mental life, and when they tried to follow out the strange evolutions whereby sights and sounds and theories blend and scatter and pursue themselves on into ever new formations, then they helped to develop this most distinctive of modern narratorial styles.

Stream of consciousness could take many forms. The main goal – the "unmediated" discourse of the mind itself – could be reached in different ways depending on the state of the mind in question, or the "level" at which a writer had chosen to pitch narration, or a writer's theory about where to locate the mind's most basic activity. Stream of consciousness might mean a very random jumble of perceptions and imaginings, or it might mean a very direct pursuit of some train of thought, as long as its narration proceeds as if unprocessed by any authorial intervention. It might look like this passage from Joyce's *Ulysses*:

> Prrprr.
> Must be the bur.
> Fff. Oo. Rrpr.
> *Nations of all the earth.* No-one behind. She's passed. *Then and not till then.* Tram. Kran, kran, kran. Good oppor. Coming. Krandlkrankran. I'm sure it's the burgud. Yes. One, two. *Let my epitaph be.* Karaaaaaaaa. *Written. I have.*
> Pprrpffrrppffff.
> *Done.*

Here Joyce gives us the contents of Leopold Bloom's consciousness in a moment of agitation and mental disarray. Leaving a boisterous bar, his guts churning with food and wine, dizzied and disoriented and preoccupied at once by his flatulence, a passing tram, grand political avowals, and his own next move, Bloom is in a particularly chaotic state of mind. For Joyce, such a state is a perfect opportunity to press stream-of-consciousness narration to an extreme, by making the various contents of Bloom's mind tumble together into nearly incomprehensible confusion. But such confusion is not in play at all when stream-of-consciousness narration takes us into the mind of Bloom's wife, Molly, as she lies awake ruminating at the end of the novel:

> Yes because he never did a thing like that before as ask to get his breakfast in bed with a couple of eggs since the *City Arms* hotel when he used to be pretending to be laid up with a sick voice doing his highness to make himself interesting to that old faggot Mrs Riordan that he thought he had a great leg of and she never left us a farthing all for masses for herself and her soul greater miser ever was.

Molly's thoughts here are unstructured and flowing but not therefore confused; in fact, they follow out focused lines of thought vigorously, if purposelessly. This, too, is stream-of-consciousness narration, however, for it has in common with the prior example a psychological immediacy. In both cases we have the contents of consciousness directly presented, without apparent authorial intervention, in the interest of making narration more true to the actual and very various movements of the mind.

Such psychological immediacy and the flux and fluidity it tended to present were the hallmarks of the modern novel, but they were by no means its only narratorial achievements. Modern writers may have wanted to let the human mind speak for itself, but they also wanted to find similar ways to speak for any possible situation: they tried in general to suit narration to all possible mixtures of inner and outer life, and to all combinations of close and distant perspectives, and so they made narration better able to run the whole range of possibilities from stream of consciousness to its very opposite.

To begin to appreciate this range, let us presume that narrative possibilities run from inward to outward – from the stream of consciousness at the most interior level to the more standard, completely detached, and impersonal kind of writing which with we are most familiar. The most typical kind of narration tends toward "outer" detachment; it tends to come from a disembodied voice, not a part of the action, who seems to know everything but never becomes itself a character. This voice speaks in the *third person* – referring to the characters as "he" and "she," and never speaking of itself as "I" – and by knowing everything, this voice seems to be omniscient. And since this voice is not that of a person involved in the story, it tends to be *objective* – with none of the subjective elements that would be so plentiful in stream-of-consciousness narration. This third-person, objective, omniscient narration would stand at the opposite end of a spectrum from the stream-of-consciousness narration. On this spectrum are many intervening possibilities – and modern fiction makes use of all of them.

If "stream of consciousness" describes the kind of narration that gives the full chaos of what goes on most deeply and immediately in the mind, the next step "outward" would take us to a kind of narration that is more deliberate, comprehensible, and coherent. This next level would be *interior monologue*, in which we feel like we are listening in on a person's running self-description. These thoughts would still not be wholly coherent, but they wouldn't descend so much into the irrational, the unconscious, or the nonverbal. Joyce described such interior monologue as a situation in which "the reader finds himself established, from the first lines, in the thoughts of the principal personage, and the uninterrupted unrolling of that thought, replacing the usual form of narrative, conveys to us what this personage is doing and what is happening to him."[5] Joyce used interior monologue in *Ulysses* principally for the self-consciously dramatic thoughts of Stephen Dedalus, which often proceed as if spoken internally for purposes of self-justification.

Once a character begins telling his or her own story – once we depart from things that seem simply thought out into things that sound externally spoken, or thought out loud – we are in the realm of *exterior monologue*. And if the story told involves the person telling it, we might call this exterior monologue *involved* (another, more technical term for this is *homodiegetic*, which refers to the way a person would be one with his or her story). If the person apparently thinking out loud is giving us a story of which he or she is not part, then the exterior monologue has become more detached (or *heterodiegetic*).

From there, before we move from *first-person* narration to third-person narration, there is an interesting middle possibility. Sometimes,

we get what sounds like third-person narration, but which nevertheless seems directly in tune with some particular character's thoughts
and feelings. This combination of the two – in which the third-person
narrator speaks with the emotional rhythms of the thoughts and feelings of the person he or she describes – is sometimes called *free indirect discourse*, because in this case the narrator is indirectly speaking the
character's mind, and doing so free of the restraint of quotes and other
distinctions. As we then move more fully "outward," into the voice of
someone speaking from a distance, we find that there are different
possible degrees of such distance. Sometimes, third-person narrators
don't just tell you what is going on; they also evaluate, comment, and
even directly address the reader. In such situations, third-person narrators are perhaps intrusively involved, despite their distance from
their characters. Then, there are unintrusive narrators, and, beyond
that, those who seem so much in another world that they have full
knowledge and full objectivity. They are not limited, and not subject
to any of the subjective involvements that come with being a part of
a story even to a limited degree.

Now, there may be other forms of narration within this range, and
there may be other ways to describe the range – ways other than this
distinction between inward and outward. It may make more sense to
say that the range here goes from extreme immediacy to extreme
intervention, or from the apparently unstructured to the deliberately
shaped. But this range and these distinctions do help us appreciate the
narrative innovations inspired by the modern writer's broadest psychological concerns. Joyce, for example, dips with unusual frequency
into the lowest stream of consciousness, presenting his characters'
most inchoate, nonverbal sensations; but just as often he tends
"outward," toward external monologue, and even toward objective,
omniscient narration. Moreover, he creates new styles of "outward"
narration as experimentally chaotic as stream-of-consciousness narration. Sometimes in *Ulysses*, the world itself seems to speak, so objectively that no person seems to be involved at all. Joyce runs this range
from inchoate personal sensation to public discourse in order to get at
the different qualities our thoughts and feelings have at different times:
sometimes (in moments of relaxation, or in moments of anxiety) our
thoughts run into "streams," but sometimes they feel almost dictated
to us in highly structured ways by whatever external circumstances

we are in (when, for example, we are taking exams, or involved in ceremonies). Fully to capture the full range of thought and feeling, Joyce runs up and down the scale of available narrative styles.

As does Dorothy Richardson, another modern novelist known for her stream-of-consciousness style. Richardson's *Pilgrimage* (a long *roman-fleuve* – a novel or sequence of novels about the same characters over a period – in thirteen parts [1915–38]) is written in what appears to be free indirect discourse modified by streaming dissolution:

> Why did the hanging garments remind her of All Saints Church and Mr Brough? . . . she must tell Harriet that in her letter . . . that day they suddenly decided to help in the church decorations . . . she remembered the smell of the soot on the holly . . .

The first sentence here combines the voice of some omniscient narrator with Miriam's own thoughts, in the style of free indirect discourse, but the *ellipses* and the flow from thought to thought indicate the flux of thinking characteristic of stream of consciousness. The combination of the two modes shows Richardson making use of the flexibility sought in the modern novelist's quest for new narrative modes.

It is this flexibility that really galvanized modern fiction. Through it, fiction developed endlessly subtle ways to characterize mental process – to recognize all the different factors that make it up. The questions to ask, then, about any particular style of narration you might encounter in modern fiction, are these: who is speaking, and how, and why? What aspect of mental life is explored by the writer's choice of narrative levels? And, perhaps most importantly, how is the writer developing a unique mode of narration by combining different levels – by finding some unique way to move up and down the scale that runs from the most inward narration to the most outward?

Flexible narration enabled writers not only to move inward but to experiment with all possible relations among inner and outer life. The main goal may have been to explore interiority, to delve into consciousness, but it was as important to test the links between the individual consciousness and its outer, social, practical worlds. To mix narrations from within and without became the most exciting endeavor, as writers came to equate modernity itself with just such a mixture. Ambiguity, plurality, heterogeneity: these in general came to seem the pattern of modern life and therefore the form for modern fiction. No single view or style of explanation could ever be adequate to the diversity of modern experience, and fiction therefore evolved toward greater inclusiveness, greater variety, and greater versatility. Such heterogeneity even diversified the very languages of fiction.

Since its inception, the novel has been a forum for different voices. Whereas other literary forms have seemed to try for unity of expression – staying with one style, one kind of talk – the novel has thrived by throwing different styles of expression together. High styles and low, big talk and small, native and foreign voices have all come together within the novel. They have come together to make novels better registers of social life, and they have come together in order to enable the novel to test the different claims made by different *discourses*. Other literary forms may stay within a single discourse – a single way of voicing cultural priorities – but the novel has gone for something more heterogeneous, a mix of priorities, something vocally diverse. In the words of Mikhail Bakhtin, the novel has always been a forum for "heteroglossia," a multitude of voices, patterning diversity into the very form of fiction. Bakhtin defined the novel as "a diversity of social speech types . . . and a diversity of individual voices artistically organized." The "internal stratification" of any nation's language – its "professional jargons, generic languages, languages of generations and age groups, tendentious languages, languages of the authorities, of various circles and passing fashions" – is the "indispensable prerequisite for the novel as a genre." The novel is a matter of the "compositional unities" that help this heteroglossia speak in structured form to the world.[6]

Heteroglossia happens in the novel when different values, arguments, and cultures are put into conflict and community through their different styles of speaking. It has been a way for novelists to test new social arrangements, to show how different cultural presumptions are encoded into the languages that express them, and to reflect the diversity which has been more and more a part of collective social life. And in the modern novel what had long been a tendency becomes more deliberate and more chaotic, as writers try hard to innovate "compositional unities" more aggressively given to diversity. *Ulysses* is the best example here. Joyce just lets all different kinds of people speak at once; moreover, he lets each chapter of *Ulysses* voice a different way of talking about the world. The various voices of Dublin send up a cacophonous chorus of aspirations and attitudes (nationalist pride; sexual longing; aesthetic idealism; religious intolerance). The voices of each of the novel's chapters speak from some different level of Irish culture (its ladies' magazines; its pub life; its literary history). The diversity here makes us think about the ways different styles of language inherently express different cultural values. And it makes us see how modern culture puts these into constant conflict and collaboration. Finally, we see how language evolves. We see linguistic creativity in action as the different voices lend to each other their various energies, or draw strength and conviction as they speak against one another.

Heteroglossia shows us language breaking up. What we might have presumed to be a single thing – the language shared by people of the same nation and culture – emerges as something plural, and discordantly so. We get variation where there had been unity. And when this variation gets most extreme, we get a texture, once again, of fragmentation. In this case, however, the fragments can be pieces of a richly progressive social plurality. Not only are the parts of the story broken apart from one another; acts of speaking break out of unified discourses into broken parts of speech. And if we combine this kind of fragmentation with that of narration, we might now get a full sense of the way fragmentation characterizes modern fiction. Narration, too, no longer proceeds in consistent patterns. Instead, as we have seen, it mixes streams of consciousness with omniscient narrators – third persons with first, and inner with outer perspectives. That inconsistency is psychological; heteroglossia, by contrast, is an inconsistency at the level of language, and, by extension, at the level of social outlook; and finally, the fragmentation we first encountered is that of structural discontinuity. Together, these fragmentations create the disjointed, wholly random and undone worlds of the modern novel. Together, they give us perhaps the clearest sense of just how the modern novel reformed itself to match the deformations of modernity.

CHAPTER 4

New Difficulties

In the modern novel's new versions of consciousness, its heteroglossia and its symbolism, its aleatory patterns and its ambiguous characterizations, we see the unique way modern writers tried to make fiction's forms a match for modernity. Modernity had brought new psychological discoveries, put new discourses into play, changed human relations; modern fiction in turn developed new forms to reflect those developments, and perhaps also to make them make more sense. At best, it even found possibilities for good form despite formlessness – languages and structures that could wrest truth or beauty out of the modern world's disorder. At least, modern fiction offered a way to pose the right questions – to call into question the changes modernity seemed to entail.

We turn now to look more closely at the way the forms of modern fiction might have made this difference – at least provoking questions, at best giving answers that could help people get imaginative control over modern life. We will see, among other things, how these forms aimed to comprehend modern *time* and *space*; what they intended by their notorious *difficulty*; and why they were committed above all to what we might call *aesthetic truth* – and with what consequences.

Ford Madox Ford noted that "what was wrong with the Novel, and with the British Novel in particular, was that it went straight forward."[1] Novels had tended to put things in chronological order, to tell their stories in linear fashion, and to Ford and other modern writers this practice seemed artificial. For even if events do happen in linear time, we tend not to experience them that way. At any moment, memories intervene, taking us back into the past even as we proceed into the future; or hopes project us forward, coloring the present with expectations of change; and other people's time frames often collide with our own to produce all kinds of temporal confusion. In recognition of these ways in which time is actually experienced, modern novelists often tried to break the sequence, to put things out of order, to work from the present back into the past, to dissolve linear time in the flux of memory and desire. Moreover, they found the potential for such temporal chaos so intriguing that they often made time itself the subject of their books. Often, they not only experiment with the presentation of time, but make it a focus for characteristically fundamental questions: what *is* time? How does it structure our lives? And how has modernity transformed it?

These were pressing questions for everyone, in these years, because time itself had demanded new attention. In the 1880s, the very measurement of time changed: it became *standardized*. To make trains run better, and to make factories more productive, clocks around the world were synchronized. As Stephen Kern writes in *The Culture of Time and Space: 1880–1918*, time therefore changed from a "heterogeneous," free pattern for private life to a system for homogeneous, public routine.[2] This change had two main effects. First, people came to see time as a force for standardization – and to resent it. A sense of freedom required some resistance to standard time, to mechanized linearity. The second effect is related to the first. People came to feel that they had within themselves a private time that was different from public time. Public time was lived by the clock; private time was idiosyncratic, and free. One inspiration here was the philosophy of Henri Bergson, who had encouraged writers to explore real inner "duration" – time as the "succession of our conscious states . . . which melt into each and permeate each other, without precise outlines."[3] This more obscure private time would become a mode for fiction, as would other changes: the world had begun to speed up, and fiction had to find a new pace in order to keep up with it; modernization had begun to leave past traditions behind, making writers wonder what meaning the past ought to have for the present; and even discoveries in physics would eventually suggest that time was not absolute, but relative – not uniform, but different depending upon your position in relation to it.

The new attitude toward time is summed up early in *The Sound and the Fury*, when Quentin Compson smashes the watch handed down to him by his father:

When the shadow of the sash appeared on the curtains it was between seven and eight oclock and then I was in time again, hearing the watch. It was Grandfather's and when Father gave it to me he said I give you the mausoleum of all hope and desire . . . I went to the dresser and took up the watch, with the face still down. I tapped the crystal on the corner of the dresser and caught the fragments of glass in my hand and put them into the ashtray and twisted the hands off and put them in the tray. The watch ticked on. I turned the face up, the blank dial with little wheels clicking and clicking behind it, not knowing any better.

When Quentin smashes clock-time, Faulkner announces a very typical modern intention: to defy chronology, to break free of linearity, to let life fracture more freely into all of its natural forms. Quentin can be taken as symbolic of the modern novelist, who wanted likewise to break free of the conventional temporal pattern, to depart from chronology, and to see how things would go if thought, feeling, and language could melt into "duration." Virginia Woolf also expressed the desire to investigate this temporal freedom, in the voice of the narrator of *Orlando* (1928):

Time, unfortunately, though it makes animals and vegetables bloom and fade with amazing punctuality has no such simple effect upon the mind of man. The mind of man, moreover, works with equal strangeness upon the body of time. An hour, once it lodges in the queer element of the human spirit, may be stretched to fifty or a hundred times its clock length; on the other hand, an hour may be accurately represented on the timepiece of the mind by one second. This extraordinary discrepancy between time on the clock and time in the mind is less known than it should be and deserves fuller investigation.

As "punctual" time became more strictly regular and linear, private time came to seem, by contrast, more erratic. As public time sped up, it seemed to demand, from writers, better ways to reproduce the rushing dynamicism that, for better or for worse, now determined the feel of ordinary life. Writers responded to these challenges in many ways, but mainly by stressing the vagaries of memory, by exploring the intensity of the present moment, and by letting the new temporalities transform the old patterns of narrative fiction.

When we remember the past, we do so incompletely, vaguely, and often in error – if we remember it at all. To explore these vagaries of memory, modern fiction writers tried to show how memory had to be a matter of difficult, creative, and even hazardous exploration. The most famous example of fiction devoted to the exploration of memory is Marcel Proust's *In Search of Lost Time* (1913–27), which revolutionized modern fiction by showing how real recollection (or true retrieval of the past) depended upon more peculiar and intense effort than people had thought. Writers of an earlier day might have presumed that the past was easily available to memory – that a writer need only think back in order to recall and to recreate the past. But Proust made it clear that the past is far more elusive, and that memory requires a far stranger process, one in which involuntary recall (when, for example, a smell or sound suddenly brings back a past moment very vividly) and hard work (involving, for example, the concentrated effort of writing and revising) only sometimes come together accurately and effectively to bring the past back to us. Proust wrote that the essences of life are strangely trapped beyond our reach, "and so it is with our own past. It is a labour in vain to attempt to recapture it all: all the efforts of our intellect must prove futile. The past is hidden somewhere outside the realm, beyond the reach of the intellect." If we are to regain it, it can only be by chance, or through the reaches of literary recall.

In general, this sense of memory as a problem came to pervade all of modernist storytelling, because stories are so often just someone's recollection of the past. In the modern novel, any such recollection happens fallibly, and the narrative result is confused and chaotic. *The Good Soldier* is the best example of this confusion. The confused protagonist tries to tell a coherent story, but since memory is faulty, he cannot just tell the story from start to finish. He has to keep backtracking, covering old ground, adding things forgotten and changing things misremembered. Toward the end of his story, he admits:

> I have, I am aware, told this story in a very rambling way so that it may be difficult for anyone to find their path through what may be a sort of maze. I cannot help it . . . [W]hen one discusses an affair – a long, sad affair – one goes back, one goes forward. One remembers points that one has forgotten and one explains them all the more minutely since one recognises that one has forgotten to mention them in their proper places . . . I console myself with thinking that this is a real story and that, after all, real stories are probably told best in the way a person telling a story would tell them.

The problem of memory here, as in much of modern fiction, destroys linearity, which had perhaps falsely suggests that memory has no problem getting the stories right.

And the *present* was no less mysterious. Just as it now seemed hard to recapture the past, it was hard accurately to convey a sense of the way time acts and feels as it passes in the present. Here the problem is not that the present is hidden from us; here the problem is that just what gives us the feel of the present – what makes us feel like we're living in the moment, that possibilities are unfolding, that things are becoming – is hard to convey in fiction. For fiction, which asks us to process words on a page, inevitably means some kind of removal from immediacy. How, then, to give readers the feel of immediate life, of the present moment, of time going by? And how to do this specifically in modern times, when present moments had grown so much more intense?

Evoking presence could mean vivid descriptions, or it could mean trying to capture the shape of a moment. It could mean giving a feel for the way things change, or trying to look behind change for what makes some moments eternal. Intense moments were perhaps the main preoccupation here, and perhaps the signature of the modern approach to time is the moment rendered at once ordinary and revelatory, at once a passing thing and a route to transcendence. There was precedent for this moment of transcendence in Romantic poetry: in *The Prelude* (1805/1850), William Wordsworth had written of "spots of time," moments in life distinguished by "deepest feeling," which "with distinct pre-eminence retain a renovating virtue" in future times of sadness or hopelessness. The modernist version of this transcendent moment reached its best-known formulations in what Woolf called "moments of being" and what Joyce called "epiphanies" – those flashes of insight achieved when, having been able to make "time stand still here," characters isolate moments from the rush of time and distill their fullest significance. Stopping time in this fashion, these moments partake of eternity, and perhaps model for us how we might find islands of meaning in the ordinary rush of time's stream.

In contrast with such possibilities, a regular linear time-sequence came to seem not just false, but oppressive, for it obliged readers and writers to follow a regular pace, and presumed simple relations between cause and effect, when in fact fiction could allow for more freedom, and more creativity, more questions. So the writers let time stop and start, leap ahead and slow down; they let time vary the way it seems to at the different moments of our ordinary lives. One way to describe this variation would be to say that modern writers made more extensive and creative use of the "speeds" always available to fiction.

There are four basic narrative speeds: scene, summary, pause, and ellipsis. *Scene* is perhaps the norm. It is the speed in which the time spent narrating is equal to time that passes in what is narrated (so it is most like a scene in the theater or in film). *Summary* happens when the narrator sums up a lot of time in a relatively shorter amount of narration. When a narration *pauses*, time stops, and the narrator takes the opportunity to fill in information. And finally, *ellipsis* is the term for what happens when a lot of time passes in a gap in the narrative – when the narration breaks, and jumps ahead, and a lot of time has passed even if no time has been spent on that time's passing.

If you think about these four speeds for a moment, you can fairly easily imagine how a deliberately conventional story might use them. Summaries might come at the beginning and end of chapters; scenes might be the main focus; pauses might come in the middle of scenes, for a narrator to fill in more background or evaluate the action; and ellipses would separate each chapter from the next. When modern fiction experiments with time, these speeds vary, in very strange ways. Sometimes, scene and ellipsis disappear altogether. Why? So that fiction can reflect the fact that there are really no moments in our lives where things fully pause or break off. (Woolf, for example, tends to try for a more seamless kind of writing, in which any breaks only take you to another place, rather than another time, and you feel that time never stops moving.) Sometimes, short scenes are full of long descriptive pauses, to reflect the fact that any thought or action can have a long history that needs explaining. In these cases a very short amount of time passes, but the length of the telling is long. And finally, in some cases, writers undo the difference between scene and summary. Their scenes are scenes of people remembering, or thinking in summary fashion about their lives. Since they are summing up, we get summary, but since we see them remembering, summary is scene. We get both at once. These are but a few examples of the ways that modern novels play with traditional narrative speeds in order to find better ways to convey the texture of modern life. Once again, the key sign of the modern is the mixing: speed varies, in ever new combinations, in order to reflect the irregularity of our real lives in time.

But not only in order to reflect it. Modern writers experimented with the representation of time in these various ways also in order to defy the temporality of modernity. Modernity seemed more and more to mechanize life. That was the problem with linearity, with public time: it seemed to restrict human possibilities, and subordinate them to the times of factories and calendars. The modernists believed that they could help restore a sense of free human possibility. The hope was that breaking linear sequences could help people toward a fuller sense of open possibilities – toward a sense of the way things could have been otherwise, and yet might change; or a truer sense of the past, in all the ambiguity memory contributes to it; or, finally, a keener sense of the richness of the present, and how one might even make time seem to stop by appreciating all of the "being" in any single moment. Or to trade the "life in time" for what E. M. Forster called the "life by values"[4] – life lived according to permanent, transcendent beliefs. When it comes to time, modern novels have a revolutionary purpose, for they aim to smash the clocks of the modern world, and break their hold on temporal freedom.

Does modern fiction have a similar purpose when it comes to *space*? Had modernity changed the nature of space in the same way it changed the nature of time, and did the changes inspire modern writers to reflect the difference? How did they do so?

Modern *city life* deeply changed the very nature of the novel. It meant a whole new set of interpersonal relationships. It meant new modes of contact: people were thrown together in new ways, without the kind of knowledge of each other they might have had in other, older places. Metropolitan perception had to be different. It was faster, more superficial, more unnerving. It saw things that were suddenly very desirable – and then suddenly very threatening. It had to deal in spaces that seemed not at all made for human life, and yet adapt to them. As the sociologist Georg Simmel claimed in 1903, metropolitan life meant an "intensification of emotional life due to the swift and continuous shift of external and internal stimuli." Fiction, to be true to this new life, had to develop new registers of intensity, speed, and flux. But it also had to work against the pattern of metropolitan life, because these stimuli were not just intensifying, but deadening. As

Simmel also claimed, "the metropolitan type . . . creates a protective organ for itself against the profound disruption with which the fluctuations and discontinuities of the external milieu threaten it." The city-dweller becomes "blasé," and so it also became fiction's job to keep the city-dweller from hardening into defensive lifelessness.[5] So one way the novel responded to the new spaces of modern life was to trace the swift and continuous shift of urban stimuli; another was to compensate for urban excess by providing readers with emotional restoration. What were others?

It became a "spatial form." Novels had tended to take one small space at a time. They were mainly temporal forms – unfolding in time, in particular spaces along the way. But the modern city expanded the spaces that fiction had to take in all at once. Any adequate cross-section of city life had to take in a lot of people and a lot of places at the same time. "Spatial form" was the way to do it. It meant stopping time, effectively, and spreading out description all over an urban space, letting the connections from one thing to the next be juxtapositions in space rather than time. One thing would lead to the next not in temporal sequence but in spatial proximity.

A good example comes in the very middle of *Ulysses*. Dublin's epic, the novel has a chapter that takes a panoramic view of the city's inhabitants. The chapter begins by following a leader of the church around town, giving us access to what thoughts he has in response to the sight of the people he serves. When these thoughts are troubled by the sight of a promiscuous young couple, our attention shifts to them, and then onward to other Dubliners, until the chapter has wandered about among a vast cross-section of the city. The things we see are not significantly sequential in time. They do not follow each other in the way events in a story typically proceed. They are proximate in space, and by moving through proximities from one to the next, *Ulysses* takes an entirely new approach to the presentation of space. Its structures become the structures of the story – whereas otherwise only individual spaces might have figured in it, as backgrounds for moments in time.

As Joseph Frank first defined it, "spatial form" is what happens more generally when writers "intend the reader to apprehend their work spatially, in a moment of time, rather than as a sequence." In this sort of spatial narrative, "the time-flow of the narrative is halted; attention is fixed on the interplay of relationships within the immobilized time-area. The relationships are juxtaposed independently of the progress of the narrative, and the full significance of the scene is given only by the reflexive relations among the units of meaning."[6] In other words, the content of the fiction is not something that unfolds in time, but something that is a spatial structure, like a painting. We are meant to consider it as a design rather than a story, and in this way space transforms fiction into a structural field. And we are meant to puzzle over the tension here between the fixed structure and the moving story – between moving narrative time and static spatial design, life in process and purer aesthetic form.

Fiction now also made space mutable. The fixed, predictable backgrounds of the past – the stereotypical settings, which served mainly to set the scene – gave way to places as inchoate as the minds that perceived them. In other words, fiction became interested in spaces for the way they varied depending upon who moved through them. In *Mrs Dalloway*, London's parks are open spaces where one person might see a threatening chaos while another finds a peaceful seclusion. Rather than stress any single landscape, Woolf chooses to show how space is relative. In *My Antonia*, Cather makes the vast landscape of the Nebraska plains a changeable factor. At first, when her protagonist is new to the place, the endlessness of the sky obliterates his sense of self; it means his insignificance: "Between the earth and that sky, I felt erased, blotted out." Later, when he feels more at home, he sees the endless sky as a symbol of some greatness in which he can play a part: obliterated before, now he thinks, "that is happiness; to be dissolved into something complete and great." Obliterating but the inclusive, the sky is not a fixed background. It is an actively changing, complicated participant in the story, subject to the same variation as human consciousness. Landscape had often played such a role in fiction, but now the *question* of its role is more directly a concern: as in *My Antonia*, its symbolic function in human "happiness" is perpetually tested and perpetually reconfigured.

But *My Antonia* is unusual for the way it presents a space in which its protagonist can eventually belong. Alienation more typically prevails, in modern fiction, and this means that protagonists tend to feel excluded from the spaces in which they move. The conflict here can mean different things for the representation of space. It can mean that spaces get personified, and given actively threatening personalities. It can mean that they get washed out, deprived of specificity, to reflect the way they fail to be habitable. Or they can get wholly remade in the mind – to become but projections of the alienated human consciousness. In any case they are rarely given in introductory description, as spaces of the past had been. That is, chapters of modern novels will rarely begin with descriptions of spaces, because of the fact that their protagonists do not inhabit space in the usual way. They conflict with it, and so appropriate description of space can no longer be the neutral, introductory scene-setting it might have been before.

And there is another reason why modern novelists would want to change their descriptions of space. As we have seen, modern writers often resist "materialism," believing that a materialist stress on objects and environments rules life out. New fiction had to trade material details for impressions, essences, things in flux, to free human character from definition solely in terms of the world of objects. Space, too, would have to recede from view. To let impressions of dynamic characters flow, to let subjective consciousness become central, and to trim fiction down to the spare essentials of thought and language, space would have to lose the fixity and solidity that had constrained fiction to the material world. And indeed it did so, just as time did, as Proust noted: "The places that we have known belong now only to the little world of space on which we map them for our convenience. None of them was ever more than a thin slice, held between the contiguous impressions that defined our life at that time; remembrance of a particular form is but regret for a particular moment; and houses, roads, avenues are as fugitive, alas, as the years." Space too would dissolve into the welter of impressions. The use of it in fiction would change, making it often that which would recede or dissolve away so that real life could return to the world of the novel.

Would these changes in the representation of space make a positive difference to modern life – the sort of positive difference modern writers hoped to make in their revolt against time? To some degree, modern writers hoped that they would. "Spatial form" would make people better able to conceptualize the modern city – to create the cognitive maps necessary to make the metropolis navigable. And the perspectival view of space could help people to understand how use makes space, how space cannot be a neutral background. But as an "outer" world, the world of space may not have been as central to the mission of modern fiction as the "inner" world of time. The modern novel, as we have seen, was largely a matter of moving inward. In that movement, it met more profoundly with time than with space. Indeed it might be possible to say that this new fiction left space behind, as strange as that may sound. As we will see, this departure, and this relative lack of engagement with public place, may have been one of the things future modern novelists would want to change.

In all of these changes to fiction's ways of enacting, describing, or patterning consciousness, time, space, there is a fundamental design upon the reader. The design relates back to the modern novel's main motivation, to try for something new. Newness would take the world and make it strange; by making it strange, it would require that people see it anew – or, see it truly for the first time. The word for this making-strange, coined by the formalist critic Viktor Shklovsky, is *defamiliarization*. Virtually every work of modern fiction aims to defamiliarize the world, and in so doing to surprise people back into real contact with it.

Modern fiction shocks us out of our complacent ways of seeing things. Unhappy with the way fiction had become too conventional, modern novelists were also unhappy with the way perception itself had become too routine. They felt that we took too much for granted – that the world had become so familiar that we no longer truly saw, felt, or understood it. So they wanted to take the familiar and render it unfamiliar, to redescribe things in such a way as to surprise and to shock, so that we would again pay real attention to them. Here is how Shklovsky described this problem and its solution in art:

> Habitualization devours works, clothes, furniture, one's wife, and the fear of war . . . And art exists that one may recover the sensation of life; it exists to make one feel things, to make the stone *stony*. The purpose of art is to impart the sensation of things as they are perceived and not as they are known. The technique of art is to make objects "unfamiliar," to make forms difficult.[7]

Such *defamiliarization* had always been the job of literary language. In its ways of describing things metaphorically and emotionally, literary language had always been about giving fresh attention to things that had fallen into ruts of perception. But with the modern novel, a few things changed, to make this defamiliarization more complete.

First of all, a style of language typically more common in poetry got applied to fiction: the style of fiction became more *poetically dense*, as writers tried more self-consciously to place stranger weight on every word and every description. And second, the fiction writer now set out self-consciously to *shock*; there was a change in the sense of mission, as writers went from feeling it was their job to present a transparent window on the world to feeling they ought to block the normal view. So a writer like Joyce, for example, now felt it important to slow down over the description of a funeral – to poeticize and sabotage it so that a reader, shocked and disoriented, could no longer look at a funeral in the same way again. And so Lawrence, in a famous scene in *Women in Love*, would now describe a rabbit as a savage, muscular beast, full of violent energy. Whereas your usual rabbit, according to hackneyed presumptions, might be soft, skittish, and harmless, Lawrence presents his rabbit "lunging wildly, its body flying like a spring coiled and released," "magically strong," a "thunderstorm": "The long demon-like beast lashed out again, spread on the air as if it were flying, looking something like a dragon, then closing up again, inconceivably powerful and explosive." The description in this case takes the familiar image of the rabbit and renders it very unfamiliar; in readers' minds, perhaps, rabbits then go from being insubstantial, cartoonish things to being things with actual, potent reality.

Defamiliarization may be the best justification for what sometimes gives modern art its bad name: its *difficulty*. We have already noted that trying for something new in fiction often meant making it a lot harder to read. There are many justifications for that difficulty, and defamiliarization is a main one. If it is necessary to shock people out of their conventional ways of seeing things, to make them aware of and not just subject to the changes modernity makes, then difficulty is a necessity.

What are some of the other motivations for making modern fiction so difficult? To answer this question it helps to know that the motivations fall into three basic categories. One is shock – the category into which defamiliarization falls, which has to do with the way difficulty forces change. A second has to do with imitation. If modern life has become more complicated, strange, and confused, then modern fiction must become as difficult, in order to reflect it accurately. And the third pertains to an entirely different agenda. Some writers felt that the future of the art of fiction depended upon a very fundamental departure from straightforward reference. That is, they felt that fiction could not be made of ordinary language, for then it would be nothing other than an ordinary form of communication. It needed to become more indirect, more a product of its own kind of language – more *abstract*. A third justification for difficulty in modern fiction was this wish to make fiction less a matter of direct reference to the world and more an abstract arrangement of artistic words, phrases, and meanings.

Joyce's funeral and Lawrence's rabbit redescribe familiar things in such a way as to shock us out of our normal preconceptions. Once we have read these descriptions, we not only see these particular things in terms of more vivid actualities, we learn to see everything this way. We absorb the shock, and all our perceptions then become more intense, more thorough, more alive. So the difficulty is justified, and even more so when we realize that the shocks of modern fiction very often came in imitation of the shocks of modern life. Many modern writers would have said that the difficulties of their fiction were not really their own inventions. Modern life was responsible – and modern fiction just responded, in imitation, in order to force people to face realities they might have been trying to deny. If *Cane* is hard to read, it is not just because Jean Toomer has decided to give us a hard time. Toomer wrote about *Cane* that "People have remarked its simple – easy flowing lyricism, its rich natural poetry; and they may assume that it came to bloom as easily as a flower. In truth, it was born in an agony of internal tightness, conflict, and chaos."[8] If such agony was its source, shouldn't that agony feature prominently in the product as well? Life now makes such conflicting claims upon an individual's identity that character can only be given in fragments; it now comes so often to crisis that plot can only move in fits and starts; it presents so many surprising appearances that literary description must often sound like nonsense. These difficulties are not fiction's creations. Fiction imitates the new "agony" of modern life, and if the result is hard to read, it is also entirely realistic. And if it seems unrealistic – if *Cane's* fragments and challenging descriptions seem made up – then perhaps that is because we have been refusing to face up to reality. The effort of a book like *Cane* may be to force us to stop simplifying. To stop simplifying, and to accept if not "agony" then *ambiguity*: perhaps the strangest thing about life for someone like Toomer was not the pain but the uncertainty, the fact that life (and therefore also the novel) seemed now impossible to unify.

This difficult imitation of modern life also derives from less dramatic changes – from changes as helpful, for example, as the advent of the telephone. Henry Green, who wrote novels like *Living* (1929) only in *dialogue*, did so in part because of the effect of the telephone on human communication:

> if [fiction] exists to create life, of a kind, in the reader – as far as words are concerned, what is the best way in which this can be done? Of course, by dialogue. And why? Because we do not write letters anymore, we ring up on the telephone instead. The communication between human beings has now come to be almost entirely conducted by conversation.[9]

Green's books are often very hard to read, because they omit communication other than dialogue; we get nothing other than the spoken words that characters exchange among each other. But this difficulty, according to Green, is warranted – by the fact that reality is ever more a matter of such strictly conversational meanings.

Unless *Cane* and *Living* also have a different mission: not to imitate reality, but to *abstract* fiction away from it. In that case, we have an entirely different justification for their difficulty.

How can fiction be abstract? Abstraction would seem impossible for the language of fiction, which is necessarily "referential." Painting is different: it is possible for a painting just to be an abstract design, which does not refer to something that exists in the real world. Not all paintings need be landscapes, or portraits. Some can be simple shapes, things in themselves, compositions of colors. But is there any equivalent in fiction? Can fiction also present merely abstract shapes, and not have its language refer to something beyond itself? Some modern fiction writers thought so – that it was possible for fiction to go abstract, and that it was even necessary, if fiction were to become something other than a slave to reality. For fiction to become truly artful, truly a matter of imaginative design and compositional beauties, it would have to give up trying to be realistic, and try instead to make its words something more like the compositions of abstract painting. This belief was relatively rare. As we have seen, for the most part modern fiction writers aimed at achieving a better realism. But in some cases, they tried to push things in another direction. When they did, a wholly different kind of difficulty resulted.

Abstraction creates much of the difficulty of *Ulysses*. The book is mainly hard to read because it tries to imitate the confusions of inner and outer life. The vagaries of consciousness and the chaos of urban life are the primary complexities. But Joyce is not only out to imitate the world. He is also out to redesign it – or to produce his own abstract composition that has much less to do with reality. *Ulysses* has eighteen chapters, each with its own formal pattern. Chapter 11, for example, takes the form of a musical fugue; chapter 13 bases its language on that of women's magazines; chapter 17 is like a catechism, a series of questions and answers, like a scientific inquiry:

> What action did Bloom make on their arrival at their destination?
> At the housesteps of the 4th of the equidifferent uneven numbers, number 7 Eccles street, he inserted his hand mechanically into the back pocket of his trousers to obtain his latchkey.
> Was it there?
> It was in the corresponding pocket of the trousers which he had worn on the day but one preceding.
> Why was he doubly irritated?
> Because he had forgotten and because he remembered that he had reminded himself twice not to forget.

This passage is representational, in that it does describe something, but it is very much abstract as well, because it is about form; it is not only describing Bloom coming home, but also enacting the form of the catechism. And the more Joyce focuses on the form, the less he tries to imitate reality. He seems hardly concerned to be describing something that might really be, and much more concerned to make some new literary shape, to create some new aesthetic style. Then, we get an abstract kind of difficulty. It is not one meant to defamiliarize or to imitate harsh new realities; it is one that happens as a result of an effort to complicate the art of fiction, to make it a forum for its own unreal designs.

Is this kind of difficulty justified? It may seem like the least valid of the three. The others try for truth and progress. They try to see reality more bravely and to make us more perceptive. But this third one may seem too self-involved, too precious. Then again, it may seem most admirably idealistic, for in his abstract artistry Joyce is trying to extend the boundaries of fictional art, and make it capable of new kinds of creativity. Fiction that devotes itself to strange new patterns with no realistic intentions may seem pointless; it may, however, also become most beautiful, most exciting, and most fun. So it often goes, with purely "aesthetic" endeavors: when writers like Joyce devote themselves solely to the abstract forms of writing, they risk pointlessness for the sake of art, meaninglessness for the sake of style. When they risk difficulty as well we sometimes want to refuse to go along with it. Perhaps art and style should mean pleasure – and perhaps difficulty is simply displeasing. Unless we enlarge our definitions of pleasure. And that is exactly what modern novelists like Joyce have wanted us to do: to take pleasure in difficulty, out of a sense that the best art is that which brings unimaginable beauty into the world.

As soon as it becomes clear that the modern novel involves both abstraction and imitation, it might seem that our definition of it has failed. How can this kind of fiction be defined in terms of something and its opposite? How can it be both real and unreal and still be one thing? Here it is necessary to admit that modern fiction is often a forum for opposite attitudes, practices, and purposes.

For example, we have noted that modern fiction has a redemptive mission. When writers like Woolf bring out the essential wonder in the ordinary elements of life, they do so in the hope of making us better able to enter this state of wonder ourselves; when Lawrence stresses the physical, and its necessary relation to thought and action, he does so in the hope of returning mental life to a state of real physical vitality. Such states would work against the degradations of modernity, in which we otherwise become subject to routine, to materialism, to "dissociated" sensibilities, and to dehumanization. But then again there are novels that stress dehumanization, with no redemptive purpose, but just a critical one. There are no moments of wonder; instead, there are just moments of defeat. In Faulkner and in Ford there are none of Woolf's "moments of being" – and no sense that we are being trained to counteract modernization with new forms of faith and idealism. Instead we get characters worn away by falsehood and disappointment, and if learning about them improves our lives at all, the process is only very indirect. So there are two tendencies here – opposite to each other, and yet equally central to modern fiction. There is the redemptive tendency, on the one hand, and the critical one, on the other.

Even when it comes to the whole question of modernity there is ambivalence. For some writers, modernity was a threat, against which fiction had to create protection. The modern novel, that is, had to work against modernization. But to other writers modernity was an opportunity – an opportunity for free creativity and more open expression. And modernization was therefore an inspiration, something to aspire to in fiction rather than something to reject. Even within single novels we see both impulses. In *Mrs Dalloway* characters wonder together at sky-writing – and yet clearly modern warfare has made a mess of the human psyche; urban change is exciting, and yet the past is recalled with a sad sense of loss. No one attitude finally prevails, even when it comes to the fundamental question of the meaning of the modernity to which the modern novel by definition responds.

But there is one constant. No matter what the purpose, and no matter what the cause, these modern novels share a strong commitment to what we might call "aesthetic truth." They all presume some vital link between fictional form and the finest justice. Whether it be in the link between defamiliarized description and revitalized perception, or between "epiphanies" and revelation, or between fragmentation and ironic insight, this commitment to aesthetic truth distinguishes the modern novel from other kinds of fiction that do not put such faith in form. As we have seen, the modern novel aims above all to do justice to the modern world. But the kind of justice it seeks is an aesthetic justice, an artful form of judgment, handed down from the topmost imagination and given in new forms for new realities.

Aesthetic truth, however, was often sought for its own sake. It could be a matter of refining people's perceptions and making them more capable of critical insight, but it could also be a matter of "art for art's sake" – of pursuing fine forms for no purpose at all. Some writers wanted fiction to become, like the finest arts, wholly gratuitous, a world of its own, not a way to get a purchase on modern reality, but a refuge from it. And as we will now see, this aspect of the faith in form, this extreme "aestheticism," would make the modern novel controversial for years to come.

CHAPTER 5

Regarding the Real World: Politics

Did their passion for aesthetic justice keep modern novelists from doing justice to the real world? Did ambiguity, difficulty, movement into "consciousness" wreck the novel's power to pay attention to outward things? Did the novel's new dispersals and dissolutions make it impossible for the novel to deal responsibly with social and political problems? Some people thought so – George Orwell, for example, who noted in 1940 that "in 'cultured' circles art-for-art's-saking extended practically to worship of the meaningless. Literature was supposed to consist solely in the manipulation of words. To judge a book by its subject matter was the unforgivable sin."[1] Had the modern novel become so concerned with art that it had become "meaningless" to the wider world?

In a moment, we will explore Orwell's complaint more fully. First, however, this chapter will stress that strange new *forms* did not necessarily mean "worship of the meaningless." The hope was that there would be no need to choose – that form and politics could come together, if advances in form could make the novel a more sensitive, responsive, and expressive form of engagement. But could the novel be both aesthetically innovative and engaged with real-world problems and issues? What were some of the ways it tried to do so?

There were many – and in a sense the combination was unavoidable. For the new forms of the modern novel were of course *provoked* by real-world social and political problems and events. Social change was one of the main provocations for the novelist's sense of new opportunity (remember Woolf's cook). The war was perhaps the main provocation for the need to question reality (for example, in the way it refuted the "idea of progress"). And other major real-world developments – in imperialism, in city life, in the rise of consumer culture – figured dominantly not only in the modern novel's subject-matter, but in all the experimental forms that sometimes seem simply "aesthetic." It was Conrad's horror of the excesses of Belgium's imperial exploitation of the Congo that led him to feel a need for the kind of "solidarity" he hoped the novel's aesthetic intensity could achieve; it was Joyce's frustration with Ireland's role as "the cracked looking glass of a servant" before its English master that prompted him to turn the novel into a broken reflection of reality. The new feel of "metropolitan perception" intensified the novel, and urban living also wholly changed the writer's job, by making life a matter of overwhelming crowds, lonely isolation, and cosmopolitan connections to the larger world of commerce and culture. So even if the modern novel often seems *autotelic* – focused inward on itself, concerned only with its own styles and structures – it was utterly formed by public problems and responsibilities.

Moreover, the new forms of modern fiction also enabled new public commitments. As we will now see, the new effort to ground fiction in the details of physical life made it better able to deal with the new sexuality that had become so controversial and essential a feature of modern life. The new sense of space and of perspective made fiction more responsive to life in regions of the world that had formerly been thought merely peripheral. Perspective also helped explore the new realities in social-class relations, and in the lives of minority groups. In these and other ways, the modern novel's aesthetic experimentation enabled new purchase on the real world.

Willa Cather, for example, brought new aesthetic distinction to the American West, and thereby argued for its cultural centrality. Seeing the western landscape through a powerful modern style of symbolism, describing it in the new "defurnished" language of aesthetic intensity, Cather made the West seem as important as more central places, and helped change the nature of "regionalist" writing. In the past, regional writing had inclined toward what we call "local color": it tended to treat the outlying regions of America and England as quaint, charming, exotic – not *normal*, but also not seriously important. Outlying regions were often described as places of peace or of adventure; their inhabitants were charming types; regional writing was for cultured people to take mental vacations, or imagine exciting places not inhabited by truly real people. But Cather (and writers like her) saw regional life very differently. She saw it for real, using modernized styles and approaches to describe regional life as something just as gritty, just as ordinary, and just as interesting as life in the centers of culture. Her places were demanding, difficult, truly inspiring places; they were populated by shrewd hard workers, sophisticated immigrants, and real problems; it took good aesthetic effort to appreciate them, and the result was a true sense of the real hardships and satisfactions of regional life. Making this kind of difference, Cather did something that was both new and socially important, and she herself says as much in *My Antonia*. Her protagonist is reading Virgil, the great Roman poet who had brought new dignity to the description of rural life centuries before. In her account of what it means to read Virgil, Cather implies that she may be his modern-day counterpart – bringing to the American West the dignity he had brought to his world long ago: " *'Primus ego in patriam mecum . . . deducam Musas'*; 'for I shall be the first, if I live, to bring the Muse into my country.' "

Real life in America's regions was one of the modern novel's discoveries. Another was the truth about imperialism – the realities of the western exploitation of other parts of the world. By 1900, Great Britain had become an imperial master of much of the world. It ruled lands everywhere – in India, in Africa, and all over the globe. But its mastery of the people of these places was not seen in the way we are inclined to see it today: whereas today we tend to reject as immoral and unfair the domination of one people by another, before 1900 the attitude was very different. For example, even John Ruskin, the marvelous Victorian art critic, could write, in 1870, that England as "true Daughter of the Sun" must "guide the human arts, and gather the divine knowledge, of distant nations, transformed from savageness to manhood, and redeemed from despairing into peace."[2] The general attitude held that Great Britain's imperial rule was or could well be a wonderful thing – a force for civilization, a moral right, something glorious. Around 1900, however, this general attitude began to change. People came more and more to question Great Britain's right to world domination, and to see as immoral and even evil the way it treated its subject peoples. Fiction played an important part in this change of mind. Not right away: for a long time, novels tended to glamorize imperialist adventure. But around 1900 they began to take a more balanced view, and, ultimately, a much more critical one.

For example, Rudyard Kipling's *Kim* (1901) shows us fiction changing – partially glamorizing imperialist adventure, but then also revealing the truth about it through the modern novel's innovative
perspectives. In *Culture and Imperialism*, Edward Said notes the change
in attitude behind this shift: "It was as if having for centuries com-
prehended empire as a fact of national destiny either to be taken for
granted or celebrated, consolidated, and enhanced, members of the
dominant European cultures now began to look abroad with the skepticism and confusion of people surprised, perhaps even shocked by
what they saw."[3] The change from taking empire for granted to becoming skeptical and confused is a change the modern novel was well
suited to document and encourage. And in *Kim*, we see it dramatizing
what Said describes as "an ironic sense of how vulnerable Europe was"
– when, for example, Kim's identity as a westerner is repeatedly
thrown into question:

> A very few white people, but many Asiatics, can throw themselves into
> a mazement as it were by repeating their own names over and over
> again to themselves, letting the mind go free upon speculation as to what
> is called personal identity. When one grows older, the power, usually,
> departs, but while it lasts it may descend upon a man at any moment.
>   "Who is Kim – Kim – Kim?"

Kim's identity becomes modern, it seems, as a result of his experience
in India, as a result of being "an insignificant person in all this roaring
whirl of India," and in showing how, this modern novel helps to
update and to complicate fiction's treatment of the problem of imperialism.

One year later, Conrad published his far more scathing account of
the results of imperialism in Africa (*Heart of Darkness*, which, as we
have seen, brought a new kind of critical intensity to the modern
novel). And then by the 1920s, skepticism about imperialism had
become a key feature of the novel's more general suspicion about
modern life. E. M. Forster's *A Passage to India* (1924) became the first
classic of anti-imperialist writing, for the way it laid bare the
hypocrisies and inauthenticity of British government in India.

Forster depicts the British in India as petty, stifling, and unjust, and
he contrasts their smallness with the relative grandeur of the Indian
landscape and Indian spirituality. And the plot makes it clear that the

British presence in India is a force for chaos and confusion rather than civilized rule. An Indian man is wrongly accused of rape; the accuser, a good British woman new to India, had been disoriented in the Marabar Caves (whose sinister mysteries are perhaps symbolic of the Indian spirit Britain could never control), and in her disorientation she thought that her friend and guide had raped her. Immediately the British establishment gears up into outraged action; hysteria and injustice follow, and by the time the man is finally exonerated, it has become clear that these two cultures cannot coexist. It becomes clear that the British presence in India is a farce – and moreover, that western presumptions of superiority make no sense at all, that "Englishmen like posing as gods" but no longer fool anybody when they do so. Forster also takes pains to evoke the different power of Indian religions and to prove that they demand concepts different from what the British could imagine. Here, we get a new indictment of imperialism, through the difference the modern novel could make. In the past, the novel had largely been "empirical": it began in the real details, and worked from there to build toward more general theories, beliefs, and conclusions. But Indian spirituality seemed to demand of Forster a more "ideal" approach – an approach that would somehow begin in a sense of mystery, in a world of abstractions. So when it comes to describing the Marabar Caves – the primeval locus of the novel's big "muddle" – Forster stresses the limits of language:

> He finds it difficult to discuss the caves, or to keep them apart in his mind . . . Nothing, nothing attaches to them, and their reputation – for they have one – does not depend upon human speech. It is as if the surrounding plain or the passing birds have taken upon themselves to exclaim "extraordinary," and the word has taken root in the air, and been inhaled by mankind.

Wanting to debunk the myth of British imperial superiority, Forster tried to evoke the truly "other" pattern of eastern reality. To do that, he had to go with the modern novel beyond a traditional "empirical" bias, and insofar as he was successful, we might say the "essential" attitude of the modern novel was instrumental in promoting political justice.

It played a similar role when it came to the problem of social class. Just as Forster and others used the modern novel to take a new view of imperialism, writers took a new view of what it meant to be rich, to be poor, to be middle class. These things had, of course, always been the subject of fiction, but the modern novel helped to get at the very foundations of what D. H. Lawrence called "class-bound consciousness," or the ways people's very minds were secretly molded by social-class presumptions. Forster, for example, famously admitted the class-bound consciousness of his set in *Howards End* (1910), his great novel about the "condition of England" at the time of modern social upheaval: "We are not concerned with the very poor. They are unthinkable, and only to be approached by the statistician or the poet. This story deals with gentlefolk, or with those who are obliged to pretend that they are gentlefolk." This statement is indicative: the poor *had* tended to be "unthinkable" for the typically middle-class novelist. But as Forster's statement also indicates, novelists had become more self-conscious about that fact, and concerned to unmask the "pretenses" of social class. And as Virginia Woolf wrote, the writer who had stood comfortably atop a tower of privilege, "scarcely conscious either of his high station or of his limited vision," found himself around 1914 far more self-conscious, and felt his tower leaning down toward the ground.[4]

D. H. Lawrence gave fiction new class consciousness. As the novelist Angela Carter has noted, his novels were unique for the way they "describe the birth of the upper working, lower middle, upwardly-socially-mobile-via-education class as a force to be reckoned with."[5] Lawrence's approach to the lives of the working classes was new for the way it involved no condescension, no hand-wringing, no superficial treatment; by contrast, it found in working-class subjects the same aesthetic complexity most novels previously found only among more elevated people. And it went even further than that. As we have noted, Lawrence wrote under the influence of the belief that physical life was what really mattered, the basis and determining thing in all our higher thoughts and feelings. This outlook made him see working-class life with no prejudice against physical labor – and instead with the belief that the life of the body is the true one, the more truly spiritual and fulfilling aspect of human being. So his fiction not only introduced other classes of experience into the modern novel; it did so with the implication that this experience was superior. Closer to the true physical basis of being, unspoiled by the high pretensions of other styles of life, honest and direct and motivated by practical need and feeling, the subjects of Lawrence's writing helped to free "consciousness" from its class-based biases.

If Lawrence helped to change thought about the lower classes, other novelists tried to lay bare fantasies of wealth and privilege. F. Scott Fitzgerald most famously documented the excesses and evils of the rich – the recklessness of America's new culture of prosperity, the way it could ruin lives, and the difficulties it created in relations between wealthy America and the world beneath it. But Fitzgerald also changed class consciousness, by exploring the fantasies that perpetuate inequitable systems, the delusions about wealth that make aristocracies seem worth keeping. In *The Great Gatsby* (1925), the rich are notoriously reckless, and the society they represent comes under a new and devastating kind of scrutiny, which reveals its emptiness and irresponsibility. At the same time, however, *The Great Gatsby* treats the rich with all the obsessive, starry-eyed admiration characteristic of Fitzgerald's culture. Fitzgerald knew that no amount of bad behavior would end America's romance with the rich, and the fantasy involved – the combination of tragic recklessness and endless appeal – was his great modern subject.

But perhaps the most innovative writer on the subject of class was a writer who managed to combine the experimentalism of Joyce with the social sensitivities of Lawrence and Fitzgerald. This was Henry Green, who wrote a series of novels that enact cross-class interactions with very extreme objectivity. As we have seen, in these novels there is hardly any description, no "consciousness," no authorial explanation or evaluation; there is mainly just dialogue – mainly just the characters themselves speaking their positions and perspectives. *Living* gives us working-class factory life directly in the voices of the people on the factory floor; *Loving* (1945) gives us life at all levels in an Irish mansion, again only in the dialogue through which masters and servants perform their complicated cultural minglings. Like Lawrence and Fitzgerald, Green is out to tell unspoken truths about class differences, and to present lower-class life in new, realistic detail. But he has chosen to find a different form to do so: he seems to think that these differences and details are all in the very language different classes actually use, to make love, to get things done, to work, to complain, to describe themselves. Here, from *Loving*, is an example of a typically terse yet revealing interchange:

"I feel we should all hang together in these detestable times."

"Yes Madam."

"We're really in enemy country here you know. We simply must keep things up. With my boy away at the war. Just go and think it over."

"Yes Madam."

"We know we can rely on you you know Arthur."

"Thank you Madam."

"Then don't let me hear any more of this nonsense. Oh and I can't find one of my gloves I use for gardening. I can't find it anywhere."

"I will make enquiries. Very good Madam."

Green seems to think that putting these languages into dialogue is the best way to enact social class in fiction, the best way to show it to you directly rather than just to tell you about it. Thinking this way, he took the heteroglossia of the experimental novel in a very different direction: whereas in Joyce and Woolf it had gone toward dissolution and fragmentation, in Green it becomes strictly external and as fully intelligible as practical speech itself. For Joyce and Woolf, experimental fiction meant subjective fiction; for Green, wanting to tell the truth about social class, and wanting to find a new form for the telling, experimental fiction had to become objective fiction to a newly extreme degree.

How formal difference helped to make a real social difference is perhaps nowhere more clear than in the difference made in novels by and for women. Just at the moment in which fiction had most clearly started going modern, women had begun to agitate with new ferocity for equal rights. The year 1910 was the one in which Virginia Woolf said "modern fiction" had become a necessity. In the following year, the suffragette movement in England found women breaking windows and committing suicide in order to try to get the vote. The change in tactics – the new energy in feminism around this time – made itself felt as well in fiction. First of all, in direct ways: women writers tried more overtly to get at women's unique experiences – and male writers more and more had to reckon with increases in female power and independence. But there was a stranger and more fascinating result, too, that had to do with fiction's treatment of *interiority*.

The modern novel served feminist interests most obviously by helping women to defy the conventional plots of social life. If traditional plots ended in marriage, the new plots (or plotlessness) of the modern novel could help modern women imagine different options. The drive of *Mrs Dalloway*, for example, is not toward social conformity, but toward the fullest exploration of "being"; it could therefore help real-world women imagine how to change the focus of their actual lives. Perhaps the most famous example of this change in focus is what happens in Kate Chopin's *The Awakening* (1899). The novel created a huge scandal by presenting a woman who, unhappy in marriage because too passionate and too imaginative, has an adulterous affair, and ultimately commits suicide rather than return to the conformity of acceptable womanhood and conventional marriage. By the time the woman, Edna, finally walks into the sea, and thinks, "How strange and how awful it seems to stand naked under the sky! how delicious! She felt like some new-born creature, opening its eyes in a familiar world that it had never known," she has enabled a new awareness in women's lives, and though her life ends in suicide, in a sense she dies so that other women will not make the mistakes that led her to that fate.

But the modern novel also served feminist interests by innovating a new form for expression of female consciousness. In a way, women's minds were a key site for modern experimentation. We see the connection at the end of *Ulysses*, where Molly Bloom's thoughts become the model for the novel's most completely "streaming" consciousness. But we first see the connection before that, in the work of a woman writer often said to be the original innovator of stream-of-consciousness writing. Dorothy Richardson's *Pilgrimage*, a multi-volume exploration of a woman's developing mind, developed a new style in order to convey the shape of a woman's thoughts. Richardson spoke of her efforts to "produce a feminine equivalent of the current masculine realism," a feminine alternative in which "the form of contemplated reality [had] for the first time in [her] experience its own say."[6] If in fact the alternative to realism – the modern novel's interest in "contemplated reality" – developed even in part as a result of Richardson's effort to find a "feminine equivalent," then we might say that a feminist effort was key to the modernization of the novel. Moreover, we might say that fiction's new alternative to masculine realism was necessary to appreciate women's ways of thinking, and that the modern novel therefore gave new meaning to women's minds. In other words, even in the apparently autotelic form of "contemplated reality," there was perhaps this important new social effect: women's minds were finally given full, unique, and inspiring consideration.

The question of the modern novel's social causes and effects is most perplexing when it comes to the fiction of the Harlem Renaissance. That movement produced many novels that were truly unprecedented: never before had African-American life been presented so accurately and honestly, and rarely had it been allowed to take center stage in fictions of real modern life. When featured in fiction before, African Americans had mainly been "characters," sources of peculiar interest, charming folk-tales, and amusing dialect. Now came the chance to see African-American life realistically, and the modern novels that did so were therefore also forces for social justice. But *Cane* – which used modernist techniques to dramatize the agonies of the African-American soul – was not the norm here. The norm was much more normal, because of the need felt among African Americans to stress normality and to create a tradition. Writers like Woolf and Joyce could break with the past and risk strangeness because they had a long tradition behind them and not so much to lose. African-American writers, by contrast, had responsibilities; they felt required to depict coherent selves and functional communities – and not to defy tradition, but to start one. Although these writers often wanted to devote themselves to pure art, and go where modern art was taking the rest of the western world, they also felt more strongly the need to stick with positive social realism – the kinds of books that would not lose themselves in experiment or call fundamental realities into question.

Here, then, the relation between modern experiment and social realities is different, and demands a different way of thinking about what it means to be modern. In *Modernism and the Harlem Renaissance*, Houston Baker addresses this difference by noting that

> the moment of the 1920s known as the "Harlem Renaissance" has frequently been faulted for its "failure" to produce *vital, original, effective* or "modern" art in the manner, presumably, of British, Anglo-American, and Irish creative endeavors. To wit, the signal outpouring of black expressive energies during the American 1920s is considered . . . as "provincial" . . . The familiar creators of Harlem . . . do not, in the opinion of any number of commentators, sound "modern."[7]

They don't sound modern, but they are so in their own way, and Baker stresses that we must consider the difference context makes. In exploring the modern fiction of the Harlem Renaissance, we have to keep in mind that the sources of experiment and its desired effects are not those of fiction by Woolf or Joyce, and that what looks traditional is often experiment by other means.

One example of this very differently modern writing is *Quicksand* by Nella Larsen (1928). *Quicksand* is about a biracial woman who is simply never allowed to live a normal life. In black society, she never feels black enough: she never wants to commit wholly to the wishes and politics of Harlem or the black university where she teaches for a time. But then of course she never feels at home in white society, either: when she goes to stay with relatives in Copenhagen, she becomes an exotic – beloved, but never really included, and never comfortable with the utter lack of black cultural life there. Caught between races, never able to fit in, she runs perpetually from one situation to the next, really just digging herself deeper into trouble. All this is described conventionally enough. This is not *Ulysses*, and it does not try for the psychic dissolutions, linguistic defamiliarizations, time-shifts, or abstractions of other aggressively experimental books. But its protagonist really embodies experimentation. Any plot based upon her would have to be new, not only because the racial questions she raises had not been raised before, but because she perpetually seeks change. No current conditions can be right for her, and in the search for better ones she drives fiction onward toward new, modern discoveries. There is an inescapable modernity, for example, in the fact that she "can neither conform, nor be happy in her unconformity," in her "indefinite discontent," which make her identity and her life's plot so fragmentary. And so there is something wholly new in Larsen's effort to reflect African-American modernity.

Even fiction written in extremely traditional forms could become modern in this different cultural context. Zora Neale Hurston wrote her fiction deliberately in the old style of the African-American folktale. She was an anthropologist as well as a novelist, and she used her research into traditional black culture as a way to re-establish a distinctly African-American style of storytelling. In her essay on "Characteristics of Negro expression," for example, Hurston reports her findings that in African-American folk language, "words are action words," and "everything is illustrated" and given to "rich metaphor and simile." These characteristics have already "done wonders" for the English language – and Hurston extends them further to give her fiction the vitality other modern writers sought by other means.[8] Since the style was "traditional," it was really the antithesis of modern; but since it brought new sensibilities, new ethics, and new plots to fiction, it created a new cultural consciousness. In, for example, *Their Eyes Were Watching God* (1937), tradition becomes radical innovation, because Hurston develops a narrative voice not heard before – a voice that speaks out of the past of folk wisdom but into a future of progressive change. The style is, after all, abstract; it is not so different from the styles of more obviously experimental fiction, because it describes things in terms of their spiritual, essential significance. For example, Hurston tends to describe objects as if they were alive and conscious; by contrast, she sees certain aspects of people merely as lifeless things. This reversal shows how she achieves, by other means, those higher meanings and skeptical insights other novelists got by trying something completely new. What was new to them came to her out of the past. But since that past was new to the world of the novel – since it was product of African-American folkways not let in before – it could produce wholly modern effects.

For Hurston and Larsen and other writers associated with the Harlem Renaissance, there always persisted a big question about the duty of fiction: should it try for aesthetic experimentation, in the interest of becoming as artistic as possible; or should it try for political significance, in the interest of advancing the causes of the race? The writers and artists of the Harlem Renaissance perpetually debated these questions about purpose of art. Was it to be beautiful, or to be useful? Should it, in other words, try always for greatness on the aesthetic front, or was it more important that it aim for the political good? Of course the dilemma was never solved. And of course these questions were asked by everybody – and would pull the novel in opposite directions for all the years to come. Art or politics; form or content; experimentation or accessibility: these dilemmas would subsequently become the action of a kind of pendulum, swinging the novel back and forth between its aesthetic and social commitments. As we have already seen, from the start people questioned the way the modern novel dealt with these different commitments. At best, they could be one – as they were for Forster, for Green, and for Hurston. Soon, however, this unity came to seem much harder to achieve, as social and political demands began to call the forms of the modern novel into question.

It was not long before the mood of the modern began to change. The impulse to try something new to redeem modernity was soon challenged. What had set out around the time Henry James championed the "art of fiction" (1884) and reached a pinnacle perhaps at the moment of *Ulysses* (1922) hit stumbling blocks when the 1920s gave way to the 1930s. Times of prosperity and peace (good conditions for purely aesthetic experiment) gave way to times of hardship, danger, and intense political demands. Due to the economic hardships of the Great Depression, and due to the rise of extreme political parties (Fascism on the one hand and Communism on the other), writers everywhere found it more and more necessary to take a political stand, even in their fiction. And as these political developments led to violence, writers thought it would be almost obscene to fritter away their time in precious aesthetic experiments. Aesthetic experimentation came to seem like an impossible luxury, at a time in which the very basis of human existence seemed to be in peril. For the modern novel, this meant (as the novelist Aldous Huxley put it) that "a reaction had begun to set in – away from the easy-going philosophy of general meaninglessness towards the hard, ferocious ideologies of nationalistic and revolutionary idolatry."[9]

One good index of the change is what happened to the fiction of Virginia Woolf. She has been one of our central modern writers, for the way she sought to disclose "life itself" through a defamiliarizing focus on ordinary "moments of being." In 1931, she published a novel that most completely met these goals: *The Waves*, Woolf's most difficult book, is pure "consciousness," and nowhere in it does the real world seem to violate the pure minds of what are less real characters than essences of humanity. But just after publishing *The Waves* Woolf turned toward something completely different. Like everyone else, she came to feel that fiction now required new social and political responsibility, and so she began to try to write what she called an "essay-novel." The plan was to "take in everything, sex, education, life," and it found Woolf "infinitely delighting in facts for a change, and in possession of quantities beyond counting"; it found her saying, "I feel now and then the tug to vision, but resist it" – very strange for a novelist whose visionary impressions had helped to define the modern novel.[10] This essay-novel – called *The Pargiters*, and not published as such in Woolf's lifetime – was as different as possible from what had come before. It depicted mundane social reality and focused on social problems, and evaluated them directly in "essay" statements of fact and opinion. This more socio-historical outlook would become typical in fiction for a number of years. Many writers would begin to seek a more essayistic, even documentary realism, out of a sense that new political exigencies demanded more direct and interventionist engagement with the world.

"Social realism" returned. But could it be compatible with the priorities of the *modern* novel, which, as we have seen, wants to stretch the limits of what counts as reality? If the new novels of social realism were out simply to describe, to document, and to criticize, could they also create new realities in the spirit of modern fiction? Some people say no: they stress a striking difference between *modernism* in the novel and the *realism* that returned with the political climate of the 1930s.

Could the best fiction have it both ways? The best writers knew that their social and political message would most effectively get the attention of the world if they truly opened up new ways of seeing and feeling about things, and if they described things in compelling new ways. To understand how the aesthetic and the political could join together in this way – and to understand why, at this moment, they would have to – we might turn to the work of the writer who best represents the political moment in the middle of twentieth-century fiction: George Orwell.

Orwell had always been something of a critic of the aesthetic bias of the modern novel. To him, extreme experiments had always seemed precious: detachment from reality, radical skepticism, and playing around with language looked to him fairly self-indulgent. Moreover, such tendencies seemed to him not idealistic, but just a privilege of wealth. Wondering about the causes of the modern attitude, Orwell wrote: "Was it not, after all, *because* these people were writing in an exceptionally comfortable epoch? It is in just such times that 'cosmic despair' can flourish. People with empty bellies never despair of the universe, nor even think about the universe, for that matter."[11] And yet in the 1930s Orwell also disliked the way things had gone too far in the other direction. He noted that the highly politicized atmosphere of the decade had made good fiction impossible. People were all too concerned to write sociological works and to pamphleteer; imaginative prose, as a result, became barren, and (according to Orwell) no good fiction got written: "No decade in the past hundred and fifty years has been so barren of imaginative prose as the nineteen-thirties. There have been good poems, good sociological works, brilliant pamphlets, but practically no fiction of any value at all . . . It was a time of labels, slogans, and evasions . . . It is almost inconceivable that good novels should be written in such an atmosphere."[12] What Orwell thought necessary was some kind of middle ground, between political responsibility and imaginative freedom. He himself achieved it, in his great imaginative works of political criticism: *Animal Farm* (1945) and *1984* (1949). In these books, he found creative means to argue political points, most notably in the choice of the form of the *dystopia* – the vision of a bad future world.

In Orwell's bad future world, totalitarianism (the threat presented in the 1930s and after by Communism and Fascism) has come to dominate the world and to mechanize every aspect of people's lives. No freedom is possible – not even the freedom to think. Language itself has been remade, in "Newspeak," to rule out the possibility of subversive thought, as we learn when one of its creators describes it:

> Do you know that Newspeak is the only language in the world whose vocabulary gets smaller every year? . . . Don't you see that the whole aim of Newspeak is to narrow the range of thought? In the end we shall make thoughtcrime literally impossible, because there will be no words in which to express it . . . The Revolution will be complete when the language is perfect.

Even the truths of history are subject to revision, all in order to guarantee full subjugation of the individual mind. Had Orwell simply meant to argue that these could be the results of totalitarian politics, he might have written an essay, or documentary fiction, but then he would have been giving in to the "barren sociology" of the fiction he disliked. Instead, he chose an imaginative form for his polemical content; dystopia was the ideal brainchild of the conflicting political and aesthetic demands of the day. Moreover, *1984* carried on the experimental tradition of the modern novel in other, indirect ways: "Newspeak" is an experimental language exactly opposite to what the modern novel had tried to develop; "thoughtcrime" is a psychological possibility exactly opposite to what the modern novel had wanted to discover. Dramatizing these negations, Orwell indirectly championed the innovations of the modern novel, at a time in which history seemed to have no time for them.

To get right to *1984*, however, is to skip over the political fictions of earlier years. By 1945, Orwell had come up with good ways to be both political and aesthetic. Earlier, it was more difficult both to try for modern innovation and yet to be politically realistic, and so the achievements of those writers able to do so are well worth noting.

Aldous Huxley's *Brave New World* (1932), for example, is an earlier attempt to do what Orwell would do fifteen years later: combine the experimental outlook with social responsibility. Another dystopia, *Brave New World* also dramatizes social dangers not by exposing them directly, but by imagining a world in which they have come fully to dominate. The new scientific approaches to cultural organization – in Fascism, in Communism, and also in the attempts in England and America to engineer a fairer distribution of wealth – are presented here in their most extreme form, as a system in which human beings are scientifically produced and systematically administered. As Huxley would later say, the book is about "the nightmare of total organization," in which "modern technology has led to the concentration of economic and political power, and to the development of a society controlled . . . by Big Business and Big Government," and in which "nonstop distractions of the most fascinating nature . . . are deliberately used as instruments of policy, for the purpose of preventing people from paying too much attention to the realities of the social and political situation."[13] Because this last problem – of brainwashing, of propaganda – seemed to him most fundamental, Huxley felt he could not just speak against the "nightmare" straightforwardly. He wanted to sound a political warning, but could not do it directly, if he wanted to compete with the "fascinations" at work in the brave new world of modernity. He had to do some "hypnopaedia" – some hypnotic teaching – himself, for "unfortunately correct knowledge and sound principles are not enough." A real "education in freedom" would require "thorough training in the art of analyzing [propaganda's] techniques and seeing through its sophistries." The key word here is "art": an aesthetic power over language was what the world needed, and this perhaps is what Huxley provides by couching his political warning in an aesthetic form.[14]

But the main trick, for the modern writer wanting also to be a responsible political writer, was to find some way to make the documentary voice an artful one – some way to make realism a transformative style of seeing. Politics would then not reduce fiction to preaching; art could advance even as the fiction advanced its ideas; the "dialectic" could continue to enrich life and art alike. One writer who did the trick was Christopher Isherwood. He was well placed to appreciate the political crises of the 1930s: he spent those years in Berlin, watching Hitler rise to power, and seeing the violence of World War II build. And he described these political developments in fiction, from a peculiar documentary point of view. The narrator of *Mr Norris Changes Trains* (1935) and *Goodbye to Berlin* (1939) at first calls himself a "camera," implying a certain direct realism, but that camera-view is always ultimately very much involved with personal lives: "I am a camera with its shutter open, quite passive, recording, not thinking. Recording the man shaving at the open window opposite and the woman in the kimono washing her hair. Some day, all this will have to be developed, carefully printed, fixed." Indeed Isherwood's narrator sees the rise of Fascism in Europe exactly as a real camera might: plainly, but also from someone's point of view, in the strange way photographs are at once just reality and also someone's choice of subject and composition. The result is a fascinating new combination, in modern fiction, of the personal and the political. We get a new sense of the requirements of subjective self-involvement, for we see how even a camera cannot really be detached from the real world. It does not depart from "objective" reality; it participates in reality, too, and can become complicit in political evil if it fails to admit it (to "develop" what it "records"). If we think back to what it meant to see things subjectively in the earlier, more deliberately experimental modern novel, we see how this represents a variation and an advance – how it makes the new political demands enhance rather than reduce the experiments of modern fiction.

The point here is that the new political novels of the 1930s were not simply realistic. If their writers took a documentary point of view, they did so with the prior decades' insights into the problem of "objectivity" in mind. Or, they did so knowing that their books would be ineffective if they were simply realistic. The novelists knew that they would have to *remake* social realism – make it more intense, different in its focus – in order to make it feel real to readers. This latter approach characterizes one of the century's most explosive works of social realism: *The Grapes of Wrath* by John Steinbeck (1939). He set out to reveal the terrible conditions into which the Great Depression had put America's agricultural workers, many of whom had to migrate in hopeless search for work and for food. Steinbeck himself knew how bad things were: he had lived and worked among the migrants in order to do his research for the book. And to some readers, the research too excessively showed: this was less fiction, they felt, than flat propaganda. Nevertheless, the book does not seek simply to protest the bad lives of migrant workers in full realistic detail. It remakes realism itself, by crossing it with something that is formally very different: the language and meaning of the Bible. It is not at all unusual for fiction to make use of biblical imagery and to model itself on biblical plots. But in *The Grapes of Wrath* there is a particularly modern tension between the real and the biblical – a tension that becomes one of the main means through which Steinbeck produces a critical view of reality. Were it not for this tension, his book might have been little different from the mass of bluntly political fiction produced in the 1930s. But the split vision and its results made for a more powerful indictment of the Depression's social disaster: indeed, it is almost as if the "mythic" irony at work in *Ulysses* (where we always compare the modern-day Ulysses to his heroical, mythic counterpart) is at work here too, and at work even more extremely, since in this case we have a much wider gap between the positive myth and the negative reality. Steinbeck's social realism makes fine use of a very modern ironic gap between the possibility of salvation and the reality of squalor. Even though it might seem plainly realistic, *The Grapes of Wrath*, like the novels of Christopher Isherwood, smuggles in modern form and characteristically modern concerns for aesthetic restitution.

In a way, then, modern experimentation continues, despite the fact that fiction seems to go political in the years leading up to World War II. Or it might be more accurate to say that experimentation could not cease. Once the first modern novelists made it clear that "reality" depended on how you saw it, that "defamiliarizing" descriptions were best at getting people's attention and changing the way they thought, that skepticism about progress was a necessary kind of wisdom in modern times, writers could no longer simply "write realistically." Even if they wanted directly to show bad social and political conditions, in order to help make vital arguments in a dark phase of history, they knew that realism was not some simple matter of saying what you saw.

But for some writers of the 1930s, the best way to engage creatively with dark realities was to mock them savagely – to take advantage of the way wicked parody could at once be an engaged and an imaginative form. The master of this mode was Evelyn Waugh, whose novels share much with those of the modernists, but have a different attitude toward modernity's "opportunities." In *A Handful of Dust* (1934), fragmentation rules, and we are limited in the modernist fashion to the perspectives of particular characters. London life, defamiliarized, is also the context here, and there is no question that the skepticism of Ford and Faulkner is out in full force. But something has changed: whereas for Ford and for Faulkner skepticism works in the service of lingering higher hopes about humanity, in Waugh's novels humanism has given way to a sense of humanity's utter sinfulness. The title comes from T. S. Eliot's *The Waste Land* (1922), and the waste land Waugh sees in modern life is one in which all values have been cheapened – in which a child might die without its mother caring, in which marriage and tradition mean nothing, in which the rich have no responsibility to the poor. But for Waugh these modern travesties are comic absurdities, and revealing them as such is a matter of ironic deflation rather than "questioning reality." The purpose is no longer to find a better form for modern reality; instead, it is to let the worst possible reality diminish fiction to bitter (if thrilling) comedy, all in order to clear the air for a return to traditional values. Waugh would ultimately speak of his objectives in terms of a reaction against modern writing – and a bid for re-establishment of the morality lost when fiction abandoned traditional moral centers:

> The failure of modern novelists since and including James Joyce is one of presumption and exorbitance . . . They try to represent the whole human mind and soul and yet omit its determining character – that of being God's creature with a defined purpose. So in my future books there will be two things that make them unpopular: a preoccupation with style and the attempt to represent man more fully, which, to me, means only one thing, man in his relation to God.[15]

Waugh's sense of responsibility – very different from but still related to that which made his contemporaries more politically engaged – ultimately meant a religious reaction against modern "exorbitance." At first, however, it meant a satirical one, which was yet one more way to limit modern innovation to "the real world."

What, then, becomes of the modern novel, in these satires and dystopias and other forms of compromise between aesthetics and politics? There are perhaps finally two views to take – two ways to see the possible survival of the modern novel into the bleaker, more political, less aesthetic years of the 1930s and beyond. First, the view that sees the modern surviving, and improving itself through a kind of correction; having become too detached, autotelic, and idealistic, the novel now chastens its aesthetic excesses and fits them out for better social responsibility. And second, the view that sees the modern failing, dying away due to changed historical circumstances; having become too detached and idealistic, the modern proves useless once the moment of aesthetic excitement has passed. Which view you take perhaps depends on what you think happens next – what happens after the political intensities of this period give way to yet other historical circumstances.

But finally we should note that some of Modernism's most extreme experiments in fiction came in or after this decade of anti-modernist activity. All through the 1930s, Joyce wrote *Finnegans Wake* (1939), which takes stream-of-consciousness narration, difficult allusion, and heteroglossia to unprecedented extremes – abandoning the "outer" world for a single night's dream which subordinates all of history to the mythical imagination. In 1936 Djuna Barnes published *Nightwood*, which devoted itself entirely to personal, sexual, and psychological eccentricity. Samuel Beckett's *Murphy* (1938), as we will see, suggests that the most important reality is that which one discovers when the mind roams free of all real-world encumbrances. And Woolf's last book, *Between the Acts* (1941), also subordinates history to what aesthetic forms can make of it – specifically, to the form of communal theater, which finds the truth about English history "between the acts" of real historical events. Here, experiment persists, unchastened and undiminished, although perhaps extended beyond Modernism. Perhaps these last experiments look ahead – to the moment in which the modern novel will get the replenishment of *postmodernism*'s new, experimental energy.

CHAPTER 6

Questioning the Modern: Mid-Century Revisions

If the politics and satires of the 1930s were not enough to discredit modern experimentation, the events of World War II were. The first world war had done much to make "civilization" seem like a lie. Nevertheless, faith in culture persisted enough to make writers believe that art could yet make up for losses. No such belief could really survive World War II, for its unimaginable atrocities could only make art seem like feeble recompense. Or, worse, itself a dangerous lie: "idealism" of a sinister kind had often justified the war's barbarism; was aesthetic idealism complicit? The most famous statement to this effect is Theodor Adorno's claim that "to write poetry after Auschwitz is barbaric."[1] To those who agreed, it seemed necessary at least to limit fiction's aspirations – to cease to hope that its aesthetic forms could make any real difference, and even to distrust them for their association with power and purity.

Some people therefore think that World War II put an end to the modern novel. Did it not prove, once and for all, that its experiments were trivial, and that fiction could not abandon its responsibilities to social life, seen plainly, with fully clear critical judgment? Did it not prove that the relative detachment of the modern novel – its movement "inward" – entailed a dangerous retreat from reality? Did it not discredit the belief that fiction could make a new form for any function, since the horrors of the war were well beyond the limits of representation? Did it not prove that fiction should not cultivate chaos, or pretend to order?

These were the questions the war raised, and they did indeed pose a nearly insuperable challenge to fiction's modern impulse. Even if

they did not put the modern novel completely in doubt, they mark a good place for us to pause to question it. Clearly, the modern novel had not yet developed the resources necessary to make it a fully satisfying response to modernity. What was missing? What was lacking in the modern novel, at the end of its first major stage of development, and how could it change to become more satisfying to the writers and readers of the future?

The modern writers often wanted immediacy – to make fiction fully able to "show" us things rather than just to tell us about them. They wanted perfect mimesis. In Joyce, Woolf, and others there is a powerful striving toward greater intensity, and no small amount of hope that modern fiction could break through the barrier that language tends naturally to place between readers and reality. Modern fiction depended in large measure on the faith that it might, in Joseph Conrad's words, "make you *see*." But could it? Could it ever get past the "mediation" of language, and deliver reality immediately to the reader? More and more it seemed that it could not, that the hope of perfect mimesis was a naive one, that even if modern fiction could present things with greater intensity, it could not every really be fully immediate. More and more, the prevailing attitude was that which Conrad's narrator Marlow in *Heart of Darkness* expresses when his storytelling seems to fail. Conrad, remember, had expressed the wish to "make you *see*," but here Marlow asks:

> Do you see the story? Do you see anything? It seems to me I am trying to tell you a dream – making a vain attempt, because no relation of a dream can convey the dream sensation . . . No, it is impossible; it is impossible to convey the life-sensation of any given epoch of one's existence – that which makes its truth, its meaning – its subtle and penetrating essence. It is impossible. We live, as we dream – alone.

Conrad, like many modern novelists, hoped that fiction could be immediate, and bind people together in "solidarity." But here Marlow expresses what they tended to realize: that fiction could not be immediate, and that hope for human togetherness on the basis of it was vain.

This does not mean, though, that modern fiction would have to give up on immediacy – that to prove itself valid, it would have to surrender this ideal. What it means is that, going forward, modern fiction

would have to combine its better mimesis with better attention to the "problematics of language," the ways that language stands in the way of immediacy. Just as modern fiction had already begun to "question reality," it would have to question language itself. The modern novel had already shown reality to be a far more complex, problematic thing than it had seemed to be in the writing of the past; now, to become the modern novel of the future, it would have to wrestle with the ways that language, too, was a problem and not just a solution.

The modern writers tried for a full range of perspectives. As we have seen, they attempted to widen out fiction's constituencies and points of view, to take in the perceptions of people the novel had not tended to include. But just how inclusive had the novel in fact become? Was the range of perspectives really wide enough? Were the treatments of other classes, other races, and other cultures really authentic? Some people thought not: they looked at the modern novel's treatment of other classes, other races, and other cultures and saw not perspective but *primitivism*. What they saw, that is, was not the authentic lives and minds of unfamiliar people, but exotics – people presented in their strangeness rather than their normality. In *Going Primitive*, Marianna Torgovnick describes this tendency to exoticize, the way modern artists often use "others" deceptively: "[These 'others'] exist for us in a cherished series of dichotomies: by turns gentle, in tune with nature, paradisal, ideal – or violent, in need of control; what we should emulate or, alternately, what we should fear; noble savages or cannibals."[2] When, for example, Joyce ends *Ulysses* in the consciousness of Molly Bloom, are we finally getting insight into the female mind, or are we getting a "natural" fantasy? When Faulkner puts a black woman into *The Sound and the Fury*, is she real, or is she a "noble" caricature? And why are there no poor people at all in the novels of Virginia Woolf, with the exception of some mysterious ideal entities that haunt the edges of reality? Questions like these made some people think that "perspective" could go a lot further.

Even worse, the modern novel seemed to threaten fiction's powers of social engagement. Modern writers had tried to delve more deeply into consciousness, to go subjective, to depict a world in flux. To some critics, they had too excessively detached the novel from the real world; they had retreated into utter interiority, dissolving social lives into the fragments and ambiguities of consciousness. Did this not have to mean that the novel would become less able to reflect social reality?

And did this not mean that the novel would stop serving a key social purpose? Georg Lukács, a Marxist philosopher and critic, thought so: in his writing against Modernism, he argued that its movement into consciousness was a retreat from responsibility, and a real danger to public culture. Lukács saw a "negation of history" in modern writing. Writers like Joyce, he thought, presented people as too "strictly confined within the limits of [their] own experience," and too lost in a "static" reality; missing was any sense of humanity's "concrete potentiality" – the way it realizes itself through engagement with objective reality. The "surrender to subjectivity," "disintegration of personality," and "disintegration of the outer world" fundamental to modern fiction were, to Lukács, false and dangerous, features of a bad "ideology" rather than authentic aesthetic choices.[3]

To Lukács and others, the modern novel would have to match its new interior aesthetic with new forms of external responsibility. It would have to find new ways to be political, new ways to be engaged, lest it dematerialize completely and become an airy, precious, and complacent indulgence. To find these new ways would be hard. How can you write both the fluid streams of consciousness and the hard edges of political commitment? How can you combine the subjective and the objective, if these are in fact opposite ways of understanding and presenting the world? These questions remained to be answered, if the modern novel were to make it past the challenges of postwar modernity.

Then again, the modern novel might have to become even more experimental. In its treatments of time and space, for example, maybe the modern novel had to do more, if it were going to fully trace out the new contours of the world. New places were beginning to come into their own, and to contribute new ways of conceiving spatial relations. New notions of history, new increases in speed, were in the making. Perhaps the problem was that the experimental novel had not become experimental enough to take these in.

And then there were also other questions about the value of the modern novel: did it really engage with the technological modernity that had seemed to be one of its main provocations? Was it too "highbrow" – too exclusive, too particular, too elitist? And why was it so unwilling just to tell a good story?

Airplanes and factories and film did, to some degree, inspire new styles of perception in the modern novel, but it is fair to say that fiction

had only just begun to respond to the challenge of modern technology. For the most part, even the modern novel still took a distant or
defensive view of it. Such a view would perhaps always have to be
part of the novel's response: perhaps it should always be the novel's
job to resist or refuse what technology advances, in order to assert
human values against mechanical ones. But the better part of the
novel's response, some have felt, must be more absorptive, more
aggressive. It must also take in the forms technology creates, make
them its own, and in so doing provide the countermeasures necessary
for us to take technology in hand. This the modern novel had not yet
done: to become fully modern, it would in the future have to innovate forms more actively involved with those of the machine and
digital ages.

It would also have to engage more openly with "lower" forms of
culture. In its aesthetic pride the modern novel seemed inattentive to
less aesthetic arts. It seemed too much geared to the cultural elite –
for those with excellent educations, fine tastes, and aristocratic priorities. Not always, of course, since many novels (especially those by
Lawrence, Joyce, Hemingway, and Cather) aimed deliberately to bring
the novel down to earth. *Ulysses*, for example, revels in the popular
songs and advertisements of its times, making aesthetic experiment
dependent upon the energies of mass and consumer culture; Hemingway happily covered bullfights and wrote in Hollywood styles. But
despite these exceptions, modern writers tended to cultivate a high
audience, and therefore to suffer from what Orwell called a "sever-
ance from the common culture of the country."[4] They would rarely
engage with pulp fictions, or encourage real interest in trashy popular
culture, or try to be fully inclusive, and to some people this seemed to
set them too much apart. Perhaps the modern novel was too precious,
too "bourgeois"; it needed to rub elbows with the cheap stuff, to absorb
the considerable energies of mass-cultural life. Breathing too fine an
air, it risked suffocation, when the robust atmosphere of life on the
ground could bring real invigoration.

And finally some needed invigoration might come with the inclusion, after all, of some good stories. As we have seen, one of the
modern novel's initial gestures was the elimination of plot. Plot was
false, plot was an encumbrance, and only without it could the modern
novel explore consciousness and present ordinary life as it really
happens. But as time passed these presumptions began to seem them-

selves encumbering. Didn't plot, after all, serve a vital cultural purpose? Aren't the shapes of plot often the most aesthetically exciting things about a novel? Don't people hunger for plot for good reasons – for the ways it gives to life just the kind of form that the modern novelists were seeking by other means? Some psychologists note what perhaps the Victorian writers – those authors of allegedly artificial plots – knew as well: that "narrative imagining – story – is the fundamental instrument of thought."[5] So perhaps the wish totally to exclude plot had been excessive. Perhaps plot could be let back in, to certain degrees, without introducing falsity or blocking narrative's access to consciousness. This was the hope of those who came to the modern novel later in its career, who would try now to make its experimental forms more flexible, and better able to engage with the fullest range of modern problems and modern needs.

Would they succeed? Although the modern novel seemed unlikely to survive the war and its aftermath, in many ways it now seems that it has. The impulse to innovate forms in the face of modernity has surely persisted – and the postwar era would produce novels as energetically modern as those of the first flowering of modern fiction. But if so, how exactly did the modern impulse it make it past resistances? If those resistances meant substantial revisions and rethinking, is it right to speak of the persistence of the *modern* novel specifically – or were the changes substantial enough to produce a new literary form? And even if the new form looked a lot like the old, is it right to call it "modern," or should we reserve that term for the specific historical phenomenon that occurred roughly 1890–1940 – before historical changes made a difference? These are the kinds of question that come up as we think about the limits of the genre – the questions we must keep in mind as we follow the modern novel into its questionable future.

In that future there is first strong dissent from everything the modern novel seemed to represent. Among, for example, the writers who in 1954 were called "the Movement," there was a deep and total sense that experimental fiction was both dangerous and dead. Novelists including Iris Murdoch and Kingsley Amis represented the popular sense that it was now necessary to return to a more strictly plain, direct, practical kind of literature, both for the sake of the good health of fiction and for the sake of the social, political, and cultural awareness of which fiction had long been a part. The modern impulse in fiction had come to seem, to them and to others, precious, pointless, and even reckless, for the way it encouraged people to get lost in self-indulgent explorations of inner lives apart from larger social responsibility. These writers felt that the experimental aspect of the modern novel would betray the more important goal: truly to help people come to terms with modern realities.

For other writers, too, reality was now the thing, if not for the reasons Murdoch and Amis gave, then for the simple reason that reality had become itself creative enough. Philip Roth said so in 1961 in his influential essay on the state of postwar American fiction. Roth pointed out that American life offered up more than enough bizarre material to keep any fiction writer busy forever. It was itself so experimental that modern fiction could not help but be so: "the American writer in the middle of the twentieth century has his hands full in trying to understand, describe, and then make *credible* much of American reality. It stupefies, it sickens, it infuriates, and finally it is even a kind of embarrassment to one's own meager imagination. The actuality is constantly outdoing our talents." But this was not to say that modern fiction ought to press forward its experimental agenda; rather, it was to call for a return to direct, conventional, plain writing, out of a sense that such plain writing would be the best lens through which to let life's real wonders appear.[6]

This anti-experimental attitude marked a kind of end to the modern novel, but also a new beginning. New demands were made of innovation in fiction. It could not get its aesthetic innovations at the expense of the forms of culture to which it ought to be responsible. Aesthetic ideals now had to balance themselves with practical need and ordinary pleasure, with social responsibility and the needs of fantasy. What were some of the ways this new beginning began? How did writers – soon after the war, suspicious of experiment, concerned to be more real – find new grounds for the writing of new fiction?

A diverse set of trends exhibits some of the dynamic ways the modern novel remade and extended itself at this pivotal moment. Writers who wanted to keep it real but also make something new did so in the following ways: in the fiction of the *Angry Young Men* and the *Beat* generation, they got their revolutionary outlook from the real world of disaffected youth; in new fictions of sexuality, they enabled change by unleashing repressed erotic energies; in new philosophical fiction, they made "consciousness" in fiction a matter of exploring the

very nature of man's fate; and, in the case of "commonwealth literature," they simply let the emergence of new world cultures create new
forms for new realities.

When the war ended, a new war began, what some called a "class
war" in modern fiction – "a conflict between two worlds: the class
world of the past and the declassed world of the future." In a 1958
essay on "class war in British literature," Leslie Fiedler noted that "the
newer English writers" were "resolved to break at last out of a world
of taste which has been, it seems to them, too long confined to the
circumference of a tea table." Impatient with precious aesthetics, "the
new writers [were] not *gentlemen* like their forerunners," and they represented "an attempt to redeem fiction and poetry in theme, diction
and decor from the demands of one social group in the interests of
another." But where would it lead? "With the weapons of crudity and
righteous anger and moral bluntness, the new writers are trying to
deliver literature from the circles which captured it early in this
century, and restore it – to whom?"[7] Because the war had finally discredited the world's ruling classes, because the lower and working
classes had become ever more conscious of the injustices that limited
their lives, and because "welfare states" turned new condescension
upon them, many young, less privileged writers began to tap their
resentment and frustration for a new fictional form. The form in question got its name, it seems, either from Leslie Paul's *Angry Young Man*
(1951) or from a play by John Osborne, *Look Back in Anger* (1956). The
"anger" in these titles brought new emotional life to socially conscious
fiction. Before, fiction that looked beneath the middle classes tended
to do so in order to idealize, to dramatize, or to polemicize; with few
exceptions, it tended to see people of lower classes as refreshingly vigorous, or inspiringly primitive, to render their lives in heroic or in
grotesque terms, or to make their miseries a focus for direct political
arguments. The new view taken in the fiction of the Angry Young Men
was far more plain and much more complex. Nothing grand, it tended
to deal in the dead ends of lives lived without much opportunity and
without much interest in grand cultural growth. Very real, it tended
to put plainly the crudities, indecencies, cruelties, and simply bleak
acts and feelings these lives may have entailed.

This fiction's new approach to working- and lower-middle-class life
dealt in no heroic emotions: its "anger" is never very specifically

justified or very ably expressed by the fiction's protagonists; instead, they are "often losers and boozers, liars, wanderers, and transients," and what you get is the quick temper, the sullen scowl, the petty furies that might in fact more realistically characterize the discontent felt by those who live at the bottom without any real sense of why or how things might change.[8] This more mitigated "anger" gives this fiction a painful precision, and the sort of blunt poetry that comes when language suits itself closely to lesser but truer emotions. A truer dialect results – not that which mimics sensationally the colorful peculiarities of the *demotic* or common way of speaking, but that which taps the energies of the emotions beneath a language whose cultural frustrations force its speakers into dynamic creativity. Here we get a variation on the sort of minimalism that an earlier generation of modern fiction had innovated in order to suggest, rather than overstate, emotional truths. It combines with the socio-political conscience of the 1930s, perhaps, to make a synthesis of spare modernist language and social realism's plots and themes.

Alan Sillitoe grew up the son of a laborer who was often out of work, and he himself did factory work at the age of 14. He didn't read much, or write anything at all, until illness during the war landed him in hospital for eighteen months. Before too long he published his first novel: *Saturday Night and Sunday Morning* (1958) reflected his personal experiences and his relation to the tradition of literature, for it not only tells the story of a factory worker, but does so according to the rebellious impulses of the worker himself. Arthur, the book's protagonist, has no "valid" motivations. After a week's work at the bicycle factory, he just gets drunk and hits on women, and though he has some wildly violent political aspirations, things stay raw. If there is any hope, finally, for decency, it comes only romantically at the end of a book more generally given to pub high jinks and visceral acts. And following these brutal doings is a style perfectly willing to treat as normal and as literary every aspect of unconscious or vomiting drunkenness, every lascivious or sleazy mistake, and to put these aspects of an ordinary life onto a scale of values different from those which had tended to guide literary plots into cleaner, more heroical outcomes. Arthur begins *Saturday Night and Sunday Morning* falling "dead drunk . . . with eleven pints of beer and seven small gins playing hide-and-seek in his stomach," down a flight of stairs at the pub, "from the top-most stair to the bottom"; he ends the novel with the thought that "there's bound to be trouble in store for me every day of my life, because trouble it's always been and always will be." In between, we get reality unredeemed by false symbolic hopes and undramatized by "consciousness," but therefore all the more true to this moment of modern rancor.

The most famous work of angry young fiction must be Kingsley Amis's *Lucky Jim* (1954). The book's anti-hero, Jim Dixon, is a junior professor out of the lower middle class who tends toward two emotions: "real, over-mastering, orgiastic boredom, and its companion, real hatred." What bores him and rouses his hatred is the pretensions and hypocrisies of cultured intellectual life. These he constantly lampoons – most often to his own detriment – as when he characterizes his own academic work in terms of its "niggling mindlessness, its funereal parade of yawn-enforcing facts, the pseudo-light it threw on non-problems." Dixon is a very funny incompetent, whose incompetence seems wholly justified by the absurdity of what counts as success and sophistication: the fact that he never fails to make a "bad impression" counts in his favor; the fact that he perpetually makes this worse is a sign of his authenticity. At one point, he has a sort of epiphany that makes it very clear how this authenticity differs from that of Amis's modernist precursors: "The one indispensable answer to an environment bristling with people and things one thought were bad was to go on finding out new ways in which one could think they were bad." Not to redeem them, or make them the basis for psychic drama or dramatic angst, but just to keep on. As an expression of anger, *Lucky Jim* is far more interested in the sheer youthful energies of pointless rebellion than in any substantial, effective critique of the establishment. It is more concerned with emotional vigor and with social absurdity; these never come together into any positive outcome for anybody, and agitate instead toward the perpetual setting-off of low-comic, slapstick explosions.

Lucky Jim is far less serious than *Saturday Night and Sunday Morning*, but the books nevertheless have some important things in common. Both strongly reject the connection in high culture between truth and sophistication, seeing truth instead as the more likely property of crudity and honest plainness; both celebrate the unproductive vitalities of youth, and draw an unexpected link between that vitality and postwar youthful disaffection; both try to find styles of expression to match their new views of youth and truth – styles that would not amount simply to some zesty dialect; both get a lot of mileage out of catastrophic drunkenness; and both assert a manic masculinity. This last shared trait is perhaps that which all Angry Young Man fiction most notably has in common: at a time in which there seemed fewer and fewer productive outlets for male striving and strength, these books seem to show us men acting out, even lashing out in order to give gladly purposeless expression to male energies that might once have been put to heroic uses.

More notorious than the Angry Young Men in England (and more fully a movement) were their contemporaries in America: the Beats. A similar cultural context – one in which cultural values seemed worn out or discredited by the war, one in which it seemed vital to give new expression to discontent – was felt as well in America, especially by a group of young poets and fiction writers who tried to turn the state of feeling *beat* into a new means of primal openness, truth, and expressive power. Jack Kerouac defined the "beat generation" as "members of the generation that came of age after World War II–Korean War who join in a relaxation of social and sexual tensions and espouse anti-regimentation, mystic-disaffiliation and material-simplicity values, supposedly as a result of Cold War disillusionment." Passionate but aimless, blasé and yet also committed to the intensities of art, and very often drunk or drugged or freaked, the Beats were a second wave of modernists: as worn out as anyone by the disasters of mid-century culture, and also disillusioned and alienated by the complacency and regimentation of postwar culture, they nevertheless felt certain that a rejuvenated and regenerated art could re-enchant the world, and they set out to prove it in part by breaking new paths for literature. These paths, spatial and emotional, took the Beats searching for authenticity and for intensity; simplicity, rejection of materialism, new mystical and otherwise heightened experience, as well as extremes of sexual and narcotic adventure were the goals, and they were goals as much in their art as in life. The movement began with a group of friends who identified with the down-and-out side of New York City, finding something real in its frank exhaustion and disaffection; it then became a full-fledged literary movement as general impulses focused into a kind of countercultural cool aesthetic. The public reading of Allen Ginsberg's poem *Howl* (1955) proved a huge and pivotal event for this counterculture – as did the publication in 1957 of Jack Kerouac's novel *On the Road*.

For better and for worse, *On the Road* shows how the cultivation of new social freedoms could reinvigorate the modern novel. The shape of life on the road demands all of the randomness, skepticism, and plotless progress of modernist narration; and the pursuits of life on the road contribute the transcendent, essential style of seeing and feeling that gave modernist randomness its higher purpose. When they all come together here, however, the result has a sort of authenticity to which few modernists could lay claim: for this transcendent randomness weaves through not just "ordinary" life but low life, and the difference is substantial.

On the Road proceeds in episodes that vary a lot but stay essentially the same. Sal Paradise hits the road with his bad-influence drifter friend Dean, and does so again and again, whenever time spent in any particular place gets played out. In its stray-dog, empty-sky movements, the realism here gets harsh, and yet it mixes with a kind of mysticism that outstrips even modernist transcendence. At one point, for example, Sal hits an ecstasy that almost parodically outdoes most modernist epiphanies:

> I had reached the point of ecstasy that I always wanted to reach, which was the complete step across chronological time into timeless shadows, and wonderment in the bleakness of the mortal realm . . . into the holy void of uncreated emptiness, the potent and inconceivable radiancies shining in bright Mind Essence, innumerable lotus-lands falling open in the magic mothswarm of heaven.

The excuse for this outlandish mysticism – in a time when literary experiment had come to seem trivial and precious – was the reality of extreme states produced by drugs, alcohol, and free, wild living. So there is no distinction between the real and the unreal, the actual and the aesthetic. This joining, so helpful to the down-and-out modern novel, happened as a result less of deliberate aesthetic experiment than of the recklessly total experiment of Beat culture. A Sal puts it, "the road is life," and even if it screws you up, that is a "holy goof," and you arrive perpetually at "the ragged and ecstatic joy of pure being."

The Beats and the Angry Young Men represented a new postwar counterculture – the alternative culture that emerged to fill the vacuum left when high-cultural values proved inauthentic and conventional "bourgeois" life lost its hold. Since the novel was funda-mentally a "bourgeois" form, however, this emergence required some serious retooling, and that is why the fiction of these writers sounded so unlike that of the past. The difference was mainly one of tone: even in the most radical and experimental novels of the past you could expect to hear some echoes of the faith and hope upon which the clas-sical novel had been built. But here, nihilism prevailed – and not the sort of noble, tragic nihilism characteristic of the modernist novel at its darkest. This nihilism was bland, blasé, and very distant from any sense of the alternative. If the earlier modernist writers went nihilis-tic, they did so with a keen sense of what they were missing – with a tragic sense of past opportunities lost. But the angry young writers of this newer generation were far more aimless; their anger was undi-rected, and their stories lacked the edge of those striving to rebuild or rediscover a lost world. Did the difference detract from the modern novel – or did it perhaps make it a more authentic register of the psychic pattern of modernity?

The answer to this question perhaps comes in fiction by writers less central to these essentially social movements. For example, Beat and Angry energy is channeled into powerfully meaningful allegory by Ken Kesey. In *One Flew Over the Cuckoo's Nest* (1962), he makes this energy the basis for social symbolism. In a mental institution, an outcast and anti-social group of men comes to symbolize, individually and together, the anger and exhaustion but also the idealism of angry-young-male disaffection. The novel's anti-hero, McMurphy, is a sort of Beat savior, defying the hospital administration and getting his fellow inmates to rediscover their lost powers of honor and virility. His character, and its power of redemption, are summed up the first time he lays a symbolic hand on the narrator, an inmate he will ultimately rescue:

> I remember real clear the way that hand looked: there was carbon under the fingernails where he'd worked once in a garage; there was an anchor tatooed back from the knuckles; there was a dirty Band-Aid on the middle knuckle, peeling up at the edge. All the rest of the knuckles were covered with scars and cuts, old and new . . . The palm was callused, and the calluses were cracked, and dirt was worked into the cracks. A road map of his travels up and down the West. That palm made a scuffing sound against my hand. I remember the fingers were thick and strong

closing over mine, and my hand commenced to feel peculiar and went
to swelling up out there on my stick of an arm, like he was transmit-
ting his own blood into it. It rang with blood and power.

McMurphy's hand is a symbol of a movement, and its transfusion of
power is what both that movement and its fiction might have hoped
for: intensity channeled through real strength and tough experience,
to bring culture back to life. To "ring with blood and power" is to tune
anger to symbolical expression, and to make this generation's war a
"restoration."

Were there Beat and Angry young women? Was there a compara-
ble women's style of writing, which expressed a specifically female disaffection or anger? Even if women could not have had the freedoms
that enabled such negative emotions to find social forms of expression,
they nevertheless mounted similar rebellions against the force of
modern conventionality. The target here was sexist ideology, rather
than bourgeois conformity and other such stifling distinctions of class.
Ultimately these rebellions would take shape in the shattering feminist experiments of later decades. At this stage, they prompted influential expressions of dawning feminist consciousness.

An apt partner to Beat fiction is a novel that also sets up a strong
dramatic contrast between a corrupt world and an idealistic young
person: Sylvia Plath's *The Bell Jar* (1963). The disaffection in question
here is specifically that felt by a brilliant young woman with few
options: Esther Greenwood, were she a man, would have had any
number of outlets for her superior intelligence and imagination, but
as a woman she can either get married or work as a typist. Such seem
to be her options when she wins a contest to become a guest editor at
a women's magazine, and these options soon pitch her into a massive
state of depression. Plath's novel then becomes ironic: institutionalized
and insane, Esther nevertheless sees things with acid clarity, and the
paradox here perfectly defines the trap that feminists would subsequently turn into an object of political complaint. In Esther's case, the
irony is merely crippling, until a good woman doctor lets her know
that her anger is not pathological but justified. Then, she recovers, but
not before Plath has endowed the modern novel with her irony's creative contribution: new with her is the voice of the angry young
woman, unique and notable for the way it sharpens feminine sweetness with a lacerating, vindictive edge, so that the gentleness and

indirection of a woman's voice become the better half of satire. For example, when Esther is asked to reflect upon the benevolence of her benefactress, who has endowed her scholarship and is one of the women who seem to offer Esther no model for happy womanhood, she says,

> I knew I should be grateful to Mrs. Guinea, only I couldn't feel a thing. If Mrs. Guinea had given me a ticket to Europe, or a round-the-world cruise, it wouldn't have made one scrap of difference to me, because wherever I sat – on the deck of a ship or at a street café in Paris or Bangkok – I would be sitting under the same glass bell jar, stewing in my own sour air.

Here we get the novel's main metaphor, and also its typical tone: always restraining anger and resentment, always a good girl, Esther makes the bell jar she stews in, but indicates she knows so in every mildly bitter word she says.

In the work of Doris Lessing, we might see finally how this generation's anger could truly renew the modern experiment. Lessing shared Plath's discontent with the roles open to women and with the effects of sexist ideologies upon their states of mind. For her, however, the experimental forms of literature become means of freedom and sources of redemptive psychic strength. *The Golden Notebook* (1962) is a novel with six sections, each devoted to a different aspect of a woman's effort to find independence and freedom. Each different "notebook" takes on a different aspect of the ideologies that perniciously shape a woman's world. A "blue" notebook ultimately tries for a sense of reality beyond these ideologies – beyond the linguistic and social rules a woman normally must follow. But the effort falls to pieces, as if to say that such a "modernist" approach can only end in madness and disaster. What's needed, instead, is what finally comes in the "golden" notebook, where a new psychic integrity takes shape. "The essence of the book, the organization of it, everything in it, says implicitly and explicitly, that we must not divide things off, must not compartmentalize": with this summary statement, Lessing indicates a wish to shape the modern novel into new unity.

Lessing's novel finally gives us a new forms for fragmentation and perspective. Taken as a broken whole, it marks a pivotal advance upon the kind of fragmentation and perspective at work in the prior generations of modern fiction. For Lessing's notebook-fragments take a more actively organizing approach to the breakdown of society. What would have been smaller pieces, in the more fully shattered works of an earlier generation's modernism, here are full facets of our broken world. They do not fit together – that is the problem for Lessing's heroine – but each of them is a fully self-conscious take on distinct versions of life. Modernism revives here, with a difference. What had been falling apart is taken in hand and investigated, reshaped. Not pieced back together, however, since Lessing does not at all want to suggest that the world has regained coherence. Not reformed, but concerted: the "notebooks" of *The Golden Notebook* show us modern fragmentation taking a new shape. These fragments are lenses, diverse ways of seeing what now fractures the modern world. The break is caused less by chaos than by *reflexivity* – the self-conscious dismantling of the parts of a book, the deliberate self-scrutiny of the workings of different ideological views. Lessing's novel shows us modernism developing, through anger, to new kind of self-awareness, addressing some of the problems that had made the modern novel insufficient to modern needs, and moving forward into styles that would soon bring the modern novel into wholly new territory.

Anger, disaffection, and worn-out resignation at first gave the modern novel new ways to respond to modernity. Modernity meant excessive rationality, materialism, and conformity, and so the modern impulse was to become brutal, rebellious, mystical, and ascetic – in plot and in theme, but also in form. Modernity, however, also meant new freedom, and in their new freedom the Beats and the Angry Young Men could hit the road or act out and let their novels do the same. Women were somewhat less free, and perhaps that accounts for the greater formal freedom found in *The Golden Notebook*. Imaginative forms – this new, self-conscious use for the fragments into which life's aspects have broken – become for Lessing the means of rebellion. Soon enough many more writers, men and women alike, would find that freedom demanded the sort of reconception of life's fundamentals that imaginative fiction could enable. Then, as we will see, the modern impulse revives, and even exceeds itself by becoming *postmodern*.

If the question for the modern writer now was how to be experimental without losing practical engagement, how to have newness without preciosity, power without naive idealism, politics without preaching, then answers came in various modes of writing that seemed to make rebellion rigorous and vigorous – in Angry fiction, as we have seen, and also when the novel spanned the heights and the depths of *existentialism* and *sex*.

Back in 1938, Samuel Beckett published *Murphy*, a novel that had seemed too unreal even for Modernism. Its protagonist is alienated beyond reason: Murphy spends much of his time sitting alone strapped into a chair, confining his body so that his mind can escape the world and become fully free of all social, cultural, and physical realities.

> He sat naked in his rocking chair . . . Seven scarves held him in position. Two fastened his shins to the rockers, one his thighs to the seat, two his breast and belly to the back, one his wrists to the strut behind. Only the most local movements were possible . . . Somewhere a cuckoo-clock, having struck between twenty and thirty, became the echo of a street cry . . . These were the sights and sounds he did not like. They detained him in the world to which they belonged, but not he, as he fondly hoped . . . He sat in his chair in this way because it gave him pleasure! First it gave his body pleasure, it appeased his body. Then it set him free in his mind. For it was not until his body was appeased that he could come alive in his mind.

Here is solipsism beyond anything found in any modernist consciousness; and here there is also a skepticism so withering that nothing seems any longer to matter or even really to exist. Absurdity has taken over, and Beckett has taken the modernist tendency to question reality to a farthest extreme. But it might make more sense to call his experiment by another name. It seems too philosophical, too absurd, and too unreal to count as modernist – since modernist fiction tends to dislike explicit philosophy and to covet more ordinary intensity. As Murphy's chair becomes a way for him to see himself as "a mote in the dark of absolute freedom," *Murphy* seems instead to become an example of the kind of fiction inspired by existential philosophy.

"Existence comes before essence": persons have no essential being, no god-given necessities, but must make themselves in the process of doing and living; according to the existentialist philosophy of Jean-Paul Sartre, they are fully, painfully free to make themselves who they are. But the freedom here is good and bad. It means total self-determination, but it was a terrible source of dread, for it means that there is nothing certain to fall back on: human realities, ideals, ethics, and actions have constantly to be made up on an individual basis. This is a total responsibility: "it puts every man in possession of himself as he is, and places the entire responsibility for his existence squarely upon his own shoulders."[9] Not to bear the responsibility is to live in bad faith – to be *inauthentic*. To pretend that life is not a very daunting matter of free choice, and to shirk the responsibility always to create the meaning of existence, is to live a lie. To exist authentically, it is necessary to embark perpetually on existential quests – quests for meaning threatened always by the intrinsic absurdity of existence. As Albert Camus put it, authenticity in the face of absurdity means that

> the absurd man . . . catches sight of a burning and frigid, transparent and limited universe in which nothing is possible but everything is given, and beyond which all is collapse and nothingness. He can then decide to accept such a universe and draw from it his strength, his refusal to hope, and the unyielding evidence of a life without consolation.[10]

Authenticity demands something like what Murphy takes to such an absurd extreme: a search beyond the false consolations of conventional life and conventional perception for the meanings true freedom can create.

If we think about existentialism in the context of the development of the modern novel, we might see how it helped the modern novel get past its problem with reality. For what we get in existentialist fiction is both extreme experiment and extreme responsibility. Indeed, the whole point of existential philosophy is to "commit." This commitment is a perfect point of connection between creativity and realism. It was strangely both pragmatic and unreal – seriously pledged and absurdly detached – and the combination gave the modern novel a way at once to speak purposeful truths and dissolve into the "nothingness" of creative consciousness.

A fine example of the combination is Ralph Ellison's *Invisible Man* (1952). The central concern here is racism, and the dilemmas it creates in the life of a young man in New York City who must choose between responsibility to racial progress and the freedom simply to be an individual self. The title's key word, "invisible," refers to a couple of things: on the one hand, it refers to the protagonist's invisibility as a black man in a white world ("I am invisible, understand, simply because people refuse to see me"); on the other hand, it refers to his chance to step "outside history," into total freedom, and give up on painful struggles toward racial equality. Already in invisibility's double meanings we can see how this story about racial identity takes on an existential cast. It is all about the anxiety one feels in a wholly random, pointless world, all about the painful necessities of responsibility created by the fact that meaning is only what one makes, even if that freedom seems a good excuse not to take action. The racial problem intensifies the existential anxieties and aspirations, for they take on an added socio-political charge. Ellison's invisible man is "free" in a truly terrible way – free from personhood, due to racism; his responsibilities, as a result, are vastly unbearable; and the temptations of inauthenticity, or invisibility, are great. But then so are the possibilities of heroism, for insofar as the protagonist here makes invisibility's freedom a positive force – mainly by associating it with the powerful immateriality of modern writing – he triumphs. "Who knows but that, on the lower frequencies, I speak to you?": in this last question, *Invisible Man* speaks the triumph of an existentialist modern novel that can *freely engage*, of what Ellison himself called "that fictional *vision* of an ideal democracy in which the actual combines with the ideal and gives us representations of a state of things in which the highly placed and the lowly, the black and the white . . . are combined to tell us of transcendent truths and possibilities."[11]

The moment of existential fiction quickly passed, but left lasting legacies. The existential dilemma would become a permanent feature of novelistic characterization. The quest for the purpose of existence would afterwards frequently mix in this fashion with a character's real-world obligations and values. And so the existential mix – its way of questioning fundamentals while forcing engagement – would set the pattern for future efforts at a pragmatic kind of experimentation. Whenever abstract questions sound over visceral or brutal events, or characters express anguish about *nothing*; when detachment seems at once a curse and a kind of sweet oblivion, within which characters must choose a definitive fate, then we see existentialism contributing its particular philosophical questioning to the modern novel's long-standing effort to question reality.

And we also see it renewing philosophical fiction more generally. Explicitly philosophical fiction had gone out of style with the advent of the modern novel. As we have seen, modern writers disliked the preachy, objective, lifeless styles that philosophical writing seemed to demand. Those writers were certainly philosophical in their own way, but their way meant philosophy by implication, or dramatic speculation, rather than any overt philosophizing. But as a result of the existential influence – its inherent drama and intensity – philosophy was able once again to become a more explicit part of fiction. In Iris Murdoch, for example, we have a writer initially influenced by existentialism but ultimately a more broadly philosophical novelist, one who made the "novel of ideas" once again a kind of modern fiction.

Murdoch was a member of "the Movement," that group of writers that demanded a revolt against precious modernist experiments and a return to a more sensible kind of fiction. But she also knew that fiction could not be plainly realistic and survive. In her essay "Against dryness," she laments the loss of a sense of fundamental and transcendent values, the absence now of a full theory of human personality and existence. "We have been left with far too shallow and flimsy an idea of human personality," she writes, as a result of the fact that "we no longer see man against a background of values, of realities, which transcend him."[12] Writers, she felt, had lost serious connections to serious explanations. Things had dried up, gone small-scale, and while the "crystalline" alternative of modernist writing had been evasive in its own way, it at least had longings toward some supreme reference. Something like it, but more morally serious, and more responsible, seemed necessary to Murdoch, and so she came up with a new kind of philosophical fiction. At first, she did so in an existential vein, but ultimately she moved beyond the excessively romantic freedom of existentialism to develop a unique philosophical style – less anxious, more practical, and yet also more engaged with re-establishing a background of values.

In *The Sea, the Sea* (1978), Murdoch takes a powerful man and sees what happens when he tries to leave reality and become master of a self-contained world of his own. Charles Arrowby has been a hugely successful stage-director, and he decides to retire to a house by the sea – to isolate himself and thereby to make his world pure and perfect. Of course he fails, and in the process we are treated to what is really a philosophical speculation about the nature of the will and the fallacies of desire. He finally realizes something like what Murdoch herself had to say about moral realities: "What innumerable chains of fatal causes one's vanity, one's jealousy, one's cupidity, one's cowardice have laid upon the earth to be traps for others. It's strange that when I went to the sea I imagined I was giving up the world." Such a statement must seem entirely unmodern, being so explicitly "viewy," and coming as it does at the end of a novel whose form is apparently fully conventional. Murdoch narrates in Arrowby's first-person, subjective voice, but we get little of the confusion and uncertainty that had been the hallmarks of modernist fiction. But even so, the philosophical mode becomes experimental, because Murdoch has remade "the now so unfashionable naturalistic idea of character": showing how "real people are destructive of myth," how "contingency is destructive of fantasy and opens the way for the imagination," and how both can "give us a new vocabulary of experience, and a truer picture of freedom," Murdoch faces the loss of fundamental values caused by modernity by proposing conceptual frameworks that might take their place.[13]

Insofar as such philosophical fictions could make the "novel of ideas" a way to experiment with form (as in the case of Beckett's existential departures, Ellison's invisible freedom, Murdoch's morality), then it also helped the modern novel to solve its problems with reality. For these were ways to arrive at the responsibility wanted by the fiction writers of the day while also pushing off into new worlds of aesthetic imagination.

Inverse to this approach was another way of getting innovation and reality at the same time. Inverse to philosophy, in a sense, was sexuality. Letting sexuality express itself in fiction, many mid-century writers got in touch with the most visceral of realities; at the same time, the dynamics of sexual desire forced fiction into new – and newly experimental – styles and techniques.

We have already seen how this began to happen in the first phases of modern fiction. In *Ulysses*, Leopold Bloom's status as an anti-hero has a lot to do with his tendency toward masochism: he likes the idea of being dominated by women, and chapter 15 of the novel is devoted to fantasies of domination by a manly prostitute: to the dominatrix Bella Cohen, who booms, "henceforth you are unmanned and mine in earnest, a thing under the yoke," Bloom cries, "Exuberant female. Enormously I desiderate your domination . . . Master! Mistress! Mantamer!" Such dark erotic fantasies made a big difference to fiction: they proved that desire can unman reason, can work against you, and dramatized the changing roles our desires force us to play. In the novels of D. H. Lawrence, sex comes to rule over thought: Lawrence's belief that modern culture had grown too abstract and too intellectual led him to physicalize his fiction, to let instincts reshape it. One main way he did so was to emphasize the power of erotic motives. His *Lady Chatterley's Lover* (1928) scandalized the world with its frank treatment of sexual desire. What was really shocking about it was the way it put erotic motives first: the story of an upper-class woman who invites the sexual dominance of a lower-class man, it suggested that sex had far more power to it than all other priorities. Sexual transgression here becomes a new way to tell the truth about human motivation. Before, it had been demonized, or sex had been repressed; once the subject of Lawrence's idealization, however, it became the essence of modern rebellion, and one of the best ways to refute the lies and hypocrisies of civilized society. Moreover, eroticism gave new patterns to fiction. Visceral inconsistency replaced reasoned progressions; explosive feeling broke the evenness of objective narration. Such changes would continue to happen as eroticism became an ever more potent way to challenge social norms and to wake fiction up to reality.

In the same year as Lawrence published *Lady Chatterley's Lover*, another book appeared that was similarly deemed "obscene": *The Well of Loneliness* by Radclyffe Hall. Hall broke the silence about lesbianism, which had hardly ever been publicly acknowledged even as a possibility. *The Well of Loneliness* shares with these other modern novels the sense that the erotic body needed to speak new truths to the world. At a more brutal level the same need is manifest in Henry Miller's *Tropic of Cancer* (1934). Miller's book is the story of an American drifter in Paris, scraping by in bohemian style, dissolving into drink, but indulging also in erotic specialties that put sex into an entirely new class of experience. The book made sex a form of dissent, a new kind of self-disclosure, and brought fiction to new heights of obscenity. To a shocked readership, when Miller's anti-hero disregards all civilized rules and expectations, and subjects himself, women, and language to the primal appetites of erotic life, he seems to reduce fiction to mere brutality. But in doing so he also fights the dehumanizing forces of modernity, by trying to get far past conventional morality to discover the desires that make people authentically human. As Anaïs Nin wrote about *Tropic of Cancer*, "here is a book which . . . might restore our appetite for the fundamental realities," by fighting against the bad detachment of modern life: "In a world grown paralyzed with intro-spection and constipated by delicate mental meals this brutal exposure of the substantial body comes as a vitalizing current of blood." For the modern novel, this revitalization meant "a swing forward into unbeaten areas": like other modern writers, Nin said, Miller wanted "to shock, to startle the lifeless ones from their profound slumber," but he did so knowing that "art is passing" because it had become blood-less. He knew, in other words, that the experiments of modern fiction could be a kind of "anaesthesia," and that only total erotic honesty could give the "blood transfusion" modern fiction needed to survive.[14]

What writers like Woolf and James had wanted of essential truth and obscure motivations is delivered here without loss to fiction's flesh and blood. In fact it is possible to say that these things are not only not lost, but aesthetically regained – and for that reason, modern sex-uality became one of the best ways for the modern novel to renew itself. It all comes down to the strange implications of the key term: sexual freedom. Freedom could encourage the higher liberties the modern novel had always wanted to take, but sexuality guaranteed the vitality the modern novel had not always enjoyed.

Vladmir Nabokov's *Lolita* (1955) is perhaps the best example of this trend – of the way the theme of shocking sexuality enhanced the vital-ity and viability of modern fiction. Humbert Humbert is a pederast: he is desperate to have sex with a pre-adolescent girl, to explore the "per-ilous magic of nymphets," and succeeds in doing so, after no small amount of maneuvering and manipulation. This would hardly seem promising material for a modern novel: the iconoclasm is typical, but too sensational, too irreedemable; this plot would seem completely at odds with the superiority and subtlety modern novels have tended to value. But Nabokov's goal is not simply to tell a shocking story. He challenges this most unchallenged of taboos not just for the sake of sensational iconoclasm, but to pursue truth anywhere, as long as it will invigorate language and art. He pushes the *aesthetic* motive to its furthest extreme – achieving in the voice of his narrator the most fan-tastic eloquence, even at the risk of the most abysmal corruption. Reflecting on the allegedly meaningless obscenity of *Lolita*, Nabokov wrote, "For me a work of fiction exists only insofar as it affords me what I shall bluntly call aesthetic bliss, that is a sense of being somehow, somewhere, connected with other states of being where art (curiosity, tenderness, kindness, ecstasy) is the norm."[15] Where art is the norm, morality is irrelevant: this is the aesthetic position, perhaps the key motivation for modernist experimentation, but pushed self-consciously to an extreme in order to test and clarify the power of art. Outlaw sexuality enables Nabokov to advance the aesthetic agenda without departing into the aesthete's notorious detachment; when Humbert Humbert realizes in despair that without Lolita, "I have only words to play with!," we realize that this is much to play with indeed, and that aesthetic bliss is our reward, at least, for Humbert's criminality.

Narrative perversity here becomes the place where experiment and reality meet. It is so also in the early fiction of Angela Carter, for whom sex is always *gothic* – always the expression of the cultural imagination's most grotesque fantasies. Sex therefore endows Carter's books with fantastic enrichments, even as it enables her to analyze the darker motives of desire. In *The Magic Toyshop* (1967), Carter makes something that ought to be charming and delightful (a magic toyshop) an elaborate metaphor for men's sadistic sexual domination of women. A young girl has been orphaned and sent to live with her uncle, whose toyshop is a scene of obscure violence and horror: severed hands turn up in drawers, family members are brutalized into muteness, and all are subjected like puppets in a grotesque parody of children's theater. At the climax of the novel, Melanie is forced to play the role of Leda to a massive puppet swan – to be raped by it, in a scene of absurd horror:

> Now she herself was on stage with an imitation swan . . . Looking up, she could see Uncle Philip directing its movements . . . The swan made a lumpish jump forward and settled on her loins. She thrust with all her force to get rid of it but the wings came down around her like a tent and its head fell forward and nestled in her neck. The gilded beak dug deeply into the soft flesh. She screamed, hardly realising she was screaming. She was covered completely by the swan but for her kicking feet and her screaming face. The obscene swan had mounted her.

The excessive symbolism here is Carter's way of getting at the horrors of female sexual subjugation. Anything more subtle might have lost just how much sexual initiation, for a girl like Melanie, really is absurd and horrid; patriarchy, Carter wants to suggest, is as excessively dehumanizing and sexually violent as this scene is silly and crude. As with Nabokov, we get a perverse imagination able at once to tell new truths and achieve rare aesthetic intensity; again, we get the modern combination, now by other (sexual) means, and without the limiting delicacy of some modern writing.

In erotic and existential fiction we get two of the new approaches to reality that enabled modern experimentation to ground itself in the fundamentals of real life. They were powerful means toward this end because of the way they could be at once so fundamental and so fantastic. They could run the range from strong social engagement (in *Invisible Man* and *The Magic Toyshop*) to bizarre lost minds (in the complicated pseudo-reason of *Murphy* and *Lolita*); they could give us both the real life of the body and the aesthetic creativity of the wildest imagination; they could widen the range of the modern fiction to novels of ideas (those of Iris Murdoch) and to stories of raw sex (in *Tropic of Cancer*). And so we see the modern novel pressing on by finding more chances for its way of shaping experience to mold modernity into livable forms.

But the novel found such chances even more abundantly by looking in places it had not gone before. For the first modern novelists, change took formal effort; to make the novel modern, it was necessary to try for new forms of description, characterization, narration, and the effort was optional, since it was possible (though to these novelists undesirable) to write traditionally despite the widespread changes of modern times. For a later group of modern novelists, however, change was not optional. Simply by virtue of living and writing in emerging cultures – in cultures emerging from imperial domination into self-determination – these novelists could only write in new ways about new things. As writers in Africa, India, the Caribbean, and other places that had not yet made the novel their own began to tell their stories, they modernized fiction – making it find ways to speak the languages and perspectives of cultures created by modernity but not yet a part of fiction's way of being new.

As a boy, V. S. Naipaul wanted to be a writer, but "together with the wish there had come the knowledge that the literature that had given me the wish came from another world, far away from our own." He came from a family of Indian immigrants who lived in Trinidad, and he would ultimately become a Nobel-Prize-winning novelist, but found at first that his "commonwealth" background kept him distant from literary culture. He loved to read Conrad and Huxley and wanted to imitate them, but "when it came to the modern writers their stress on their own personalities shut me out: I couldn't pretend to be a Maugham in London or Huxley or Ackerley in India." "The books themselves I couldn't enter on my own. I didn't have the imaginative key": the modern novel lacked the range to reach him, and he could not unlock it until travel and education in London and Oxford closed the distance. But then Naipaul turned around and closed the distance in another way. From London, he discovered the theme and the voice that would make him a writer and also help change the future of the novel. At first unable to write (still without the "imaginative key"), Naipaul realized his material had to be the "mixed life" of the city streets of Trinidad, mixed further with "the ways and manners of a remembered India," and captured in a "mixed voice" – Indian, Spanish, British. The mixed life in the mixed voice became Naipaul's first novels, *The Mystic Masseur* (1957) and *Miguel Street* (1959), early advances in the modern novel's progress into other worlds.[16]

This was the phase of "commonwealth" fiction – a moment between anti-imperialist writing written by outsiders (Conrad, Forster) and the later moment in which more fully "postcolonial" novelists would really develop wholly new political concepts and languages. It was an interim phase of first experiments, from English-speaking nations in the first phases of postimperial independence – from India, independent in 1947, and countries in Africa that began to fight for and get independence throughout the 1950s and 1960s. It was the first moment of a change that would prove crucial to the life of the modern novel, by creating a new demand for fiction's experimental means of reckoning with modernity's upheavals.

A key novel here is Chinua Achebe's *Things Fall Apart* (1958), the book that was among the first to shift the international focus of fiction to make it include new cultural forms and new political perspectives. *Things Fall Apart* is the story of imperial adventure into Africa, a familiar story – but told now from the point of view of the colonized. The book focuses on one heroic Ibo warrior and leader, Okonkwo, who has a tragic flaw: his father had been an embarrassment, a lazy man who never worked hard enough or attained honor sufficient to take the "titles" that made Ibo men great. Determined to make up for his father's inadequacies, Okonkwo becomes too rigid, too single-minded, and too proud, so that when white men come to his land he is unable to adapt. "His whole life was dominated by fear, the fear of failure and of weakness," and ironically that fear makes him unable to succeed – unable to help his clan change with the times. The inability here is, in part, heroical: Okonkwo resists the encroachments of white rule, at a moment in which the willingness to adapt would lead to the ruin of Ibo culture. But his inflexibility is also weakness, for it leads to his suicide – an utter disgrace according to Ibo values. Focusing on Okonkwo, Achebe presents a complex account of the "contact" between African and western cultures. Had he simply described a wholly good character ruined by imperialism, his novel would have been politically effective but two-dimensional; had he described a faulty Ibo culture giving way easily to imperialism, he would have made no difference to the tradition of books that had been, for some time, describing Africa as if it had no valid cultures of its own. But by combining these two approaches – stressing both the strengths and weaknesses of Ibo culture – Achebe gets at the complexity of the situation of "contact" and the worthy complexity of African peoples. For his treatment of them describes the full range of cultural attributes; it allows them weakness as well as strength, and above all the sort of ambiguity in cultural traditions that reflects a rich history and a rich tradition of legal, economic, and spiritual development.

Another notable "commonwealth" novel is Naipaul's best early book, *A House for Mr Biswas* (1961). It tells the story of a man's effort to build himself a suitable house amid a culture both rich and repressive – the culture of the Indian immigrant community on the Caribbean island of Trinidad. Ultimately he succeeds, and even if the house he builds falls far short of his hopes, its symbolic meaning is unquestionable. "As a boy he had moved from one house of strangers to another" – and since then it had been one decaying, clumsy, rented or borrowed house after another, living shabbily or in someone else's space. But finally he gets his "own portion of the earth," and the satisfaction is vital:

> How terrible it would have been, at this time, to be without it: to have died among the Tulsis, amid the squalor of that large, disintegrating and indifferent family; to have left Shama and the children among them, in one room; worse, to have lived without even attempting to lay claim to one's portion of the earth; to have lived and died as one had been born, unnecessary and unaccommodated.

Clearly, the house symbolizes a kind of postimperial emergence, from a "large, disintegrating and indifferent" empire into one's own place on earth. But the house also becomes more specifically an allegorical symbol for the emergence of the "commonwealth" writer. Houses had long been symbols for fiction itself – in, for example, Henry James's treatment, in his preface to *The Portrait of a Lady*, of "the house of fiction" – and Naipaul falls into that tradition by having Mr Biswas simultaneously seek his house and a career as a writer. But Naipaul also make that tradition new, for this "house of fiction" raises different questions: what should it be like, this "house" built with few resources by a man out to defy both the expectations of his immigrant culture and the possibilities open to the immigrant entrepreneur? What fiction can be built by him, or by Naipaul, trying to cobble together the means to make it from what material comes to Trinidad, and from the "mixed" material passed down through the different cultures that live there? As the novel attempts to answer these questions, it tries to customize the materials of fiction for new cultural structures, and in the process it makes fiction accommodate new modern needs – those of a Mr Biswas, now, who "had lived in many houses," and found it all too easy to "think of those houses without him."

The great virtue of commonwealth fiction for the modern novel was an unprecedented justification of the aspiration to face modernity with new forms. It gave this justification because "modernity" was perhaps nowhere more palpable than in the former colonies of the world, where ambiguous change was the essence of every aspect of life. It did because new forms were natural to writers starting whole new traditions, and so clearly at work in such things as the "contact" novels and house-fictions of writers like Achebe and Naipaul. And it did because these novels had such enlarging effects on the political consciences, the psychologies, and the aesthetic boundaries of the cultures that the writers wanted to change. Many people object to the naming these novels "commonwealth fiction," because that name implies that the writing done in these other places is one thing and subject to the British empire. Salman Rushdie, for example, thought the term "unhelpful and even a little distasteful," for the way it created a "ghetto," the effect of which was to "change the meaning of the far broader term 'English literature' . . . into something far narrower, something topographical, nationalistic, possibly even racially segregationist." And indeed this writing would not fully come into its own until it went more fully "post"colonial in later decades. But "commonwealth" does mark a first stage of emergence – a stage in fiction we might usefully place after "imperial" but before the "post-colonial" in the sequence of modern fiction's advancement into global cultures.[17]

CHAPTER 7

Postmodern Replenishments?

The new energy of "commonwealth" fiction made an ironic contrast with what was otherwise often considered a moment of literary "exhaustion." In the commonwealth, writers were vigorously beginning to make their experiences the source for innovative new kinds of writing – writing which, in turn, would aid good cultural change. Elsewhere, however, writers were facing a sense that the purpose of literature had been exhausted, and that as a result, innovation had become purposeless.

John Barth described this situation in his essay on "The literature of exhaustion" (1967). He noted that modern experimentation, which had once made fiction both exciting and important, now went on for no clear reason, with no good effects. Writers had started simply playing around, or showing off; there were plenty of new tricks, but these seemed to be little more than tricks, just experimentation for the sake of shock, surprise, or cleverness. And then on the other hand there were writers writing as if modernism had never happened – just offering up traditional descriptions of traditional situations, and failing entirely even to enter the twentieth century. Things had devolved mostly into a "literature of exhausted possibility", of "used-upness," a "tradition of rebelling against tradition." Where were the writers who could purposefully experiment, who could really entertain people with innovation, and find the right path between "exhausted" trickery and traditional writing?[1]

Ultimately, Barth would find them: over a decade after writing about "The literature of exhaustion," he would write about "The literature of replenishment," declaring that fiction had revitalized its experimental mission and begun again to advance the cause of the modern novel. In the meantime, however, the fate of the modern novel was uncertain. These were the years of the "postmodern": postmodernism introduced into fiction a new, extreme kind of experimentation, a skeptical outlook far more severe than that of the modernists, and a stunning challenge to the notion that fiction or art of any kind could have redemptive effects. At first, postmodernism seemed to mean the end of the modern novel, but ultimately it was a "replenishment"; at first, it threatened an end to any faith in "representation," but ultimately it would turn out to solve many of the problems left unsolved by the modern novel in its first phases.

What were the signs of the "exhaustion" that seemed to characterize postmodernism in its first moments? What were its causes, and how did its effects jeopardize the modern novel? How could postmodernism have "replenished" modern fiction – if, as its name indicates, it succeeds the modern?

Recall that the modern novel began in a special set of mixed feelings. In the face of modernity, it was wary but also welcoming – sure, in any case, that fiction ought to try to deal with modernity by dramatizing its new freedoms and pleasures, or criticizing its problems, or even redeeming what modernity seemed likely to destroy. Writers believed that fiction could change the way people thought, that as "the one bright book of life" it could revitalize them, spread sympathy, and help return aesthetic and ethical complexity to worlds going cold with technology, rationality, materialism. There was skepticism, but it too worked in the service of this kind of idealism. All this changed – gradually, as we have seen, in the political fervor of the 1930s and in the aftermath of the war, but finally with the advent of postmodernism.

Postmodernism happened when people lost faith in this idealism, and other idealisms like it. Faith, of course, had been on its way out for a long time, but now all structures of positive thinking seemed to collapse; principles gave way to paradigms, any remaining certainties gave way to total relativism. The causes were many, but we might generalize by saying that they were all the bad things about "modernity" redoubled and ruthless: technology now was the atomic bomb; materialism now was a consumer culture of insidious influence; alienation now was the very plan of suburbia; "civilization," largely discredited after World War I, was now a total lie, a pretense masking only a lust for power. And what had been good about modernity seemed good no longer. Its freedoms and its controls both now seemed too total. They seemed to mean now that there was nothing beneath it all – no traditional substance upon which to rest beliefs, true emotions, or valid aspirations. This loss of "foundations" mainly meant an "incredulity toward metanarratives" – a now total loss of faith in the larger stories by which people had tended to think, live, work, feel, and write.[2]

Gone were the *grand narratives* people had lived by and the foundations upon which their values had rested. If you felt this way, as many writers and thinkers did, what kind of fiction could you or should you write? With the guiding narratives and stable foundations gone, could you any longer do what the modern novelists had done? That is, could you believe that there was any point to trying for something new in the hope of making a difference, if even the myth of "making a difference" had been debunked?

And could you really believe that there could be anything "new" at all? "Exhaustion" also meant everything had already been done, that art was out of options. Everything seemed tired, predictable, played out. Originality was a naive, romantic dream. Or worse, it sounded like an aesthetic pretense, meant not to create something new but to show off, to exert power. For art itself was another thing debunked by postmodern skepticism. Its aspirations toward beauty, meaning, and wisdom now seemed to be false cover for something else: aristocratic or political privilege. Rather than beauty, art seemed to be after a way to make people believe that those in charge of culture deserved to be in charge, because they had special kinds of taste, creativity, and knowledge.

Truth, too, seemed exhausted. The modern writers had wanted always to question it – to see things from different perspectives, to doubt the conventional wisdom, and even to suggest that truth lay beyond our powers of perception and knowledge. But even at their most skeptical, modern writers had always thought it worthwhile to try for truth. And their whole enterprise rested on the faith that improved powers of "representation" would mean improved chances for getting truth right. But now modern skepticism got pushed further – further enough to undermine totally the possibility of "representation." The modernists had wanted immediacy; postmodernism seemed to prove that we could only get "mediation," since there was no reality beyond the reach of thought and language. Postmodernism only "put forward the unpresentable in presentation itself," and denied "the solace of good forms" that had been the point of modern writing.[3] All it could do was "dramatize the theme of the world's non-interpretability."[4]

What was left for modern fiction? Without faith in originality, art, representation, goodness, without the solace of good forms – in its exhaustion, what could it become?

Could the novel now only express total, negative skepticism? If there were no sure meaning in the world, maybe it would be best just to think of the world as a big game. If you could not truly represent anything, why not make that failure your subject? If art had been falsely aristocratic, why not force it down to earth? And if there were no longer any way to be original, maybe it would be best just to spoof what there already was. These were four ways fiction could respond to the postmodern condition. Play, parody, reflexivity, and deflation seemed to be what was left to the "literature of exhaustion." Fiction would become fiction about the failures of fiction; it would be fun, but finally empty, and it would aim above all to deflate any pretensions to meaning, faith, and truth.

Take for example B. S. Johnson's *Book in a Box* (1969). Here was a book out to mock the very possibility of a book, by breaking up its parts, undoing its typical form, and making it a random kind of game in which chapters might be chosen purposelessly in any order. The point was to become self-conscious about the expectations we bring to books, even before we get on to reading them. And the reading procedure – now random, totally in question, as you picked your way through – was meant to mirror the randomness of a world without foundations. Not to represent anything (there could be no sure connections between what was in a book and the outside world) but to throw you back on your expectations about reading, and show you how they must fail. Or take *Pale Fire* (1962), another book by Vladimir Nabokov, which is less a novel than a parodic game of interpretation. The subject of the novel is a famous poet's long poem, and the effort to interpret it made by a scholar with a deranged obsession. The poem, it seems, is simple enough, but the scholar believes it contains a vast and historically crucial secret allegory: he believes the poem is about him, and the history of the nation of which he is the exiled king. *Pale Fire* is consequently a parody of the effort to find meaning in literature. We get, in other words, a novel not after some true reality, but all about the doomed process of producing and interpreting fiction itself. We get the sense that there is no truth behind fiction, that fiction is really just all about its own falsity. "Life itself" is just "commentary to an abstruse unfinished poem," and the idealistic aims of the modern novel are tantamount to paranoid delusions of grandeur.

These are excellent books, and not what John Barth deplored, but they are nevertheless examples of what made him worry about the exhaustion of fiction. Postmodernism, it seemed, dead-ended the modern novel, by taking away its basic premises. Modern fiction could not work without two beliefs: first, that "representation" was worth the effort (that it might be hard, and even doomed to fail, but must be tried); and second, that the effort could result in some good effect, whether it be beauty, truth, solidarity, perceptivity, justice, or the vitalization of language. Postmodernism debunked these two beliefs, leaving only one aspect of modern fiction. All that was left was the desire to try something new. Without those two other beliefs, however, experimentation became a very different thing. Now, it became a game, and a game all about its own uselessness.

But this is far too bleak a picture of the effect postmodernism had on fiction. Barth soon abandoned his concerns about the "exhaustion" of the novel, finding proof that postmodernism had heralded a "replenishment." For him, the postmodern meant a "synthesis or a transcension" of the antitheses of modernist and pre-modernist modes of writing, in which "the ideal postmodernist novel will somehow rise above the quarrel between realism and irrealism, formalism and 'contentism,' pure and committed literature," to combine all the most vital aspects of all the novels of the past.[5] Barth discovered early what turned out to be true: all those tendencies that seemed to mean the death of the modern novel (as well as an end to much of faith and meaning) actually meant its enrichment. The extreme skepticism, the tendency toward parody and play, the distrust of grand narratives, the reflexivity: all of these things became marvelous resources for modern fiction, and ultimately widened the range of its powers to make sense of the modern world. In some purely technical sense, postmodernism may have marked an end to the modern impulse in fiction, but in effect it made for a new beginning.

What follows here is an account of what postmodernism did for modern fiction. This account aims mainly to define the postmodern approach to fiction and to give examples of it. But it will also do two things to emphasize the ways postmodernism advanced modern fiction: it will stress how postmodernism reinvigorated the key styles and features of the modern novel (defamiliarization, consciousness, fragmentation, etc.); and it will also stress how postmodernism solved many of the modern novel's key problems. Earlier, we saw that people came to criticize the modern novel for a number of things: for example, its naive hope of "immediacy," the limits on its perspectives, its disengagement, and its persistent traditionalism. Once postmodernism came into play, these problems got addressed, and in what follows here we will see how.

The first generation of modern novelists had worked hard to "match word and vision." More than anything else they wanted to make language a better, more self-consciously adept register of immediate reality. Of course they knew there were limits, and often they let on in their fiction that these limits worried them (at the end of *The Good Soldier*, for example, when the novel's narrator laments the fact that he just can't speak the truth). Nevertheless they pushed on, for what defines modern fiction more than anything else is the idealistic pursuit of new words that might match new visions of new worlds. But by the moment of postmodernism, the match seemed impossible. The world seemed too wild – and experimental language seemed to feeble, or too strong. This failure of reference, this end to representation, made some writers so skeptical that their fiction just enacted failure: it presented language in crisis, stressing its pointlessness, playing with disaster. To other writers, however, the failure of reference presented a new opportunity to enrich the language of fiction.

To these writers, the failure of immediacy meant new interest in *mediation*. In other words, it meant marvelous new interest in the medium of language itself, in the act of representation, as a thing of its own. If, as the modernists had discovered, language no longer catered to reality – if it's function was no longer only to be a transparent window on what it showed – did this not make it free? Did this not mean that language could now become even more of a focus of experiment, of innovation, of excitement? Many writers took this failure of language as an opportunity to pay far more attention to it, to make language abstract – truly to discover its powers and properties and much more creatively to play with its possibilities. What Joyce had done with the abstract wordplay of *Ulysses* and *Finnegan's Wake*, novelists would now do in fictions of all kinds. So what was for some just a crisis was to others – to those who yet felt the modern impulse to try productively for something new – a chance to make the language of fiction a fantastic new world of its own, and "the jubilation which result[s] from the invention of new rules of the game."[6]

The medium becomes the playful message in Anthony Burgess's *A Clockwork Orange* (1962). The novel is a dystopia: like *1984*, it presents us with a nightmarish future world, in this case one in which lawlessness has taken over. Also like *1984*, Burgess's novel worries about a lawless future. Soviet control seems to be a large part of the problem, for the novel's lawless characters speak a Russianized English, a language called NADSAT. We might be reminded of *1984*'s Newspeak – except for the fact that NADSAT is a much more dominant aspect of the novel and a lot more fun.

The title of the novel refers to the way excessive social planning – the welfare state, for example – reduces humanity to machinery. A "clockwork orange" is a mechanical life, made that way by a combination of technological modernity and technocratic government: the title refers to "the attempt to impose upon man, a creature of growth and capable of sweetness . . . laws and conditions appropriate to a mechanical creation." Critical of this dehumanizing social "improvement," Burgess bases the novel on one of the key postmodern ideas: that the "grand narratives" of social progress are in fact oppressive, dangerous distortions. The specific clockwork orange in question here is Alex, the novel's protagonist. At first a juvenile delinquent, he is made into a model citizen by a medical process (the "Ludovico Technique") that makes him incapable of violence. It also makes him unable to appreciate art; it also makes him inhuman, because incapable of *choice*, and we therefore see that the allegedly civilizing efforts of modern society must utterly fail. But along with this dark message we get an exuberant medium: Alex's language, NADSAT, is itself an important and dynamic subject of the novel.

Here is an example of it, from the beginning of the novel:

There was me, that is Alex, and my three droogs . . . Our pockets were full of deng, so there was no real need from the point of view of crasting any more pretty polly to tolchock some old veck in an alley and viddy him swim in his blood while we counted the takings and divided by four, nor to do the ultra-violent on some shivering starry grey-haired ptitsa in a shop and go smecking off with the till's guts. But as they say, money isn't everything.

Here Burgess's postmodernism has led him to bring language fantastically to life, but to a life of its own; not to imitate reality, but to express its own complications. Or even to obscure reality: Burgess claims to have invented NADSAT in order to put distance between his readers and his "pornographic" subject-matter: "Nadsat, a Russified version of English, was meant to muffle the raw response we expect from pornography. It turned the book into a linguistic adventure."[7] So the problematics of language becomes the issue, both to make us value the distance between words and things, and to make us enjoy the arts of which language is capable once it is no longer so directly responsible for "reality." We might best appreciate the benefits here by recalling what modern writers had wanted to do with defamiliarization. Whereas earlier modern novelists had used words to defamiliarize things, a writer like Burgess defamiliarizes the words themselves, making us more conscious of the true matter of meaning.

This consciousness of fiction itself – this attention to the way the language of fiction comes in between us and reality – is the main change postmodernism brought to the modern novel. Not only does the problematics of language become the subject of fiction. Storytelling itself becomes an issue. Whereas before, modern writers had tried to efface their narrators, going directly into consciousness and getting rid of any intrusive omniscience, now they found it important to do the opposite. Narration became a theme within the novel. Now, writers felt it necessary to write about writing, to tell about the telling of stories, because the whole possibility of fiction had been thrown into question. Fiction became *metafiction* – stories about stories, fiction about fiction, novels within novels.

Metafiction typically gives us narrators who constantly think about the ways they are telling their stories. Sometimes, such narrators may be writers themselves, trying to write a work of fiction and meditating constantly on the problems they face in doing so. In its most experimental forms, metafiction can involve a deep questioning of the possibility of truth in fiction, or an obsession with the power fiction has over our lives. Whatever the form of its preoccupation, metafiction shifts the focus back from *showing* to *telling*. The first modern novelists had shifted things in the other direction, leaving behind the conventional plots of storytelling in favor of radical immediacy; their priority, as we have seen, is *mimesis*. Now, however, there was a total self-consciousness about what telling entails, a deliberate exploration of *diegesis*. David Lodge makes the difference between mimesis and diegesis a helpful way to know the difference between modernist and postmodernist priorities:

> The classic realist text, we may say, was characterized by a balanced and harmonized combination of mimesis and diegesis, reported speech and reporting context, authorial speech and represented speech. The modern novel evolved through an increasing dominance of mimesis over diegesis. Narrative was focalized through character with extensive use of "pictorial" reported speech or delegated to narrators with mimetically objectified styles . . . what we see happening in postmodernist fiction is a revival of diegesis: not smoothly dovetailed with mimesis as in the classic realist text, and not subordinated to mimesis as in the modernist text, but foregrounded against mimesis. The stream of consciousness has turned to a stream of narration.[8]

This last difference is key: whereas the modern writer wanted to "mime" consciousness, as if fiction were a transparent window into it, the postmodern writer focuses on the intervention of narration itself.

Metafiction's return to diegesis produced John Fowles's *The French Lieutenant's Woman* (1969). Set in 1867, the novel tells the story of a man who gives up his conventional, respectable life in order to pursue a "fallen" woman – a woman who seems to have a scandalous past. The details of the lives they lead richly explore Victorian culture and its presumptions about decency, sexuality, and love. And this exploration is made explicit by an intrusive narrator, who fills in all the historical and social detail. Nothing unusual, and nothing apparently postmodern, until it becomes clear that this apparently conventional narrator is not conventional at all. As much as he is master of the historical facts of the story, he is undone by the variety of possible ways he might present them. He is persistently conscious of the fact that everything depends upon his choices – how the different options open to him might frame things fictionally in different ways. At one key moment, the narrator asks about his mysterious heroine, "Who is Sarah? Out of what shadows does she come?," and then answers,

I do not know. This story I am telling is all imagination. These characters I create never existed outside my own mind. If I have pretended
until now to know my characters' minds and innermost thoughts, it is
because I am writing in (just as I have assumed some of the vocabulary
and "voice" of) a convention universally accepted at the time of my
story: that the novelist stands next to God. He may not know all, yet he
tries to pretend that he does. But I live in the age of Alain Robbe-Grillet
and Roland Barthes; if this is a novel, it cannot be a novel in the modern
sense of the word.

Fowles implies that a "modern" novel would never extend to this
degree of self-questioning, denying the existence of the contents of the
story, calling it all a pretense. Modern writers were aware that writing
was a matter of conventions; but a postmodern writer like Fowles
makes those conventions his explicit concern, so that the story is as
much about how a story might be told as it is about the particular
events in question. This is the essence of metafiction – this creative
uncertainty about the means of storytelling itself, this self-conscious
exploration of fiction-making, this questioning not just of reality but
of fiction's power to imagine. It made fiction so much a matter of
inquiry that it became a "borderline discourse between fiction and
criticism."[9]

But doesn't this excess of questioning defeat the purpose of fiction?
If fiction is all about itself, and no longer about mimesis, how can it
effectively capture the outside world, or interest those of us who aren't
writers ourselves? Fowles might have answered that his self-conscious
questioning was a very powerful *assertion* of the power of fiction. *The
French Lieutenant's Woman* is not just about the different choices a novelist might make in setting up a story. It is also about the fact that any
reality, any historical event, is a product of fiction. Fowles noted that
"One cannot describe reality; only give metaphors that indicate it. All
human modes of description . . . are metaphorical. Even the most
precise scientific description of an object or movement is a tissue of
metaphors."[10] The point is not that everything we think is really just
all made up. Rather, the point is that we always see reality through
fictional frameworks. There is always some metaphor, some style of
plotting, some style of description and characterization, at work in any
view we take of the world. So when modern novels become metafic-

tions, they aren't only playing games. They are also exploring the way we make up our worlds. Experimenting with fictions about fictions, metafictional novels also explore the very basis of our realities.

The first modern novelists had been interested in the subjective view of reality, and they had therefore turned inward, to discover the workings of the individual consciousness. Now, novelists pushed the subjective even further – to the point where reality itself became a fiction. And this meant there was more to do when it came to the exploration of individual consciousness, for now the activities of consciousness became reality's source. There is a reversal here: consciousness is no longer what responds to reality, but what produces it. There is no reality before states of mind frame it, process it, make it into stories. Far from undermining the power of fiction, this reversal puts fiction first, and gives it a lot more to do. It even puts fiction before history. In this way of thinking, history too becomes a product of fiction – of the way stories put a reality that really cannot be said to exist before stories make it up. The category of "historical fiction" changes dramatically, for now history is a fiction, or is something wholly subject to the imagination.

This new dominance of fiction over history is a basis for E. L. Doctorow's approach to US history in *Ragtime* (1975), a "historical novel" about the exuberance and villainy of early twentieth-century America. Doctorow takes extreme liberties with historical fact, putting real historical figures into fictional situations, arranging encounters that never happened, in order to make history itself more meaningful. That is, Doctorow stresses the fictionality of great historical figures, to stress the fact that they are always really mainly products of the cultural imagination; it is no violation to make them up, since they are really fictions anyway. When, for example, Doctorow fictionalizes an encounter between J. P. Morgan and Henry Ford, he does not have to worry about the truth, for these men are not in history as real people:

> Morgan brought [Ford] to the great West Room of the Library. Here they took chairs on opposite sides of a fireplace that was as tall as a man. It was a good day for a fire, Morgan said. Ford agreed. Cigars were offered. Ford refused. He noticed that the ceiling was gilded . . . Morgan let him take it all in.

Here we have made-up facts about real people stated as if true, not because Doctorow thinks for sure that they happened, but because he knows that such imaginings are all we really have of truth even about real-historical figures. Moreover, we have an impressionistic style of description, which had been developed to get at "life itself," but now sketches out deliberate fictions.

This focus on fiction itself could also make writers want to rewrite the fictions of the past. Rather than create something entirely new, some writers thought it more important to rework something old, partially out of a sense of "exhaustion," but mainly out of a sense that our present realities are really made up of the fictions of the past. It seemed less important simply to take on current events and problems than to take on the whole cultural imagination as developed in the world's old stories. The most famous example here is Jean Rhys's *Wide Sargasso Sea* (1966). Here, Rhys rewrote the story of *Jane Eyre* (1847), with a particular interest in exploring the very influential fiction of ideal womanhood promoted in the Victorian novel. Knowing that this ideal still had influence, Rhys decided to rewrite it, from another point of view.

In *Jane Eyre*, the heroine is haunted by a "madwoman in the attic": a governess soon to marry her wealthy employer, Jane Eyre hears insane howling from the darker parts of the house soon to be her own, and finds it occupied already by her lover's first wife, a crazy woman hidden away and unknown to the world. The contrast between the two women could not be stronger, and for a time it seems that female madness might win out over female virtue. Ultimately, however, the madwoman dies, Jane's goodness triumphs, and women readers are taught a lesson. That lesson is what Jean Rhys set out to revise. *Wide Sargasso Sea* tells the story from the "madwoman's" point of view: we see her from childhood, menaced by life in colonial Antigua, and exploited by the man who would become the hero of *Jane Eyre*. We see that what makes a madwoman is not her womanhood, but sexism, imperialism, and other forms of injustice and inhumanity. And we see this because Rhys knows the powers of fiction. She knows that *Jane Eyre* has long determined the way people think about Creole women, and so she writes to remake the fictional norm, and to give culture another way to imagine Creole women's lives.

If originality ceases to matter to these postmodern writers, it is not because they have given up on the modern impulse toward innovation and change. Rather, it is because they have taken a new approach to it, in which making up new things is less important than exploring the very processes of making up. More often than not this means returning to prior scenes of invention, as Rhys returned to the scene of madness in *Jane Eyre* to turn it into a different kind of story.

Nevertheless it is true that the postmodern influence on fiction meant less earnest engagement with new realities. Parody was more the norm, for so many writers had decided to give up on any sincere and serious effort at aesthetic redemption. The angst with which the first modern writers faced the world, the intensity they brought to bear on modern problems, gave way to something very different: dark irony gave way to light, sincerity gave way to cynicism, angst went more blasé, and in general fiction became a forum for more playful ways of dealing with the problems of the world. As Gerald Graff puts it, "the tragic quest for meaning and justification, for transcendence, gives way to a glorification of *energy*."[11] And in the place of novels in search of the meaning of "life itself," we get "the game-novel, the puzzle-novel, the novel that leads the reader . . . through a fairground of illusions and deceptions, distorting mirrors and trap-doors that open disconcertingly under his feet, leaving him ultimately not with any simple or reassuring message or meaning but with a paradox about the relation of art to life."[12] But playful parody did not really mean taking things less seriously, or taking them more lightly. It meant finding a different way to question reality – not in earnest, now, but in travesty, farce, and a more total kind of doubt.

One master of postmodern play is Thomas Pynchon, whose novels suggest something crucial about this form of unseriousness: that it may after all be the best measure of modernity, and at the same time the best source of formal ingenuity. *The Crying of Lot 49* (1966) is an absurd treatment of a deeply serious problem. The problem is the feeling people had, in the Cold-War and consumerist cultures of the day, that all was controlled by nameless, unknown powers, that strange governments and conspiring corporations were constantly doing secret and evil things to enhance their hold on the world. The problem, in other words, is that of realistic paranoia – the justified but unprovable and therefore insane sense that individuals have lost control of their lives to secret evil systems. As the novel's unlikely heroine Oedipa Maas discovers, "Tristero's Empire" is a massive, centuries-old conspiracy, controlling everything, and its "legacy was America"; freedom is an illusion, for every innocuous place or person around her turns out to be in Tristero's control. Or are they? She thinks she has discovered the conspiracy – but it might *just* be paranoia, and what then?

> For there either was some Tristero beyond the appearance of the legacy America, or there was just America and if there was just America then it seemed the only way she could continue, and manage to be at all relevant to it, was as an alien, unfurrowed, assumed full circle into some paranoia.

We never find out the "truth" – the novel ends before Oedipa's questions are answered – and so we are left in what Pynchon implies is the postmodern condition: both sure and unsure that our lives are not our own, continuing as if freedom does and does not exist. The absurdity here is in the way Pynchon presents the problem – not as a serious concern, but as the crazy possibility, obsessed over by an ordinary woman, that a vast conspiracy composed of postal workers, playwrights, and big business has infiltrated every aspect of life. An unserious approach to a serious problem, it would seem, and no useful critique of modernity – until you see that Pynchon has perfectly captured the absurdity of modern paranoia. He not only gets the best measure of this key symptom of modernity, he find a fantastic new source of formal ingenuity, because paranoia turns out to be a maker of the wildest descriptions and the strangest leaps of thought. In the paranoid imagination, we get more intense versions of the defamiliarization and fragmentation we have seen in prior writers, but with a difference: here, they connect better than ever, if unseriously, to real-world problems.

The kind of fragmentation common in modern fiction here changes, as do the other things modern novelists had done to experiment with the composition and organization of words, phrases, and sentences. Mainly, experimentation on this level becomes more playful. Modernist deformations had been meant to reflect negatively the fragmentation of the world, or to try to remake language so that it could be a better register of real chaotic experience or essentially plural truth. Fiction written under the influence of postmodernism, however, deforms prose more for its own sake and for the fun of it. For example, this fiction shows a marked tendency toward digression. Narrators go off at tangents, breaking the flow of the story, and introducing new elements that fail to cohere together. Whereas before such digression would have been a symptom of madness, or a reflection of life's incoherence, here it goes on in enjoyment of storytelling's extreme complexity. Again we have exploration and expansion of the resources of storytelling itself. What had been a function of modernist mimesis becomes an expansion of postmodern diegesis. Unserious, the practice is nevertheless purposeful, for the way it maps out the real tendencies within our habits of telling the world into being.

How else did postmodernism expand the inventive capacities of the modern novel? Think, first of all, about character. In the modern novel, we have had a tendency to make characters anti-heroical, dispersed, and solipsistic; now, we get an even more total negation of all that had seemed to make characters integrally human. Some novels written under the influence of postmodernism would not even give their characters full names; limiting them to initials only (*G., V.*) became a way to reflect the fact that there was no longer any basis for identity, and that in its place there was now only a random and utterly changeable set of characteristics. Also more utterly undermined was the sense of time. In the modern novel, time went subjective; in defiance of clock-time, modern writers stressed the vagaries of personal time, the unlinear tricks of memory. Postmodern novels took things further by seeing unlinearity everywhere: now, not only personal time but public time melted into flux, as writers stressed the ways that it, too, had no basis in reality. And finally, when it comes to styles of narration, postmodernism turned modern flexibility into fully free play. Recall that the modernists had run up and down the scale of narrative possibility, choosing whatever forms were necessary to convey subjective, psychological truths. Postmodernism put a new twist on the scale: now that narration had become self-conscious, and all about itself, the difference between the "interior" and the "exterior" could no longer hold tight. Just who spoke and why therefore became a matter of boundless speculation.

But postmodern play also brings experimental fiction down to earth. It takes pains to include within its hybrid mixtures of different forms of mediation those that might have been considered beneath the modernist writers. Very often, modernist form excluded popular forms – deliberately, in order to make fiction a kind of refuge from the cheaper entertainments and low plots of the new kinds of writing perpetually turning up on the modern scene. Modernist fiction, that is, would become a realm of high art, to protect culture against the debasement of "mass culture." Postmodernism, on the other hand, tended to deny the distinction between high and low culture. Its refutation of the grand aspirations of western culture included refutation of aesthetic distinction, as "art has come to be seen as a form of complicity, another manifestation of the lies and hypocrisy through which the bourgeoisie has maintained its power."[13] As we have seen, this could mean a distressing kind of end to art – a capitulation to consumer culture's trivia. But it could also mean a democratization of art, in which the valid appeals and energies of allegedly lower forms of culture could make their way into great literature. It would mean that the modern novel could now more happily follow the example of new forms of writing and entertainment – that it could, for example, pattern itself after cinema, or television, or journalism, and that it wouldn't have to do so with the sort of cynical irony that might have accompanied reference to these things in earlier fiction.

A good example of a novel open to mass media is Don DeLillo's *White Noise* (1985). Here we have a book utterly caught up in the postmodern condition. Everything comes mediated to the Gladney family, who get by on images and products, on shopping and television, and live lives determined by a consumerist society. Not entirely at ease with it all, they nevertheless find what comfort they can take in shopping and television preferable to the anxieties that would otherwise consume them. For such things are all that is available, now, to make sense of the world and to distract attention from the big problems of death and disaster. When those problems assert themselves, however, DeLillo's characters must put new pressures on their mediated realities. And then DeLillo pays compelling attention to the way mass culture determines modern life. Whereas we might expect disgust with it – whereas we might expect a novel like this one to present television and shopping as decadent and degrading – instead we get a fascination with the mysterious, almost religious appeal of products and advertisements and radio voices. At one moment, Jack Gladney's sleeping child says the words, *"Toyota Celica,"* and Jack thinks,

> The utterance was beautiful and mysterious, gold-shot with looming wonder. It was like the name of an ancient power in the sky, tablet-carved in cuneiform. It made me feel that something hovered. But how could this be? A simple brand name, an ordinary car. How could these

near-nonsense words, murmured in a child's restless sleep, make me sense a meaning, a presence? She was only repeating some TV voice . . . Whatever its source, the utterance struck me with the impact of a moment of splendid transcendence.

DeLillo understands that such TV words somehow link up to transcendence, and so he takes them seriously throughout *White Noise*. The result is a more balanced, inclusive, and sympathetic vision of the whole of culture – not just admiration for and preservation of the higher forms of art and culture, but appreciation for the lower forms that fill the white-noise background to modern life. This appreciation does not extend to any fully postmodern play – DeLillo wants something more for his characters and for us – but here we see the modern novel letting in the low, at least to take on some of its strange power.

Giving up on purely high aesthetics also meant that fiction could once again include fantasy, the supernatural, the unreal. For a long time, the focus on essential and immediate realism in the modern novel had ruled these things out. Magic, ghosts, fantastic worlds: these things are nowhere in the modernist novel, mainly because writers like Woolf, Faulkner, and Joyce wanted so exclusively to make fiction a heightened register of everyday reality. But now fiction could once again accommodate the unreal, and it did so for any number of good reasons. The main reason, once again, was to explore the powers of fictionality. Whatever the mind could make up, whatever its storytelling capacities could imagine, was now fair game, because writers wanted to trace the furthest edges of fiction's capabilities. Also, they wanted to see reality, too, from a different perspective. They now wanted to stress the fact that because reality had become so astonishing, no realism could really reckon with it effectively. This is a paradox, but a vital one: realism could no longer reflect reality, because reality had become unreal, and so it was necessary to fantasize in order to evoke the feelings and problems the modern world now created.

Fantasy captures reality in *The White Hotel* (1981) by D. M. Thomas. The novel begins with a made-up exchange of letters between the psychoanalysts Freud and Ferenczi about the case of "Anna G.," a woman Freud has allegedly cured of hysteria. She had suffered from hysterical pains in her breast and abdomen; exploring her psyche and her past, Freud discovers why, and accomplishes the "release of repressed ideas into consciousness." The cause is discovered, and the symptoms are largely cured. But it ultimately becomes clear that this novel is not a psychological one after all; it is about history. Years after her analysis, "Anna G." is murdered at Babi Yar, the notorious site of one of the Holocaust's worst mass killings. Her mortal injuries there are to her breast and abdomen – so that those "hysterical" pains turn out not to have been psychic symptoms, but symptoms of history. They come not from the psychological past, but from the historical future; they speak not of personal problems, but of historical disaster. Trading psychology for history, and doing so through this fantasy of clairvoyance, *The White Hotel* shows how postmodern "unreality" might improve upon the modern novel's power to tell the truth. It implies that psychology – the modern novel's main preoccupation – cannot be true to history, unless postmodern fantasy broadens its horizons. Its leaps are not merely playful, as Thomas's narrator finally tells us:

> The soul of man is a far country, which cannot be approached or explored. Most of the dead were poor and illiterate. But every single one of them had dreamed dreams, seen visions and had amazing experiences . . . If a Sigmund Freud had been listening and taking notes from the time of Adam, he would still not fully have explored even a single group, even a single person.

To explore so many lives and histories, Thomas implies, the novel needs resources beyond the psychological, and it needs fantasy in order to get to the far country of the soul of man.

So under the aegis of postmodernism, respectable fiction could once again be fantastic (and had to be, in order to get at the truths formerly sought only realistically). And it could, once again, just tell a good story. Perhaps the most crucial change that happens in the modern novel as a result of the postmodern influence is a return to plot. This might seem unlikely, given what we have learned about postmodern parody and play, but stress on diegesis, while often very extreme, just as often meant the return of an old-fashioned kind of plot. It would go along with ironies, tricks, and complications of all kinds, but nevertheless plot could once again give the modern novel the feel of the fiction against which it had rebelled. Perhaps it is best to think about this as a sort of reconciliation. The modernists had rejected plot because of the way it forced fiction into artificial conventions. They had disliked the way plot compelled writers to falsify reality. But once postmodernism took its new view of conventions – deciding to ridicule them through exaggeration, rather than rejection – those conventions could return. Plot could return to the modern novel now not as an agent of convention, but a way to break convention after all. For the reader, this return has meant an ever fuller range of pleasures: now, in the modern novel we get all the pleasures of radical experimentation along with the pleasures of a good story.

These postmodern changes: do they mark the end of the modern novel? Diegesis, unseriousness, fantasy, mediation, plotting – are these signs of the end of a form of literature that had, after all, aimed at mimesis, earnest redress, reality, plotlessness, immediacy? Some say yes, and therefore define the postmodern as something opposite to the modern impulse. If they are right, the modern novel lasts from 1900 or so until no later than 1965, when postmodernism becomes the dominant sensibility in literary fiction. But in our examples of less extreme forms of postmodern writing we have seen signs that the modern impulse has not been killed but replenished – not ended but reformed or even advanced, so that the modern novel does not end around 1965, but continues as an ongoing project into subsequent decades.

CHAPTER 8

Postcolonial Modernity

Gertrude Stein's Modernism came in part from her psychology experiments. As we have seen, discovering "automatic writing" was crucial to discovering modern ways to plumb the depths of the mind, and Stein used what she found there to innovate one of the modern novel's most difficult and abstract styles. But there were other inspirations as well – particularly the work of the Cubist painters, and above all the work of Pablo Picasso. He helped to make painting modern around 1907, when he began to paint in a strange new abstract style: in such paintings as *The Women of Avignon*, he depicted the human form not in realistic detail, but in jumbled masses of flat planes and crude shapes. What inspired him was African sculpture, which had recently become a newly influential presence in European museums. African sculpture inspired Picasso's Cubism; his Cubism inspired Stein's modern fiction; and if we follow this line of influence backwards, we see again how much the forms of the modern novel were shaped by the expansion of culture into the wider territories of the world. Or, rather, we see how a certain new feature of that expansion was responsible: as we learn in *The Empire Writes Back: Theory and Practice in Postcolonial Literatures*, "Europeans were forced to realize that their culture was only one amongst a plurality of ways of conceiving of reality and organizing its representations in art and social practice."[1] The plurality of the modern novel, its questions about reality and its interest in finding new styles of representation – these were matters of aesthetic form, but first they were matters of encounter with new worlds beyond Europe and America, encounters in which westerners were finally forced to see other cultures as real alternatives.

Edward Said says much the same thing in *Culture and Imperialism.* "The formal dislocations and displacements in modernist culture . . . [are] a consequence of imperialism": things like modern irony, fragmentation, and even the hope of making fiction redemptive were consequences of challenges to western control over the world.[2] No account of the modern novel can overlook the way peripheral cultures and situations made this fundamental contribution to its forms. But the reverse is true as well. Accounts of the development of peripheral cultures – of their emergence from imperialism into independence, of their postcolonial movement from peripheries to centers of their own – do well to take into account the contributions made by the modern novel. For the forms of modern fiction have helped emerging cultures to imagine new possibilities, to rewrite the language of oppression, to give new shape to time and to space. They have played an active part in postcolonial progress, for many of the same reasons other modern writers have thought fiction might redeem the modern world.

The kind of influence African sculpture had on the writing of Gertrude Stein has since become much more direct. Since 1907, African writers have themselves modernized fiction, by shaping it to the needs of different cultures and different modern objectives. And other postcolonial writers have likewise replenished the novel's modern impulse by making it an ever more vital factor in cultural change. They have done so in large part because the forms of modern fiction (especially once those forms were replenished by postmodern energies) were already well suited to their needs. Ready for linguistic diversity, for questioning realities, for making life new, the novel promised to help in the fight for cultural success. How it did so – how the novel contributed its forms to postcolonial progress, and how it was reshaped and renewed in the process – is the subject of this chapter, which explores how postcolonial fiction has given the modern novel a role in global modernity.

Jean Rhys's *Wide Sargasso Sea* rewrote *Jane Eyre*, we have noted, in order to rewrite the fiction of the ideal woman. But the revision had another target as well. *Jane Eyre* only briefly mentions that its "madwoman" comes from the Caribbean, from a colony of Great Britain. It could mention such a thing only in passing because it was written from within the imperial mindset; in much of English literature written from *Jane Eyre* to *Heart of Darkness*, colonial people were less than peripheral concerns, a distant backdrop for the English stories. They often figured like *Jane Eyre*'s madwoman: as distant, mysterious, unknowable caricatures, people without substance, without identities or cultures other than those that enriched or intrigued their colonizers. When imperialism came to a crisis, this began to change, although it was still something Chinua Achebe could complain about, as he did, when writing of *Heart of Darkness*, that Conrad used "Africa as setting and backdrop which eliminates the African as human factor . . . reducing Africa to the role of props for the break-up of one petty European mind."[3] When the empire gave way to the commonwealth, this role changed more, and writers like Achebe and Naipaul began to supply the other side of the story – to write fiction from the point of view of the mysterious periphery. And then the "commonwealth" mentality gave way to the *postcolonial*, and things changed completely. The postcolonial situation, the situation now of struggle in newly independent nations for full cultural self-determination, led to a new kind of writing, one in which writers not only wrote from the periphery, but wrote against the very ideas and attitudes that had put them there. They rewrote *Jane Eyre*, for example: in *Wide Sargasso Sea*, Jean Rhys makes the "peripheral" story central, so that people could finally see where that madwoman came from, and why – how the neglected story of colonial life was really vital to the truth.

But Rhys did not just retell the old story in the same way, with the omitted information put back in. She knew she needed a new style for the new story, or else the imperial mindset might not change. Had she just made a different story the central one, the idea that some stories are central where others are not would persist. So she developed a new form, in which no story is central, in which the story moves from person to person unannounced, so that we never feel centered in any most important point of view. This kind of innovation was typical of writers like Rhys. Those writers in the Carribean, in India, in Africa and elsewhere who had begun to describe their cultures more authentically and extensively from the inside soon came to realize that such description really required of them a whole new way of thinking about fiction. It was not enough, they found, to apply the old rules of fiction to their new identities, concerns, and subjects. Those old rules seemed to have built into them the very colonialist presumptions that had tended to exclude "commonwealth" writers in the first place. Certain presumptions about the way human selves develop, certain western spiritual, political, and economic priorities, and even the west's fundamental habits of thought and language came to seem contrary to the things these writers needed to say. As Canadian writer Dennis Lee put it, "the language was drenched with our non-belonging."[4] And so they set about remaking the novel so that it could better express non-western beliefs, feelings, habits, and priorities.

The result is the postcolonial novel. The term refers to fiction written by people of formerly colonized cultures, in which "those people who were once colonized by the language are now rapidly remaking it, domesticating it . . . carving out large territories for themselves within its frontiers."[5] More than that, however, it refers to a mindset, a theory, and a style – to a departure from the colonial way of thinking as well as the colonial political situation, and to a new kind of writing based upon the departure.

Postcolonial fiction is "post" in two ways. First of all, it deals with what happens to colonized peoples and places after colonialism has ended. It describes the positive and negative developments in places such as Nigeria, where the end of imperial rule meant new possibilities of cultural self-determination but also a kind of chaos – both the pleasure and thrill of freedom and the pain of developing indigenous cultural and political systems. In this sense, the postcolonial condition is a question: what will the newly independent nation become? And the fiction devoted to asking this postcolonial question works very crucially as a form of experiment, providing answers to the question in such a way as to test them.

The postcolonial condition, however, is also a mindset – a way of thinking, or, more specifically, a state of mind now free of the presumptions and attitudes and even the language that made imperialism possible, desirable, and effective. To be postcolonial means to know that the attitudes of both the colonizers and the colonized entailed wrong presumptions in many areas – about human nature, about economics, about political rule. Having rejected these presumptions, the postcolonial attitude involves an effort to replace them. Here again fiction helps: postcolonial fiction is all about designing plots whereby the old presumptions give way to newer, better, fairer ones. As the peoples of postcolonial nations and former imperialists alike try to reconceive international relations and rethink the identities of non-western life, postcolonial fiction has served as a kind of crucible. For its structures and styles have had to develop out of the old into the new, much in the way that postcolonial societies themselves have had to try to make the shift into fully viable self-realization.

To become postcolonial, in other words, fiction has had to accomplish changes like those that have had to take place at the level of politics, government, and social planning. For it had been steeped in the cultural logic that had allowed imperialism to work: as we have seen, its plots and attitudes had tended to discourage dissent and to promote western middle-class values. But not entirely: the novel had also had styles and attitudes ready to work against imperialism, when the right moment came. The challenge fiction faced at the moment of postcolonial independence was to find a way to put its skeptical, oppositional, contrary, subversive, exploratory, and reframing tendencies to work in the service of those writers and thinkers trying to write and think a way into true cultural change.

This, then, is how the modern novel helps in the postcolonial project. It aids in the effort to go postcolonial, by rewriting the political fictions that helped to create and maintain the imperial dynamic. How exactly has this rewriting taken place? Sometimes, very literally. As we have seen in the case of *Wide Sargasso Sea*, the rewriting sometimes involves taking old books, written within the imperial aesthetic, and changing them, to tell the other side of the story. It has been a matter of "appropriation," to seize the story, "re-place it in a specific cultural location, and yet maintain the integrity of that Otherness, which historically has been employed to keep the post-colonial at the margins of power, of 'authenticity,' and even of reality itself."[6] Beyond such appropriations, there are many other postcolonial changes that have remade modern fiction. One fertile preoccupation has been the moment of independence – the event with which postcolonial nations have come into being. Many postcolonial novelists have focused their attention on the problem of any such moment, stressing the fact that no such transformation can happen right away; others have even gone as far as to question the very temporality behind the belief that it could. Always concerned with time, the modern novel could help explore the temporality of nationhood. Similarly, it was ready to help in a number of other ways: its talent for mixing languages helped explore the *hybridity* at work in cultures now necessarily part western and part indigenous; its focus on alienation helped understand the state of *exile*; its openness helped to follow the *migrant identities* forced by postcolonial unrest; its insight into the means of mimesis – how we make up our worlds – meant insight into the *mimicry* in which colonial people often felt obliged to engage; and its stress on consciousness helped detail the alternation within the *double consciousness* created in people part of both the imperial world and the unique decolonized culture.

For our purposes, it is important to focus upon the way these post-colonial tendencies dovetail with – and then also remake – the inventive tendencies ready in the modern novel. Again, the modern novel has helped cultural decolonization with its styles of defamiliarization, of heteroglossia, of shifting temporalities, of questioning the relationship between the individual and society, of perspective, and of revealing the presumptions to authority in any act of speaking. And in the process, new life has come to its once-new forms.

We see this reciprocity at work in *A Grain of Wheat* (1967) by Ngugi wa Thiong'o. Ngugi (the first name is the surname) is well known for his reflections on the problems African cultures face as they try to "decolonise the mind." Getting past colonialism, he says, means much more than just attaining political and economic self-determination. For the very *minds* of colonial peoples have been determined and structured by the languages, priorities, and habits of their oppressors. It is not as if there were some purely African mind just waiting for liberation to once again become itself; rather, the African mind has become largely a product of western intentions, and to decolonize itself it has to find ways to regain its own authentic mentality. It must engage in "an ever-continuing struggle to seize back [its] creative initiative in history through a real control of all the means of communal self-definition in time and space." These means are mainly those of language. "The choice of language and the use to which language is put is central to a people's definition of themselves in relation to their natural and social environment, and indeed in relation to the entire universe," and yet in the face of imperialism, "writers who should have been mapping paths out of that linguistic encirclement of their continent also came to be defined and to define themselves in terms of the languages of imperialist imposition."[7] Great attention must be paid, Ngugi says, to the forms and habits of expression that have been the footholds of oppression. These forms and habits must be rewritten and rethought – varied and revised so that they can be reshaped and stretched to cover and include both old and new African needs.

A Grain of Wheat shows this rethinking and revising getting started. The novel tells the story of various lives in Thabai, a Kenyan village, four days before Uhuru, or independence. What should be glorious days, however, are not, as the novel's different protagonists reflect upon the terrible ways in which the events leading up to independence have embittered or ruined them. For the years before independence in Kenya saw brutality and betrayals of many kinds, as the "Emergency" declared by the British cracked down on rebel "Mau Mau" forces, and people's loyalties were tested beyond reason. When independence came, it therefore could not be the great beginning for which people had hoped; too much had been betrayed – and too much corruption seemed to continue into the future of black rule. "Life was only a constant repetition of what happened yesterday and the day before"; "the coming of black rule would not mean, could never mean the end of white power": in order to convey these ironies, and in order to convey a sense of the ironic difference between Uhuru celebrations and his protagonists' regrets and resentments, Ngugi plays with the presentation of *time*. The modern novel's gift for temporal disorder becomes, in this postcolonial novel, a way to stress the vast, tragic difference between past dreams and present realities – between hopes for the future and the past truths that undermine them. The temporal shocks help to "decolonise the mind." They undo the smooth sequences that might make a reader presume easy progress from past oppression into the independent present; they stress the illogicalities and breaks that make past and present fit poorly, and in so doing they shake readers out of the bad logic through which some would have wanted to make independence sound easy.

We get another angle on the effort to shake the mind of imperialist ways of thinking in the work of white South African novelist Nadine Gordimer. In *July's People* (1981), she imagines a disastrous future for South Africa, in which the rebellion against the apartheid regime has become an all-out war. The members of a prosperous white family have to flee their home, and they find shelter and protection in the remote village of the man who has been their faithful household servant for years. Living now under his protection, and ultimately subject to him, the white people have to change the way they think about him:

> The decently-paid and contented male servant, living in their yard since they had married, clothed by them in two sets of uniforms, khaki pants for rough housework, white drill for waiting at table, given Wednesdays

and alternate Sundays free . . . he turned out to be the chosen one in whose hands their lives were to be held; frog prince, saviour, July.

Now in his hands, they have to see him, finally, as a complete and even superior human being, rather than as the two-dimensional black underling he had been for them before. And this does not just mean getting to know the real man: it means facing hard cultural differences, and realizing how much their happy lives had depended upon wrong power relationships and unwarranted privileges.

Taking us through this process of postcolonial awakening, Gordimer dramatizes the difficulty and the necessity of retraining the mind and removing from it the bad presumptions that have enabled racial injustice. Toward this end, she makes use of certain techniques long available in the modern novel, and suits them to new purposes. Psychological fragmentation, rendered in disjunctive phrases and paragraphs, reflects the trouble her characters have in piecing together their past of privilege with their present disempowerment. And she lays very effective stress on the subjective meaning of objects: that characteristic complication, present since the days of Joyce and Woolf, here helps Gordimer to show how the real meaning of such things as cars, keys, clothes, and even toilet paper really depends upon the personal contexts in which we use them. Once those contexts change – as they do for Gordimer's white family in the black village – then such objects change as well and must be redescribed. Though fictional, this redescription is in fact essential to a political process in which "whites of former South Africa will have to redefine themselves in a new collective life within new structures," changing the "hierarchy of perception" that endorsed the bad political hierarchy of the past.[8]

These novels by Gordimer and Ngugi emphasize how the methods of modern fiction have helped postcolonial progress. If such things as psychological fragmentation and revealing the subjective "hierarchy" of objects show how minds might go postcolonial, then it becomes clear that fiction's techniques for rediscovery can recreate political consciousness. But we must see this the other way around as well: the need to decolonize the mind renewed the modern impulse in fiction, by giving it a new, crucial reason for being.

All this comes together – indeed, all of postmodernism, too – in what may be the most important work of postcolonial fiction: Salman Rushdie's *Midnight's Children* (1981). Here, the moment of India's independence in 1947 becomes the focal point of a massive allegorical treatment of Indian history. The novel's protagonist, Saleem Sinai, is born at the very moment of Indian independence, and this makes him stand for India – for better and for worse:

> I was born in the city of Bombay . . . once upon a time. No, that won't do, there's no getting away from the date: I was born in Doctor Narlikar's Nursing Home on August 15th, 1947. And the time? The time matters, too. Well then: at night. No, it's important to be more . . . On the stroke of midnight, as a matter of fact. Clock-hands joined palms in respectful greeting as I came. Oh, spell it out, spell it out: at the precise instant of India's arrival at independence, I tumbled forth into the world . . . I had been mysteriously handcuffed to history, my destinies indissolubly chained to those of my country.

Saleem's life story becomes the story of his nation. But the result is deliberately absurd. Once it becomes a real human story, the "birth of independent India" proves itself to be impossible; it becomes a sort of postmodern joke, in which failure, fragmentation, and magical disasters dominate. The joke of "independence" becomes, for Rushdie's novel, inspiration for rampant postmodern excess, parody, and play. This in turn becomes the basis for a whole new way of thinking, not only about modern political realities, but about the nature of the way we make fictions about emerging worlds.

Because Saleem is born at the moment in which India becomes an independent nation, people come to see him as representative of the hopes for India's future. Rushdie then makes him a way to explore the nature of those hopes. Saleem takes on all the features people might have liked the new India to have; he is strangely responsible for all kinds of major events; and his body eventually suffers for all of India. Like postcolonial India itself, his body begins to fragment – to break apart, just as India divided into two nations and then fragmented further into cultures that after all could not hold together: "Please believe me that I am falling apart . . . I mean quite simply that I have begun to crack all over like an old jug – that my poor body, singular, unlovely, buffeted by too much history . . . has started coming apart at the seams." And like postcolonial India Saleem becomes subject to new political tyrannies and economic disasters. This fabulous connection between the individual character's story creates a marvelous new way to make the novel's traditional connection between the individual and society. Typically, novels question this relationship – and perhaps ultimately find ways for even the most rebellious individual to fit in. *Midnight's Children* forces a total fit, and in so doing questions the possibility that the social whole can be an adequate context for truly individual lives.

But what makes *Midnight's Children* most important to the development of the modern novel is the way it combines the political agenda of postcolonialism with the styles of postmodernism. The key point of connection here is metafiction. Saleem is not just a character in the novel. He is the novel's narrator – or, more accurately, its author: he is trying to piece together the story of his life, which is also the story of India. The harder it gets, the more we learn both about the difficulties of telling a whole story and about the difficulties of encompassing modern India or imagining its independence. Saleem is racing against time. His body, like the nation of India, is falling apart, and it seems as if his survival and the survival of the country depend on his power to put it all into a narrative. So we learn about the constructive powers of storytelling; we learn about its relationship to the existence of selfhood and of nationhood; and we learn, also, about the points at which storytelling in the modern novel must fail to be adequate to postcolonial needs. In other words, things work both ways: metafiction in *Midnight's Children* is all about the political fictions of postcolonial independence – their power, their tricks, their failures; and India itself is, in turn, all about fiction – what its status as an independent nation does to the way people imagine themselves, their worlds, and the connections between them.

Since the publication of *Midnight's Children*, postcolonial modernity has continued to modernize the novel – making it a better vehicle through which to diversify and expand cultural consciousness. Ben Okri's *The Famished Road* (1994) is a surprising example of how the novel has developed to meet new needs. Here we have another very symbolic character: the novel's protagonist is an abiku child, the kind of child who, according to Nigerian folklore, really belongs to the spirit world, and, in trying always to return there, brings sadness to the families into which it gets perpetually born:

In that land of beginnings spirits mingled with the unborn. We could assume numerous forms . . . The happier we were, the closer was our birth. As we approached another incarnation we made pacts that we would return to the spirit world at the first opportunity. We made these vows in fields of intense flowers and in the sweet-tasting moonlight of that world. Those of us who made such vows were known among the Living as abiku, spirit-children. Not all people recognised us. We were the ones who kept coming and going, unwilling to come to terms with life.

But in *The Famished Road*, the abiku decides to do what he can to remain in the world of the living. And yet the spirit world does what it can to tempt him back. Right away, as a result of this plot dynamic, we get a new mode for the modern novel: realism gets lost to a degree that is rare for a novel, as the abiku spends so much of his time swept up in spiritual visions and wandering along the spirit road. We see what Nigerian folk-culture might do for the western form of the novel. The novel's materialism – resisted throughout the twentieth century, but always likely to return in unexpected and powerful ways – gets completely undone by the abiku's utter detachment. What's more, this materialism gets re-evaluated. A spiritual essence, the abiku longs for the material world, and so we see it differently. We see it not as the hindrance or cheapening thing other modern novels have made it out to be, but as an understandable limitation of human life, something indeed tragic but not beyond redemption.

The great significance of the abiku's spirituality does not really become clear until the end of *The Famished Road*. Then, we finally see what his struggles have been trying to tell us. He symbolizes independent Nigeria's struggles to be born. Just as the abiku departs again and again out of the real world back into unreality, so do possibilities for Nigerian emergence into the real worlds of modernity:

> The spirit child is an unwilling adventurer into chaos and sunlight, into the dreams of the living and the dead. Things that are not ready, not willing to be born or to become, things for which adequate preparations have not been made to sustain their momentous births, things that are not resolved, things bound up with failure and with fear of being, they all keep recurring, keep coming back, and in themselves partake of the spirit-child's condition. They keep coming and going till their time is right. History itself fully demonstrates how things of the world partake of the condition of the spirit-child.

But this connection is not quite what it would seem. Okri does not see this as a failure. For it is not really a negative thing that Nigeria should fail to enter into the world of modernity, if the failure is really a matter of staying in the world of spiritual ideals. Nigeria is waiting for the right moment to be born; in the meantime, it is, like the abiku, adrift in a state of more ideal possibility. And that state contrasts powerfully with other ways of thinking about postcolonial Africa, in which the continent is all failure and disillusionment, and its problems in becoming modern are just disasters. In Okri's way of thinking, there is a whole world behind the sad reality, which will one day embody itself in actual progress, perhaps, but which, in a larger way of thinking about things, makes the present seem less significant.

The shift in thinking here – from tight focus on a disastrous post-colonial present, to a longer and transcendent view of more extensive possibility – is a marvelous way of "decolonizing the mind." It con-tributes, to a present-focused and materialistic attitude, a transcendent and timeless correction. And as with *Midnight's Children* we get the sense that the modern novel helps, in its form, to bring this alterna-tive attitude into existence. Here, this happens as a result of a strange fit between the spiritual story of the abiku and the more realistic ten-dency built into the novel as a form. The abiku's perpetual return to the spirit world perpetually defeats plot; moreover, his character never builds. Folk tradition therefore sits uneasily with novelistic conven-tion. But it works well with the unconventionality of the modern novel, and indeed renews it, by finding in African religion new reasons for plot and character to change. So we might say about *The Famished Road* what we have been finding about postcolonial fiction more gen-erally: it shows us how the modern novel has migrated to new places, sustaining itself by contributing to the making of new and better realities.

What is true about the postcolonial modern novel is often also true wherever language and representation have been key to the develop-ment and self-realization of marginal cultures. It is true as well for the fiction of minority groups *within* western cultures. Here, too, we have efforts to represent and dramatize the problems and possibilities of hybridity, in everything from language to custom to personal identity. We find efforts to rewrite the standard plots of the dominant culture to reveal the bad presumptions within them and to find space beyond them for alternatives. Again, we get unprecedented variations of perspective, and new ways of negotiating the authority given to narratorial voices.

But one key difference makes "multicultural" fiction a realm of unique expansion for the modern novel. Multicultural writers have had to take a greater interest in coexistence, diversity, and cultural exchange; they have unique concerns with the necessity to live within, alongside, or in spite of the dominant culture – as opposed to the more emphatic need fully to "decolonize" or enact full independence. The questions to ask, then, include these: what about the modern novel appeals to the minority writer as he or she makes the effort to create a good balance between cultural difference and cultural assimilation? To what use does he or she put the novel's way of clarifying the relationship between the individual and the social whole? How does the novel's power to mix languages help the minority writer to find means of description, explanation, and testimony that balance alternative cultural requirements? How do its ways of challenging grand narratives with its "local" propositions help the minority writer to debunk exclusive attitudes about national culture? And it is then necessary to ask the reverse kinds of questions, about the way the modern novel changes as a result: once the multicultural writer has made use of them, how do the modern novel's techniques of perspective, reconciliation, and "local" treatment improve? How, more specifically, might minority customs diversify the role the modern novel plays in social ritual? Or how might the minority sense of the sacred find a new "higher reference" for fiction?

Maxine Hong Kingston's *The Woman Warrior* (1976) dramatizes the difficulties of the multicultural demands placed on a young Chinese-American woman, who must find a way to remake her Chinese heritage so that it can meet the needs of a modern American woman. Kingston's heroine finds herself in a classic multicultural perplexity: her Chinese heritage is rich with inspiring stories and ennobling role-models, but also rife with sexist limitations; her American present, while perhaps better suited to her womanhood, would have no place for the heritage that is necessarily so much a part of her identity. Her task is to create a new identity, out of what the different cultures provide – and to do so despite the fact that the powers of these competing cultures necessarily dwarf those of her own young sense of selfhood. What makes her able to do so – and what makes *The Woman Warrior* a particularly modern approach to the question of multicultural identity – is the power of storytelling. She comes from a culture in which this power links women back to strong mythic histories. Her mother has this power of "talk-story," and passes it on to her: "Whenever she had to warn us about life, my mother told stories that ran like this one, a story to grow up on. She tested our strength to establish realities." But those stories leave her unsure "how the invisible world the emigrants built around our childhoods fits in solid America"; and they would restrict her to traditional Chinese roles. And so she ultimately revises them, retaining the power but losing the limitation. The novel ends, "Here is a story my mother told me, not when I was young, but recently, when I told her I also talk story. The beginning is hers, the ending mine." In the conflict and continuity between mother and daughter – this struggle between tradition and change that is also a modernization of the power of storytelling – Kingston gives the modern novel a symbol for the struggles that would help to enable new cultural identities and also pattern a multicultural literary form. Here, and in the many novels that would pursue this approach to fictions of identity, storytelling itself becomes the ground upon which new identities are built – and the ground into which new multicultural layers are laid down.

Often this new ground is broken by the arrival of *oral* culture in the world of written fiction. In Louise Erdrich's *Love Medicine* (1984), for example, the storytelling methods of native-American Ojibwa culture dissolve novelistic structures of perspective into a communal mode of fiction, with surprising results for such fundamentals as plot and time-sequence. Once the burden of the story is shared, no single authority fixes its key points in time or space; these spread around, and the openness that results is a key feature both of this one novel's main theme and of a new time-sense available to fiction in general. Another novelist steeped in indigenous oral culture is Leslie Marmon Silko, whose *Ceremony* (1977) makes Laguna tale-telling a basis for something even more ambitious: a new kind of "ceremony," able symbolically to rescue American cultures from the witcheries of destructive modern technology. *Ceremony* mixes various forms of ritual and poetical discourse, to tell the story of a Laguna man whose experience in World War II has left him cursed and ill. His illness, shared apparently by the land as well, is the sort of thing his people might once have cured with traditional ceremonies; now, however, its modern aspect makes a new ceremony necessary. This demands a quest, and its success ultimately leads beyond the ceremony itself to the discovery of larger problems and larger solutions. The ultimate witchery plaguing all cultures is the mass destruction threatened by nuclear technology; the larger solution, in a sense, is a recognition of the way all cultures are linked together in the face of this common threat. This final multiculturalism gives *Ceremony* a remarkable trajectory: the novel generates a ceremony out of Laguna tradition and new resources, as we see in its mixed forms of oral and written telling, and then it broadens this ceremony to include redemptions like, but more diverse than, the positive effects the modern novel had long been hoping to achieve. We get a novelistic pattern supremely rich in "higher reference": one that finds a new way for the modern novel to act as a redemptive ritual through its ability to plot diverse cultures together into a single ceremonious story.

Such has been the multicultural novel's larger advantage. Not only has it told the stories of marginalized peoples, and not only has it proven a fine means for minority writers to experiment with mixed identities and to remake old forms for modern purposes, it has offered up to the larger culture allegories for modern redemption. The fragmentations within the minority psyche and within the marginalized community have turned out to reflect, at different levels and often in more immediately painful ways, the fragmentations of modern culture more generally. So when multicultural novels propose fictions through which fragmented minority psyches and communities might heal themselves, we also get ceremonies that imagine ways also to draw modern cultures in general back from the brink of chaos. When you recall that such ceremonies had always been the goal of the modern novel – that so many modern novels had hoped to make fiction a way to imagine new forms for new communities – you can appreciate the extent to which multicultural fiction, in its efforts to solidify minority identities, also builds upon the novel's powers to imagine redemptive structures of all kinds.

Keri Hulme's *The Bone People* (1984), for example, is at once a hymn of hope for the future of New Zealand and a triumph for fiction's redemptive take on modern crisis. Once again, we have a novel that works well at different levels: in its style and feeling, it is almost a kind of ritual poem, and it beautifies novelistic prose with elements of Maori phrasing; in its outlook, it draws the realism typical of novels up and down into spiritual heights and depths, as spirits intervene to make grim stories suddenly go good; its characters introduce wholly new human possibilities – of, for example, womanhood utterly unconcerned with sexuality, and utterly disempowered imperialists; and its plot moves with matchless force from total chaos to a remarkable, positive new beginning. *The Bone People* has three characters, who seem at first to promise a fine nontraditional multicultural family, but who deteriorate into strife, violence, and madness. In all this we have not only a new story about the human failures forced by modern dislocation and anguish, but an allegory of the situation in New Zealand: these are representatives of the country's warring factions, whose competing interests seem perpetually to lead to disaster. And finally we have even more. *The Bone People* pulls out of its nose-dive into chaos on the wings of ancient help – the help of the "bone people," an ancient tribe whose legacy, symbolized in a stone, marks a place for a new cultural beginning. Overleaping the recent history of social strife to reach for a better model for multicultural diversity, the novel finds a way to ground a better future in better traditions. It finds the cultural point of reference around which different cultures might gather, and not just in terms of its plot. That finds New Zealand's different cultures coming together as a multicultural "family" under the aegis of ideals they can be willing to share in common; but *The Bone People* is itself such an ideal, as well, for it models such sharing, and weaves together the story-selves of different cultures into another "ceremony" for modern redemption.

That *The Bone People* and *Ceremony* could enact these ceremonies says surprising things about the adaptability of the modern novel's mission. It seems very unlikely that a form innovated in order to find a way to shape the life of middle-class London, or to mime the fragmentation of the African-American culture of the 1920s, should connect up to multicultural ceremonies among the Maori or within Chinese-American families decades later. And perhaps it does not: perhaps these forms are not the same form, and it makes no sense to class Woolf and Hulme, Toomer and Kingston, in one category. Perhaps the novel is a loose enough form of writing to contain very different forms of expression, and perhaps that openness ought to discourage us from enclosing together books that hardly resemble each other at all. Unless putting them together can explain them better by bringing out something they do have in common, despite differences of years and cultures and languages. If they are all in fact modern novels, then they share a belief that the ceremonies of innovative story-making can resist or undo or take advantage of the loss of traditional structures of society, belief, and feeling. They share this vital idealism, and even at the risk of neglecting the more important differences among them, we can learn a lot about their cultural purpose by seeing how it makes them alike.

Conclusions

Four Contemporary Modern Novelists

If it is true that the modern novel has survived – into the postmodern, the postcolonial, to be renewed and replenished by them – can we see some *contemporary* novelists continuing and replenishing what we saw in some of the *first* moderns? Are there writers writing today with some of the same motives – vying with modernity through experimental writing, in the hope that such writing might make a difference? Many writers today align themselves with the modern tradition, and here are four examples – four contemporary writers who often seem to want to continue what was begun by their modernist precursors. Many things make them modern (even though they are writing in the year 2000 rather than 1900), mainly their tendencies to explore subjective "impressions" of reality; to cultivate the life of literary language; to rebel against moral and creative convention; and to open fiction always to the truth of change.

Philip Roth was at first among those who wanted to turn the novel away from formal invention toward a more straightforward kind of realism. His essay on the state of American fiction around 1960 called for writers to take from the extremities of American culture all they needed of invention: the American "here and now" was enough, he thought, to make fiction a truly modern enterprise (see p. 104). And it has been enough to make his own fiction extraordinary. Especially in *Goodbye, Columbus* and *Portnoy's Complaint*, Roth has made American desire – sexual, cultural, political – the subject of powerful skepticism. More recently, however, he has allowed key aspects of the modern impulse to launch his fiction into new realms of invention, after all. Specifically, the metafictional view and the alternative patterns of purely physical urges have made his fiction a source of new forms for the American cultural imagination.

In much of his recent fiction, Roth has focused on characters very much like himself. In fact, his characters are sometimes writers, living lives hard to distinguish from his own, and the focus here gives him the chance to take a serious metafictional view of the ways that desires create reality. Most clearly in *The Counterlife* (1987), he experiments with the different fictions our desires force us to take for reality: here, a novelist like Roth himself gives us a set of contradictory stories, each of which elaborates upon different possibilities. But these metafictions tend to have a unique obsession: how do the imaginative fictions of desire try to fight against the cruel realities of physical mortality? How, in other words, do these opposite aspects of our physical being together generate the overall, half-real and half-imaginary, stories of our lives?

The obsession reaches its apotheosis in *American Pastoral* (1997). Here, Roth's familiar narrator, a writer named Nathan Zuckerman, takes on the making and unmaking of a vital American myth. A school reunion gets him thinking about the young man who had been the local hero – everybody's idea of the perfect American male. "The Swede" (called that because of his perfect blond good looks) seems to have had the ideal life. Jewish, he has nevertheless been able to cross over, and live the life Roth's narrator himself dreams of living. But Zuckerman discovers some flaws, some problems, and on the basis of the impressions they produce in him, spins out a speculative story very different from that of all-American perfection. On the basis of minimal information, he decides to "think about the Swede for six, eight, sometimes ten hours at a stretch, exchange my solitude for his, inhabit this person least like myself, disappear into him, day and night try to take the measure of a person of apparent blankness and innocence and simplicity, chart his collapse, make of him, as time wore on, the most important figure of my life." In Zuckerman's story, the Swede raises a daughter who becomes a terrorist – defying in every way the ideal life the Swede has tried to build for himself. She destroys him, in Zuckerman's version of the story, "transports him out of the longed-for American pastoral and into everything that is its antithesis and its enemy, into the fury, the violence, and the desperation of the counterpastoral

– into the indigenous American berserk." But we never know if the story is actually "true": it could be Zuckerman's jealous wish, to see perfection spoiled – to see the Swede suffer. And so this story becomes an extended "impression" rather than a reality. For that reason, however, it becomes a more essentially truthful document of American desire, of American fantasy. Roth makes the subjective reality the truer one – and *American Pastoral* is therefore a modern novel, experimenting with subjective truths in order to explore the fantasies and fears American modernity inspires.

Roth, then, is one contemporary novelist still committed to the modern enterprise. Another is Toni Morrison. In the speech she gave when she accepted the Nobel Prize for Literature, Morrison told a story. In the story, some young people visit a wise old woman, to ask her a question. They carry in their hands a bird, and ask the old woman whether it is alive or dead. The wise woman chooses to answer the question in a strange way. She tells them that whether or not the bird is alive, it is in their hands. For Morrison, the story is an allegory, in which the bird stands for language, and the old woman represents the writer: the writer is one who alerts the world to the way language and its powers rest in their hands. Morrison goes on to explore a theory about language that contains important connections to the past of the modern novel, and a strong affirmation of its future. Language lives always in danger of dying, through misuse and exploitation; it is always available to violent, racist, or mindless misappropriation, which make it act in suicide. Writers save its life, by turning it in the other direction, toward imagination and possibility, and by so doing they save us: "Word-work is sublime . . . because it is generative; it makes meaning that secures our difference, our human difference – the way in which we are like no other life. We die. That may be the meaning of life. But we do language. That may be the measure of our lives."[1] In this theory about literary language, Morrison reveals herself to be a modernist, in the tradition of Woolf and Faulkner, but also to be a modern writer with a newer sense of the way that a more fantastic imagination can help create new and better realities.

In *Beloved* (1987), Morrison makes the supernatural the means of adding to language the story of slavery that had been heretofore excluded by the bad kind of relationship between language and power. In its racist misappropriations, the language of power left no room for the remembrance of those who died, in slavery, beyond official history.

To change the official story so that it can now better include the stories of slaves, Morrison resorts to supernatural fantasy: Beloved is the ghost of a baby killed by her own mother, Sethe, who chose to end her baby's life rather than have her grow up in slavery. The event actually happened, but Morrison reimagines it, in order to supply the statements and expressions necessary truly to do justice to it and to the effects acts like it have had upon African-American culture. Beloved returns twenty years after her death to haunt her mother, and to compel recognition and remembrance. As a result, the reasons for the infanticide come out – as do the fully imagined implications of the deed and what it symbolizes for the state of African-American motherhood. What Morrison achieves here is a remarkable restitution, in line with her theory about fiction's service to language: what had been an historical trauma (a painful gap, a killing silence) gets answered through the supernatural power of a language that undoes death by speaking for the creative imagination.

Without what creative language does in and through the imagination, history would remain a matter of trauma; the vitality of culture would drain away, into what ignorance and violence would prefer to make of it. Morrison's writing embodies this conviction, and in so doing champions modern fiction as few writers have ever done: she justifies as never before the effort to try something new, in the face of modernity, for the betterment of the world. And she is not alone, for many other contemporary writers are willing to avow such literary idealism – to make such explicit connections between literary innovation and the health of culture. For example, Jeanette Winterson: not only in her novels, but in her writings about the purpose of fiction, Winterson has also championed the modern impulse to make the language of fiction a redemptive force.

Oranges Are Not the Only Fruit (1985) makes a hybrid of two very different things: evangelical Christianity and lesbian sexuality. You might expect that the second would follow and rule out the first – that lesbian sexuality would mean rebellion against traditional values. And to some degree, that is how it goes in Winterson's novel. Her heroine comes to see the hypocrisy and narrowness of the beliefs according to which she has been raised, and her modern self-realization is all about defying those beliefs in favor of liberating eroticism. But although Winterson's heroine is an iconoclast, she does not quite leave evangelicalism behind. In fact, its passions and excesses segue fairly well into those of her new sexuality, and its structures (the chapters of the Bible) give shape to the novel itself. There is a hybrid here, a fantastic mixture of the discourses of religion and eroticism, and in it we see how tradition and modernity might mix in a new kind of revolutionary selfhood. The hybrid gives new life to a modern aspiration: modulation of traditional faith enables authentic consciousness, all in a new, bold language for sexual desire – all the product of Winterson's intention to "create an imaginative reality sufficiently at odds with our daily reality to startle us out of it."[2]

Winterson writes with the full confidence that the novel, in this sort of innovation, can create better realities. For her, writing is a kind of prophecy; it anticipates life, articulating the feelings and needs that would remain frustrated and ineffective, were it not for the writer's unique sensibility. Here we have most manifest the survival and extension of the modern novelist's hope to give better imaginative shape to modern possibility. In *Oranges Are Not the Only Fruit* and Winterson's other novels, we have most clearly the continued effort on the part of the modern novel to sketch out the emotional structure necessary for people to have powerful feelings at all. For Winterson would say that passion – what comes surprisingly in the combination of evangelical traditions and erotic subversions – can come to a world otherwise muted and pinched by modern priorities only through the experimental language of fiction. And she has said that thinking this way makes her an inheritor of the modern novel:

> To assume that Modernism has no real relevance to the way that we need to be developing fiction now, is to condemn readers and writers to a dingy Victorian twilight. To say that the experimental novel is dead is to say that literature is dead. Literature is experimental. Once the novel was *novel*; if we cannot continue to alter it, to expand its boundaries without dropping it into even greater formlessness than the shape tempts, then we can only museum it. Literature is not a museum it is a living thing [sic].

Winterson is committed to "a fresh development of language and to new forms of writing," out of a sense that language is "something holy."[3]

Far less rapturous is the South African novelist J. M. Coetzee, whose experience of the political turmoils of apartheid and its aftermath has ruled out most forms of hope. Steeped in the impossibly grave situation of postcolonial South Africa, Coetzee has a perfect awareness of the obstacles there to justice and to happiness; steeped in the literary tradition of the modern novel, he has a perfect sense of just how far its forms might go in making a positive difference. What results, in his fiction, is a remarkable application of fictional invention to political exigency – something that entails uniquely provocative use of fiction's resources.

The Life and Times of Michael K. (1983) is a story about a very simple man, whose needs and feelings are few and mild. He finds himself, however, in the midst of the dystopian South African world. Chaos has shaken him out of his humble job (as a gardener) and the very modest home he shares with his ailing mother. A state of siege casts him out onto the road, in search of refuge on the farm where his mother grew up. But the search comes to nothing – and all along the way, police and doctors and abusers of all kinds prevent Michael from a very plain goal: all he wants is to cultivate a small subsistence garden, and live on what meager resources the land itself provides. In the brief moments in which Michael is able to do so, Coetzee dramatizes the purest human contentment:

> he was learning to love idleness . . . as a yielding up of himself to time . . . He could lie all afternoon with his eyes open, starting at the corrugations in the roof-iron and the tracings of rust; his mind would not wander, he would see nothing but the iron, the lines would not transform themselves into pattern or fantasy; he was himself, lying in his own house, the rust was merely rust, all that was moving was time, bearing him onward in its flow.

That this simple, free being is impossible makes *The Life and Times of Michael K.* an ironically harrowing allegory of South African life: all Michael wants is to be left alone, and yet he is never free from the "help" others force upon him. And the allegory gets unique complexity, and a revolutionary effect, from a powerful set of modern qualities. First of all, alienation: Michael K.'s inability to find home anywhere draws heavily on the homelessness of a century of modern protagonists. Second, perspective: uncomplicated and purely innocent, Michael can make no sense of the world in which he finds himself –

a failure that becomes a very successful way to stress that world's absurdity.

The allegory produced gives us the plight of modern humanity, but perhaps also the more politically specific plight of modern South Africa. What Michael would be alone – allegorically, what South Africa would be if fully free – is something we struggle hard to know. There is a doctor in the novel who tries to understand Michael's motivations, and tries to get him to eat enough to survive; when the doctor can't, and as he wonders why Michael would refuse help, we are forced to conceptualize a South Africa that would subsist on its own, free of false complication, authentic in purely its own way. To the extent that we can do so, and thereby achieve heightened political consciousness, Coetzee has managed a remarkable combination of modernist, existential, and postcolonial priorities. He has formed a novel capable of such extremes of aesthetic invention and political commitment that we can hardly doubt that, in its contemporary instances, the modern novel has gathered its strengths for a vital future.

The Future of the Modern Novel

But even if we say that postmodern and postcolonial challenges have enriched the modern novel, demanding new political engagement and formal complexities, and even if we say there are yet modern novelists writing today, finding ways for us to make ourselves more at home in modernity or to take aesthetic refuge from it, we might still need to ask: can the modern novel now be *modern enough*? For those postmodern and postcolonial challenges – those things that made the world so much more chaotic and diverse, thereby stretching the modern novel's representational capacities to new limits – have lately gone much further. Technological change and geopolitical conflict have become complicated in ways the first modern writers probably could never have predicted. We have entered a state that some call *globality*. Within it, does the modern novel have a future? Can it really continue to develop credible new forms of perception, thought, and social awareness – and can it really still make up a credible response to modernity? Or has modernity now truly left it behind, having become too total for any purely literary form to match or resist it, and having chosen more technologically advanced forms of information to be its representatives?

Let us define globality in two basic ways – as a strange new *geopolitical unification*, and as the ascendancy of a total or global kind of *information age*.

International power, which once centralized itself in the hands of particular powerful nations that had hands in the workings of less powerful governments worldwide, has now dispersed itself all around the world. The world now is defined by "supraterritorial, technologically-led worldwide economic and cultural integration."[4] And power is no longer national, but multinational, in the hands of elites like global corporations and international finance organizations. This is the negative way to see the new world order in which boundaries no longer apply – in which the globe has been unified, but in a kind of *neo-imperialism*, and not therefore made a place in which all are equal and all is peace. Indeed for some theorists *"globalization* conjures up . . . a spectacle of instantaneous electronic financial transfers, the depradations of free-market capitalism, the homogenization of culture, and the expansion of Western, by which is usually meant American, political hegemony . . . widening economic inequality, worsening ecological degradation, intensified ethnic rivalry, spreading militarism, escalating religious nationalism, and other ills."[5] The more positive way to describe this state of geopolitical globality is to say that cultures have now completely mixed: in any major city of the world, populations are now diverse, and people have access to "world cultures" all around the globe. Globality brings a "complex, overlapping disjunctive order that cannot any longer be understood in terms of existing center–periphery models," and therefore promises positive change.[6]

How might we expect the modern novel to respond to this ambiguous new geopolitical unity? Would we expect it to use its powers to model diversity, perspective, and fragmentation to challenge the "totality" whereby global elites come to dominate the world? Would we expect it to use those powers to feature the aesthetic benefits of globality's cultural mixings – to produce veritable carnivals of heteroglossia, in which we might see world voices mingling into marvelous new languages for the imagination and for justice? Or would we predict that vast new global politics would have to outstrip the relatively moderate capacities of the modern novel – and that the full plenitude of world voices would be too much for its narrative modes to handle? Has world culture, in other words, entered into a situation in which the modern novel (as a form for dealing with modernity, with significant effects on the individual and cultural imagination) will have become obsolete?

And if the new world order is not enough to make it so, wouldn't global technologies? Linked to the postnational make-up of the world is the way information circulates across it. If borders seem less distinct now, and old divisions less important, it is largely because information technologies have bound the world together into new communities. New media technologies – capable of breathtaking "immediacies" and unimaginably flexible forms of storytelling – disseminate creative productions around the world in vast quantities and at breakneck speeds. For this reason, "discussions of globalization and culture rarely deal with literature, but focus instead on those mediums that transmit culture electronically, which are imagined as having an especially powerful and even determinate impact on social and individual identities." And for this reason, it seems perhaps "pointless to worry about literature" – pointless to wonder about the power and impact of a form like the modern novel, which would be nothing by comparison.[7] For many of the things modernist novelists had wanted to do or to change are perhaps done and changed far more readily and effectively in these much more dynamic forms; and any effect the modern novelist may have wanted to have is far outdone by the impact of charismatic new visual and computer technologies. We might say that "human character has changed" again, for now "the interface relocates the human, in fact *redefines* the human as part of a cybernetic system of information circulation and management."[8]

Technology has drawn human character into new realms of innovation and change; the "new world order" has drawn politics into new realms of hybridity, community, and conflict. We find ourselves in the new situation of globality. And here we have to wonder: can the modern novel extend its reaches yet again to connect with new worlds of change? Can it incorporate modern technologies, evaluate and interpret them, absorb what lessons they teach about the nature of human thought, perception, and action? Can it make sense of changing social and political life, when they now expand to encompass and reorient so many new cultural possibilities and "ills"? Will globality make the modern novel a more interesting, dynamic, and powerful form of writing, or will it leave the modern novel behind? Will the novel yet be able to face modernity in ways that will galvanize its forms and guarantee its necessity?

There are some reasons to think so – and some examples of modern novels that have made globality both the opportunity for new developments and the object of newly effective criticism. First let us consider the reasons why the modern novel might yet be itself a relevant technology, and then turn to those books in which we see it remaking its power to remain one.

In an article on globalization and the future of English literature, Paul Jay outlines a new plan for literary study. Given the changes entailed in globalization, Jay argues, we need to focus on the way literature may or may not involve itself in the developments of a new kind of consciousness; we need to wonder how fiction might help in creating the kinds of minds and personalities able to thrive in new global contexts:

> Global mass culture creates a postnational context for reimagining, organizing, and disseminating subjectivity through all the devices formally associated with literary (or cinematic) narrative. National scripts regularly give way to globally disseminated media scripts that engage the imagination complexly. This process suggests that we need to turn our attention away from a simple preoccupation with how national literatures function in relation to historically homogeneous cultures and toward an examination of how postnational literatures are instrumental in the formation of subjectivity in deterritorialized and diasporic contexts.[9]

Jay's theory here – that globality changes the way literature shapes how people imagine their identities, responsibilities, and powers – suggests that the modern novel might yet play a role in the way individuals and cultures make their larger imaginative frameworks. Even if the novel was first made for "historically homogeneous cultures," it can go "postnational," and, moreover, it can shape postnational consciousness; it can form the way people think and feel about lives spread beyond territories and gone "diasporic" or worldwide.

We get a remarkable example of just such a "postnational subjectivity," and a surprising example of how cultures might now mix in individual novels, in the work of one peculiarly global writer: Kazuo

Ishiguro. Both Japanese and British, Ishiguro has a keen sense of the things his two cultures share, and he makes the combination the basis for a unique critical sensibility. In *The Remains of the Day* (1989), Ishiguro writes about an English butler, a man who recalls his years of faithful service to an important English aristocrat. The aristocrat had tried to influence English policy in the years before World War II – not positively, it turns out, for he had tried to get the English government to appease the Nazis. Nevertheless, Ishiguro's protagonist had served him well, always putting his professional duties before personal ones, and never questioning his master's authority. But now, years later, he begins to see that all this was a mistake. Once he admits that his master had been wrong, he also has to admit the error of blindly faithful duty, and to see that he has really wasted his own life by giving it over so absolutely to service to another: "You see, *I trusted*. I trusted in his lordship's wisdom. All those years I served him, I trusted I was doing something worthwhile. I can't even say I made my own mistakes. Really – one has to ask oneself – what dignity is there in that?" This ending is tragic, and additionally powerful for the way it seems to be about many things at once. One man's tragic failure is one theme; but then also the failure of an English way of life is another; and, surprisingly, the similar but distant failure of a Japanese style of duty. Ishiguro seems to be writing not only about a tragic English temperament, but about a tragic Japanese one – out of a sense that the English and the Japanese have in common an excess of blind obligation, one that can lead to personal and to general disaster. Something about the way Ishiguro can combine two cultural critiques into one suggests a "global" difference; he seems to write with a world audience in mind, and with a sense that he can draw at once on different cultures and subsume them into the making of a fictional theme.

Here, then, we have a "deterritorialized" outlook, a hybrid subjectivity, and perhaps proof that the techniques of the modern novel are well suited to global complexities. And to complexities of the deepest kind – not just those of simply factual cultural diversity, but those of a deeper, stranger kind of mingling, this mixing of cultural temperaments deep within a theory of moral duty. If modernity now means combinations of cultural styles, perhaps the modern novel yet has within it powers of subjective perspective, skepticism, and "dialogism" that can show us exactly how the global subjectivity of a writer like Ishiguro might be formed.

On the technological end of things, the challenge is different. For even if the modern novel still has these powers to explore, explain, and shape consciousness, even if nothing else has come to the fore that might match it in this regard, its technological powers now seem strictly limited in comparison with those of new media forms. For example, the media form known as *hypertext*: as a style of storytelling hypertext seems to be everything the modern novel has been and much more. If the modern novel has been flexible, fragmentary, open, diverse, and in general a mode of questioning, hypertext is these things, too, and much more so. In hypertext we very well may have a form that has superseded the modern novel, by doing what it does, only better.

Hypertext is what has become of narrative fiction in the cyberspace, in the storyspace of the computer. In that medium, fiction is made up not of pages, but of *lexias*. And these units are not things that follow, as pages did, one after the other; lexias are of course threaded together in any number of ways, by the dynamic links among them. How their story goes depends upon the desire of the reader. Once begun, the hypertext story can link in many different directions, producing any number of different plots. The reader becomes the story's author, and the multiform plots he or she produces can exist all at once, or take shape in different readings at different times. Whereas once fiction was something made actively by a writer and then consumed passively by a reader, now it is something much more extensively interactive. Whereas once fiction was a limited selection of information, now it is encyclopedic – for there are in fact no effective limits on the amount of information that can extend and enrich the hypertext fiction's various plots. There are these advantages, and then other things hypertext has over the modern novel specifically: notoriously immersive, it can make readers feel a vital part of an immediate environment; notoriously kaleidoscopic, it can do full justice to a pluralistic universe; and, finally, so definitively digressive and lacking in closure (since a hypertext story can change from reading to reading), hypertext completely reflects the true openness and contingency of real life.

Michael Joyce's *Afternoon* (1987) was one of the first full hypertext fictions, and it remains an excellent example of the strengths of the form. Navigation through the story begins with the information that the narrator may have seen his former wife and his son dead by the side of the road. Was it them? Has he been, in some way, responsible for their deaths? Are they even dead? All this remains to be discovered, but it can be discovered in different ways, or not discovered at all, depending upon the way the reader navigates his or her way through the lexias of the text. It is possible to take a short route through and learn nothing; it is possible to probe more thoroughly, and to follow the story through to some kind of completion, but even then there are lexias not visited, and closure only comes to the degree that you feel satisfied by what you have learned. If you are not satisfied you can of course try the story again. In any case, however, built into the storyspace are devices that shape your progress. For example, you cannot quickly learn things that the narrator himself would be afraid to find out. The program prevents it, blocking you from progress in certain directions until you have somehow earned the power to proceed. This and other such tendencies are what made *Afternoon* vital to the progress of hypertext. What might otherwise be a random game, a gratuitous clicking-around among different parts of a text that might never hang together and never give real narrative satisfaction, here becomes a fully literary experience. The openness of hypertext is combined with a compelling structure, and so we get all the advantages of the medium without the merely technological tricks that might make it just a game.

In *Hamlet on the Holodeck: The Future of Narrative in Cyberspace*, Janet Murray explains these advantages, and concludes that hypertext partakes of "the most powerful representational medium yet invented," and that it is therefore likely to leave others behind. She quotes D. H. Lawrence's praise for the novel, and then says that amid new global realities, hypertext and other cyberspace narratives are necessary to do what the novel did for Lawrence:

> D. H. Lawrence argued that "the novel is the highest example of subtle inter-relatedness that man has discovered. Everything is true in its own time, place, circumstances, and untrue out of its own time, place and circumstance." The novel can put things in their place, can let us figure out what is right and wrong by offering us specific context for human behaviors. But in a global society we have outgrown our ability to contextualize. We are tormented by our sense of multiple conflicting frameworks for every action. We need a kaleidoscopic medium to sort things out.[10]

Once upon a time, the modern novel could hope to reflect "multiple conflicting frameworks" and help us to understand and manage them. But now, in globality, that multiplicity has grown so much more tormenting that we need a new medium in order to understand and manage it. Has the modern novel therefore had its day?

Will hypertext fictions ultimately replace the novel? Will we become so used to their openness, interactivity, dynamicism, their multiform plots and their encyclopedic range of reference, that novels, more conventionally composed of more closed sentences and uniform plots, will seem retrograde? Has hypertext outmoded the modern novel?

Or will hypertext fictions always be *too* open to satisfy the needs that modern novels fulfill? The great flexibility of the form might make it a different form altogether. Recall that modern novels have long been about striking a balance between the flux of the world and the solace of forms – what Henry James called "notation" and "reference," what Frank Kermode called "contingency" and "concordance" (p. 21). Never fully contingent even when very fragmented and dispersed, modern novels have always tried to mime disorder but not so much that it becomes formless – and to test forms that might be orderly and yet not so orderly that they falsify the "contingency" of modern life. If hypertext is fully "contingent" – all subject to chance, fluidity, play – then perhaps it does not abduct fiction into the world of the digital future, but instead makes an extreme but marginal game out of what fiction will continue to do within the pages (paper or otherwise) of the modern novel. And perhaps it will therefore be an influence rather than a replacement.

Or, perhaps, a warning. For hypertext is a special kind of chaos: one secretly subject to the will of the machine. Its promiscuous possibilities happen within cybernetic systems. Should we worry about this combination? Some novelists seem to think so, and they have therefore made this combination the crux of the global novel. For in every way, globality seems to involve just such a combination, freeing people, things, and information to move about with unprecedented speed and in unprecedented mixtures, but then making that happen within systems that seem, more than ever, controlling. To face this new modernity – this planned play, this systematic promiscuity, which takes place both among cultures and within the digital media – the modern novel has taken on a new form. The new form gives us, on the one side, a sheer diversity of objects, events, and people, mingling them with careless abandon; on the other side, however, is a nearly parodic sense of the planned, the inevitable, the cybernetic.

Two of the most acclaimed novels of the end of the twentieth century are defined by this combination: David Foster Wallace's *Infinite Jest* (1996) and Zadie Smith's *White Teeth* (2000). These are both global novels – in their encyclopedic scope, their worldwide diversity, their technological edge, and their eagerness to take it all in.

The title of Wallace's book suggests a postmodern parody: *Infinite Jest* would seem to prepare us for that kind of dispersive playfulness, and indeed Wallace began writing under the influence of writers like Don DeLillo and John Barth (who, as we have seen, found ways to make postmodernism a vitalizing force for fiction). But Wallace takes us beyond the endless jokes of postmodernism and into the realm of the global by returning to the everyday and yet doing so on a massive, futuristic scale. *Infinite Jest* is set in a near-future moment in which disaster has made a wasteland of much of America and mass culture has taken over everything. Even the names of years are now given to corporate sponsors; the novel's present moment is "the year of the depend adult undergarment." And there is in circulation a video that incapacitates anyone who watches it – bringing the narcotic effects of television to a new extreme. Here we have the ingredients for a postmodern satire of consumer culture, or a post-apocalyptic dystopia, and these we get, to a degree. And yet more than these we get torrents of erudition, and sentences too richly ingenious to reflect a world drained of meaning; we also get a degree of realism that seems odd, given the book's fantastic tendencies. The combination calls to mind what Philip Roth had said about the new reality of American fiction back in 1961. Roth had claimed that American realities had become bizarre enough to make fiction experimental without additional formal effort. Wallace might have argued the same – now about the global system within which America has played so dominant a role. For that global system floods fiction with information, and Wallace here channels it into endless sentences, pages of footnotes, limitless obscure pharmaceutical and technical terminology – into a text that is at once explosive, realistic, and sharply designed. That combination, finally, is what seems to make the global difference, and to place Wallace's novel at the dawn of this new age.

If *Infinite Jest* globalizes the parodies of DeLillo and Barth, *White Teeth* does the same with the postcolonial postmodernism of Salman

Rushdie. Like Rushdie, Smith has chosen to make the absurdities of cultural diversity a comic way to explore and explode myths of identity. And like him she chooses to do so mainly at the level of linguistic excess – letting manic loquacity mimic the necessary insanity of the cultural identities of the moment. But Smith's world is more diverse, and less likely to fall apart. It is more diverse because it gives us hybridities and then third terms – confrontations of the Indian and the English but then the further complication of yet other cultures and mixtures. *White Teeth* is mainly the story of two families, those of Archie Jones (who is English) and Samad Iqbal (originally from Bangladesh). Archie is married to a Jamaican woman, and Samad perpetually worries about the bad English cultural influence on his children, and in the complexities that result from these attractions and repulsions Smith gives us globality in microcosm. The novel's scenes perpetually reflect – and yet also question – this tendency:

> It is only this late in the day that you can walk into a playground and find Isaac Leung by the fish pond, Danny Rahman in the football cage, Quang O'Rourke bouncing a basketball, and Irie Jones humming a tune. Children with first and last names on a direct collision course. Names that secrete within them mass exodus, cramped boats and planes, cold arrivals, medical checks. . . . Yet, despite all the mixing up, despite the fact that we have finally slipped into each other's lives with reasonable comfort . . . it is still hard to admit that there is no one more English than the Indian, no one more Indian than the English.

The "mixing up" here is typical of the novel and its globality, but typical also is the sense of what happens "despite" the mixing up: the strange cultural affiliations globality cannot undo. Conscious of these, Smith shows us how the modern novel might give us a valuable critical purchase on globality. Moreover, she takes on the technological side of globality, mocking the way it would "eliminate the random" from life. She makes fun of one character's plans to make the perfect mouse: "The FutureMouse© holds out the tantalizing promise of a new phase in human history where we are not victims of the random but instead directors and arbitrators of our own fate." In this extensive parody of genetic engineering, Smith indirectly mocks the routinization at work in global technologies (and in hypertext), and thereby carves out a place for the modern novel. For as she implies, it must still be a form for vital *human* questioning, even once (and especially when) technological modes of information become the dominant thing.

Encyclopedic, exuberant, infinitely creative, and sharply real, *Infinite Jest* and *White Teeth* certainly seem to keep the modern novel alive. To some, however, they have been cause to worry about the future of the novel. One critic sees in their encyclopedic exuberance a bad kind of "hysterical realism" – something that might be a symptom of fiction's last desperate bid for attention.[11] Other novelists preferring something more traditional call for a return to some more spare, simple, straightforward style of writing: the "New Puritans," not unlike the "Movement" of an earlier decade, speak against the aspirations of the modern novel, and advocate a return to simpler methods.[12] And one contemporary of Wallace and Smith sees their fictional worlds as places so dispersed, processed, and fragmented that they make the novel wholly irrelevant. Jonathan Franzen, author of *The Corrections* (2001), worries that new technologies and cultural situations have rendered the novel unable to help now in our imaginative shapings of selfhood and society. What he therefore prefers, as *The Corrections* indicates, is a more "tragic realism," one that faces our new societies in a different, less exuberant way. His vision of the future of the novel places it back in a more traditional role, and in a more traditional form – not to flee from the future, or to give up on the creative imagination, but just to give up on "modern" pretensions. Or some of them, anyway – the more "redemptive" pretensions: "Expecting a novel to bear the weight of our whole disturbed society – to help solve our contemporary problems – seems to me a particularly American delusion. To write sentences of such authenticity that refuge can be taken in them. Isn't this enough? Isn't it a lot?" Franzen here presents a different challenge to the modern novel. Whereas globality might spoil its powers truly to matter, he wonders if those powers are even worth having – if it might not always have been better for the novel just to give us refuge in authentic sentences about matters of lesser weight.[13]

And yet Franzen also implies that the hopes of the modern novel are still valid. He speaks of the way fiction helps us in our life-saving "pursuit of substance in a time of ever-increasing evanescence"; and he admits that "even for people who don't believe in anything they can't see with their own two eyes, the formal aesthetic rendering of the human plight can be (though I'm afraid we novelists are rightly mocked for overusing the word) redemptive."[14] Here we are back where we began, in a sense – back to the balance Henry James long ago hoped the novel could strike, and to the kind of redemptive patterning Frank Kermode called essential to the life of the narrative fiction.

So perhaps the best way to answer the question about the future of the modern novel is not to say whether the novels of the future are likely to be modern ones, but instead to stress the need, even in the "global" future, of what modern novels have always tried to offer. What have been the essential characteristics of the modern novel, and how might they be necessary to our future?

Modernity confronted the modern novelist, as it confronts us today, with a flood of facts, with an excess of sights and sounds and information. Facing this flood, the modern novelist stressed the need for fiction to become more selective, to boil things down to more essential impressions, epiphanies, and dynamics. When Virginia Woolf looked at the excess of factual details in the conventional novels of her time and called upon her fellow novelists to pare things down to essentials, she did so in the hope that fiction might cut through the excess of modern experience and get at what really mattered. Such a hope must only be more powerful today, when the information inundating us has grown to a far more massive flood. The ecology of modern fiction, its techniques for winnowing modernity down, its powers of concretion and concision, may very well be vital in the future. As may be its feeling: D. H. Lawrence knew that modernity meant alienation of abstract intellect from the life of the body, and what worried him has surely become more of a problem, in the information age. What Lawrence expected from the novel – that it would return the mind to involvement in real physical being, through its plots and figures for sensuous life – is something we might also still need from the form.

If our future is to be all about information, and we are to live ever more *mediated* lives, then it would be good to keep in mind what the modern novel has discovered over the course of the century of its existence: that immediate reality, or a full sense of connection to present life, is a valuable and yet completely elusive thing. As we have seen, the first modernist writers tried for immediacy, out of a sense that fiction could become most vital and most artful if it could make people feel connected to the present life of the moment. And as we have also seen, such efforts tended mainly to end in a sense of failure – in a sense that language and experience must always be matters of mediation. This sense subsequently became a source of great interest and ingenuity in the postmodernist style of modern fiction, from which we might carry away important lessons about our future lives amid new media technologies. Like the narrator of *The French Lieutenant's Woman*, we might become importantly conscious of the way any reality is what our forms of thought (our media technologies) allow us to see and to believe.

And then there are the inner realities, as well: perhaps the main talent of the modern novel, and the main thing we might want to preserve, is its power to question the margins and contents of the self. Just what makes an individual, if anything does at all, has been modern fiction's main preoccupation. What distinguishes the self from the world, enabling a person to deviate from the norm or enjoy personal agency; what defines the particular perspective of a particular kind of person; how consciousness cobbles together its contents: these are some of the key questions through which modern fiction has helped us to determine the very nature of selfhood. If selfhood is now to disperse across the globe – as cultures migrate, as people intermix, as media and information technologies turn the mind into a web – we might do well to keep trying to explore and describe selfhood in the ways of modern fiction. What *Midnight's Children* does to the self of its protagonist, we might try in the future to do to our selves: try to give them a form, through the shaping and breaking powers of modern fiction, and see how the result reflects the needs of our times and our lives.

Any number of other techniques and concerns could come up here, and the point is not to name them all, but rather to stress some of the ways that contemporary society can help us see what is yet important about the modern novel. Its future depends less on the future writing of new modern novels than it does on our perpetual appreciation of what it has permanently contributed to the modern cultural imagination. What it has mainly contributed, we might say, is the awareness that modernity confronts us – will now always confront us – with perpetual change and rupture, and that the survival of culture nonetheless depends upon the extent to which the imagination and its powers of representation can match change with a creativity of forms.

Notes

INTRODUCTION: MODERN *HOW*?

1   Arnold Bennett, "Is the novel decaying?," in *The Author's Craft and Other Critical Writings of Arnold Bennett* (Lincoln, NE: University of Nebraska Press, 1968), p. 88.

2   Virginia Woolf, "Character in fiction" (1924), in *The Essays of Virginia Woolf: Volume Three, 1919–1924*, ed. Andrew McNeillie (New York: Harcourt Brace Jovanovich, 1988), p. 426.

3   Charles Baudelaire, "The painter of modern life," in *Baudelaire: Selected Writings on Art and Artists*, trans. P. E. Charvet (Cambridge: Cambridge University Press, 1972), p. 403.

4   Henry Adams, *The Education of Henry Adams: An Autobiography* (1907; Boston: Houghton Mifflin, 1961), p. 231.

5   Marshall Berman, *All That Is Solid Melts Into Air: The Experience of Modernity* (New York: Penguin, 1988), p. 15.

6   Stephen Spender, *The Struggle of the Modern* (Berkeley, CA: University of California Press, 1963), p. xiii.

7   Ibid., p. 84.

8   D. H. Lawrence, "Why the novel matters" (1925), in *Study of Thomas Hardy and Other Essays*, ed. Bruce Steele, *The Cambridge Edition of the Letters and Works of D. H. Lawrence*, eds James T. Boulton and Warren Roberts (Cambridge: Cambridge University Press, 1985), pp. 195, 197.

CHAPTER 1: WHEN AND WHY: THE RISE OF THE MODERN NOVEL

1   Henry James, "The art of fiction" (1884), in *Henry James: Literary Criticism*, vol. 1 (n.p.: Library of America, 1984), p. 47.

2 Henry James, "Preface to *The Princess Casamassima*," in *The Art of the Novel: Critical Prefaces*, intro. Richard P. Blackmur (New York: Charles Scribner's Sons, 1946), p. 62.

3 William James, *Principles of Psychology* (1890), in *The Writings of William James: A Comprehensive Edition*, ed. John J. McDermott (Chicago: University of Chicago Press, 1977), p. 33.

4 Judith Ryan, *The Vanishing Subject: Early Psychology and Literary Modernism* (Chicago: University of Chicago Press, 1991), p. 4.

5 Joseph Conrad, "Preface," in *The Nigger of the "Narcissus"* (1898; London: Penguin, 1987), pp. xlvii–xlix.

6 Henry James, "The new novel" (1914), in *Henry James: Literary Criticism*, vol. 1, pp. 129–33.

7 Frank Kermode, *The Sense of an Ending: Studies in the Theory of Fiction* (London: Oxford University Press, 1966), pp. 145, 133.

8 Paul Fussell, *The Great War and Modern Memory* (London: Oxford University Press, 1975), p. 8.

9 Modris Eksteins, *Rites of Spring: The Great War and the Birth of the Modern Age* (New York: Doubleday, 1989), p. 211.

10 Virginia Woolf, "Character in fiction" (1924), in *The Essays of Virginia Woolf: Volume Three, 1919–1924*, ed. Andrew McNeillie (New York: Harcourt Brace Jovanovich, 1988), p. 422.

11 Alain Locke, "Foreword," *The New Negro* (1925; New York: Macmillan, 1992), p. xxvii.

12 Eksteins, *Rites of Spring*, p. 218.

13 Virginia Woolf, "Modern novels" (known as "Modern fiction") (1919), in *The Essays of Virginia Woolf: Volume Three*, p. 33.

14 Ford Madox Ford, "Techniques," *Southern Review* I (July 1935), pp. 20–35 (p. 22).

15 Ford Madox Ford, "On Impressionism," *Poetry and Drama* II (June, December 1914), pp. 167–75, 323–34 (p. 174).

16 See D. H. Lawrence, "The novel and the feelings" (1924), in *Study of Thomas Hardy and Other Essays*, ed. Bruce Steele, *The Cambridge Edition of the Letters and Works of D. H. Lawrence*, eds James T. Boulton and Warren Roberts (Cambridge: Cambridge University Press, 1985), pp. 202, 205.

17 Willa Cather, "The novel démeublé" (1924), in *Not Under Forty* (New York: Alfred A. Knopf, 1970), pp. 43–51.

18 T. S. Eliot, "The Metaphysical poets" (1921), in *Selected Prose of T. S. Eliot*, ed. Frank Kermode (London: Faber and Faber, 1975), p. 65.

19 "Class conferences at the University of Virginia," quoted in *The Sound and the Fury*, ed. David Minter (New York: W. W. Norton, 1994), p. 236.

CHAPTER 2: "WHAT IS REALITY?": THE NEW QUESTIONS

1 Ian Watt, *The Rise of the Novel* (Berkeley and Los Angeles: University of California Press, 1957), p. 32.

2 Eugene Jolas, "Suggestions for a new magic" (1927), in *Modernism: An Anthology of Sources and Documents*, eds Vassiliki Kolocotroni, Jane Goldman, and Olga Taxidou (Chicago: University of Chicago Press, 1998), p. 312.

3 Interview, April 15, 1957, in *The Sound and the Fury: A Norton Critical Edition*, ed. David Minter (New York: W. W. Norton, 1994), p. 237.

4 Virginia Woolf, "Character in fiction" (1924), in *The Essays of Virginia Woolf: Volume Three, 1919–1924*, ed. Andrew McNeillie (New York: Harcourt Brace Jovanovich, 1988), pp. 434–5.

5 F. T. Marinetti, "The founding and manifesto of Futurism" (1909), in *Manifestos*, ed. Mary Ann Caws (Lincoln, NE: University of Nebraska Press, 2001), p. 187.

6 Perry Meisel, *The Myth of the Modern: A Study in British Literature and Criticism After 1850* (New Haven, CT: Yale University Press, 1987), p. 2.

7 E. M. Forster, *Aspects of the Novel* (New York: Harcourt Brace Jovanovich, 1927), p. 26.

8 Gustave Flaubert, letter to Louise Colet (January 16, 1852), in *The Letters of Gustave Flaubert, 1830–1857*, ed. Francis Steegmuller (Cambridge, MA: Harvard University Press, 1980), p. 154.

9 Aldous Huxley, *Point Counter Point* (New York: Doubleday, Doran, 1928), p. 192.

10 Arthur Symons, from *The Symbolist Movement in Literature* (1899), in *Modernism*, eds Kolocotroni et al., p. 135.

CHAPTER 3: NEW FORMS: RESHAPING THE NOVEL

1 Lionel Trilling, "On the modern element in modern literature," in *Varieties of Literary Experience*, ed. Stanley Burnshaw (New York: New York University Press, 1962), p. 428.

2 Franco Moretti, *The Way of the World: The Bildungsroman in European Culture* (London: Verso, 1987), p. 15.

3 Hugo Von Hofmannsthal, *The Lord Chandos Letter* (1902), trans. Russell Stockman (Marlboro, VT: Marlboro Press, 1986), p. 21.

4 Erich Auerbach, *Mimesis: The Representation of Reality in Western Literature* (1946; Princeton, NJ: Princeton University Press, 1968), p. 552.

5 Quoted in Dorrit Cohn, *Transparent Minds: Narrative Modes for Representing Consciousness in Fiction* (Princeton, NJ: Princeton University Press, 1978), p. 16.

6 Mikhail Bakhtin, "Discourse in the novel," in *The Dialogic Imagination: Four Essays*, ed. Michael Holquist, trans. Caryl Emerson and Mikhail Bakhtin (Austin, TX: University of Texas Press, 1981), pp. 262–3.

CHAPTER 4: NEW DIFFICULTIES

1 Ford Madox Ford, *Joseph Conrad: A Personal Remembrance* (London: Duckworth, 1924), p. 192.

2 See Stephen Kern, *The Culture of Time and Space: 1880–1918* (Cambridge, MA: Harvard University Press, 1983), pp. 10–20.

3 Henri Bergson, *Time and Free Will: An Essay on the Immediate Data of Consciousness* (1889), trans. F. L. Pogson (London: George Allen Unwin, 1910), p. 100.

4 E. M. Forster, *Aspects of the Novel* (New York: Harcourt Brace Jovanovich, 1927), p. 28.

5 Georg Simmel, "The metropolis and mental life" (1903), in *Georg Simmel: On Individuality and Social Forms*, ed. Donald N. Levine (Chicago: University of Chicago Press, 1971), pp. 325–6.

6 Joseph Frank, "Spatial form in modern literature" (1945), in *The Idea of Spatial Form* (New Brunswick, NJ:Rutgers University Press, 1991), pp. 10, 17.

7 Viktor Shklovsky, "Art as technique" (1917), in *Russian Formalist Criticism: Four Essays*, trans. Lee T. Lemon and Marion J. Reis (Lincoln, NE: University of Nebraska Press, 1965), p. 12.

8 Jean Toomer, letter to Waldo Frank, n.d. (September 1923?), in *Cane: A Norton Critical Edition*, ed. Darwin T. Turner (New York: W. W. Norton, 1988), p. 156.

9 Henry Green, "Communication without speech," *Listener* (November 9, 1950), pp. 505–6.

CHAPTER 5: REGARDING THE REAL WORLD: POLITICS

1 George Orwell, "Inside the whale" (1940), in *A Collection of Essays by George Orwell* (New York: Doubleday, 1954), p. 234.

2 John Ruskin, *Lectures on Art* (1870), in *The Works of John Ruskin*, vol. XX, eds E. T. Cook and Alexander Wedderburn (London: George Allen, 1905), p. 43.

3 Edward Said, *Culture and Imperialism* (New York: Vintage, 1993), p. 189.

4 Virginia Woolf, "The leaning tower" (1940), in *The Moment and Other Essays* (New York: Harcourt Brace Jovanovich, 1948), p. 138.

5 Angela Carter, "D. H. Lawrence, scholarship boy," in *Shaking a Leg: Collected Writings* (New York: Penguin, 1998), p. 53.

6 Dorothy Richardson, "Foreword," in *Pilgrimage I* (Urbana: University of Illinois Press, 1979), p. 10.

7 Houston Baker, *Modernism and the Harlem Renaissance* (Chicago: University of Chicago Press, 1987), pp. xiii–xiv.

8 Zora Neale Hurston, "Characteristics of Negro expression" (1934), in *The Gender of Modernism: A Critical Anthology*, ed. Bonnie Kime Scott (Bloomington: Indiana University Press, 1990), pp. 175–87.

9 Aldous Huxley, *Ends and Means* (New York: Harper and Brothers, 1937), p. 317.

10 Virginia Woolf, Wednesday November 2 1932, in *The Diary of Virginia Woolf*, eds Anne Olivier Bell and Andrew McNeillie, vol. 4 (New York: Harcourt Brace Jovanovich, 1982), p. 129.

11 Orwell, "Inside the whale," p. 235.

12 Ibid., p. 246.

13 Aldous Huxley, *Brave New World Revisited* (New York: Harper and Row, 1965), pp. 2, 29, 15.

14 Ibid., p. 85.

15 Evelyn Waugh, "Fan-fare" (1946), in *The Essays, Articles, and Reviews of Evelyn Waugh*, ed. Donat Gallagher (Boston: Little, Brown, 1983), p. 302.

CHAPTER 6: QUESTIONING THE MODERN:
MID-CENTURY REVISIONS

1 Theodor Adorno, "Cultural criticism and society," in *Prisms* (1967), trans. Samuel and Shierry Weber (Cambridge, MA: MIT Press, 1981), p. 34.

2 Marianna Torgovnick, *Going Primitive: Savage Intellects, Modern Lives* (Chicago: University of Chicago Press, 1990), p. 3.

3 Georg Lukács, "The ideology of Modernism," in *Realism in Our Time* (New York: Harper and Row, 1962), pp. 21–5.

4 George Orwell, "England your England" (1941), in *A Collection of Essays by George Orwell* (New York: Doubleday, 1954), p. 279.

5 Mark Turner, *The Literary Mind: The Origins of Thought and Language* (New York: Oxford University Press, 1996), p. 4.

6 Philip Roth, "Writing American fiction" (1961), in *Reading Myself and Others* (New York: Farrar, Straus and Giroux, 1975), p. 120.

7 Leslie Fiedler, "Class war in British literature," (1958), in *The Collected Essays of Leslie Fiedler*, vol. 1 (New York: Stein and Day, 1971), pp. 410–11.

8 Elaine Showalter, "Lad-lit," in *On Modern British Fiction*, ed. Zachary Leader (Oxford: Oxford University Press, 2002), pp. 60–76.

9 Jean-Paul Sartre, *Existentialism and Humanism* (1946), trans. Philip Mairet (London: Eyre Methuen, 1978), p. 29.

10 Albert Camus, *The Myth of Sisyphus* (1942), in *The Myth of Sisyphus and Other Essays*, trans. Justin O'Brien (1955; New York: Vintage, 1991), p. 60.

11 Ralph Ellison, "Introduction," in *Invisible Man* (1947; New York: Vintage, 1981), p. xvii.

12 Iris Murdoch, "Against dryness" (1961), in *The Novel Today: Contemporary Writers on Modern Fiction*, ed. Malcolm Bradbury (Manchester: Manchester University Press, 1977), pp. 23, 26.

13 Ibid., p. 31.

14 Anaïs Nin, "Preface," in *Tropic of Cancer* (1934; New York: Grove Press, 1961), pp. xxxi–xxxiii.

15 Vladimir Nabokov, "On a book entitled *Lolita*" (1956), in *Lolita* (New York: G. P. Putnam's Sons, 1980), pp. 316–17.

16 V. S. Naipaul, *Reading and Writing: A Personal Account* (New York: New York Review of Books, 2000), pp. 9–10, 25–6.

17 Salman Rushdie, "'Commonwealth literature' does not exist" (1983), in *Imaginary Homelands: Essays and Criticism, 1981–1991* (New York: Penguin, 1992), p. 63.

CHAPTER 7: POSTMODERN REPLENISHMENTS?

1 John Barth, "The literature of exhaustion" (1967), in *The Friday Book: Essays and Other Nonfiction* (Baltimore: Johns Hopkins University Press, 1984), pp. 64–5.

2 Jean-François Lyotard, "Introduction," in *The Postmodern Condition: A Report on Knowledge* (1979), trans. Geoff Bennington and Brian Massumi (Minneapolis: University of Minnesota Press, 1984), p. xxiv.

3 Jean-François Lyotard, "What is postmodernism?," in *The Postmodern Condition*, p. 81.

4 Christine Brooke-Rose, "Where do we go from here?," *Granta* 3 (1980), p.163.

5 John Barth, "The literature of replenishment" (1980), in *Essentials of the Theory of Fiction*, eds Michael J. Hoffman and Patrick D. Murphy, 2nd edition (Durham, NC: Duke University Press, 1996), p. 283.

6 Lyotard, "What is postmodernism?," p. 80.

7 Anthony Burgess, "*A Clockwork Orange* resucked" (1986), in *A Clockwork Orange* (New York: W. W. Norton, 1986), p. x.

8 David Lodge, "Mimesis and diegesis in modern fiction," in *Essentials of the Theory of Fiction*, eds. Hoffman and Murphy, pp. 362–3, 369–70.

9 Mark Currie, "Introduction," in *Metafiction* (New York: Longman, 1995), p. 15.

10 John Fowles, "Notes on an unfinished novel," in *Wormholes* (New York: Henry Holt, 1998), p. 16.

11 Gerald Graff, "The myth of the postmodernist breakthrough," in *The Novel Today: Contemporary Writers on Modern Fiction*, ed. Malcolm Bradbury (Manchester: Manchester University Press, 1977), p. 227.

12 David Lodge, "The novelist at the crossroads," in *The Novel Today*, ed. Bradbury, p. 105.

13 Graff, "The myth of the postmodernist breakthrough," p. 217.

CHAPTER 8: POSTCOLONIAL MODERNITY

1 Bill Ashcroft, Gareth Griffiths, and Helen Tiffin, *The Empire Writes Back: Theory and Practice in Postcolonial Literatures* (London: Routledge, 1989), p. 156.

2 Edward Said, *Culture and Imperialism* (New York: Vintage, 1993), p. 188.

3 Chinua Achebe, "An image of Africa: racism in Conrad's *Heart of Darkness*," in *Heart of Darkness: A Norton Critical Edition*, 3rd edition, ed. Robert Kimbrough (New York: W. W. Norton, 1988), p. 257.

4 Quoted in Ashcroft et al., *The Empire Writes Back*, p. 142.

5 Salman Rushdie, " 'Commonwealth literature' does not exist" (1983), in *Imaginary Homelands: Essays and Criticism, 1981–1991* (New York: Penguin, 1992), p. 64.

6 Ashcroft et al., *The Empire Writes Back*, p. 77.

7 Ngugi wa Thing'o, *Decolonising the Mind: The Politics of African Literature* (London: James Curry, 1986), pp. 4–5.

8 Nadine Gordimer, "Living in the interregnum," in *The Essential Gesture: Writing, Politics, and Places* (New York: Alfred A. Knopf, 1988), pp. 264–5.

CONCLUSIONS

1 Toni Morrison, Nobel lecture (December 7, 1993): www.nobel.se/literature/laureates/1993/morrison-lecture.html.

2 Jeanette Winterson, *Art Objects: Essays on Ecstasy and Effrontery* (New York: Alfred A. Knopf, 1996), p.188.

3 Ibid., pp. 153, 176.

4 Martin Shaw, "Globality as a Revolutionary Transformation," in *Politics and Globalization*, ed. Shaw (London: Routledge, 1999), p. 163.

5 Giles Gunn, "Globalizing literary study," *PMLA* 116.1 (January 2001), pp. 16–31 (p. 19).

6 Arjun Appadurai, *Modernity At Large: Cultural Dimensions of Globalization* (Minneapolis: University of Minnesota Press, 1996), p. 32.

7 Susie O'Brien and Imre Szeman, "Introduction: the globalization of fiction/the fiction of globalization," *South Atlantic Quarterly* 110.3 (Summer 2001), pp. 603–26 (p. 611).

8 Scott Bukatman, *Terminal Identity: The Virtual Subject in Postmodern Science Fiction* (Durham, NC: Duke University Press, 1993), p. 192.

9 Paul Jay, "Globalization and the future of English," *PMLA* 116.1 (January 2001), pp. 32–47 (p. 39).

10 Janet H. Murray, *Hamlet on the Holodeck: The Future of Narrative in Cyberspace* (Cambridge, MA: MIT Press, 1997), pp. 282–3.

11 James Wood, cited in Daniel Zalewski, "Hysterical realism," *New York Times Magazine* (December 15, 2002), p. 98.

12 See Nicholas Blincoe and Matt Thorne, "Introduction: the pledge," in *All Hail the New Puritans* (London: Fourth Estate, 2000), pp. vii–xvii.

13 Jonathan Franzen, "Why bother (the *Harper's* essay)," in *How to Be Alone* (New York: Farrar, Straus and Giroux, 2002), p. 84.

14 Ibid., pp. 88, 91.

Index